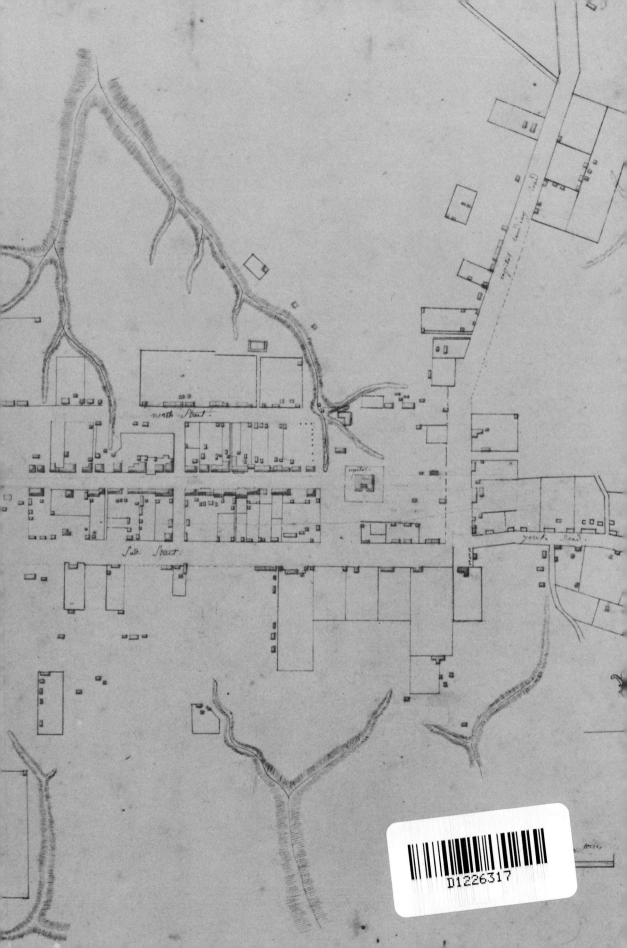

*The Eighteenth-Century Houses of Williamsburg*

*Williamsburg*
*Architectural*
*Studies*


The Public Buildings of Williamsburg
by Marcus Whiffen

The Eighteenth-Century Houses of Williamsburg
by Marcus Whiffen

Tidewater Towns: City Planning in Colonial
Virginia and Maryland
by John W. Reps

# The
# *Eighteenth-Century*
# HOUSES
## of *Williamsburg*

*A Study of Architecture and Building
in the Colonial Capital of Virginia*

By MARCUS WHIFFEN

The Colonial Williamsburg Foundation
*Williamsburg, Virginia*

© 1960 by
The Colonial Williamsburg Foundation

Revised edition, 1984
Second printing, 1985

Distributed by The University Press of Virginia, Charlottesville, Virginia

Library of Congress Cataloging in Publication Data

Whiffen, Marcus.
 The eighteenth-century houses of Williamsburg.

 Includes index.
 1. Williamsburg (Va.)—Dwellings.  2. Architecture, Colonial
—Virginia—Williamsburg.  3. Architecture, Domestic—Virginia—
Williamsburg.  I. Colonial Williamsburg Foundation.  II. Title.
NA7238.W4W5  1984      728.3′7′097554252  83-20955

ISBN 0-910412-05-7

Printed in the United States of America

*To the Memory of*
*SINGLETON PEABODY MOOREHEAD*
*(1900–1964)*
ARCHITECT
*Whose Scholarship Enhanced the Restoration*
*of Williamsburg for Thirty-five Years*
*and*
*Whose Eye for the Subtleties of Colonial*
*Design Was Unexcelled*

# Contents

## PART III

# Illustrations

# *Foreword*

A new edition of a classic in any field usually brings to mind a steady succession of supplements and offshoots. Yet Marcus Whiffen's study of Williamsburg domestic architecture continues to be the best and most comprehensive work on the subject. It is of great value, of course, for southern and specifically Virginian building traditions. The scope of the work, however, is much broader than a regional study. Rather, it constitutes a major contribution to our knowledge of the eighteenth-century practices of all builders in the English-speaking world. Here in an exact but entirely readable format, the author presents the gradually developing picture of building construction procedures which emerged as typical of the time, adaptable to the place and climate, but always orderly and suitable. The study concludes with a careful scrutiny of individual buildings, analyses of the most representative houses, and the variations they play on an old and excellent, tight and precise, little theme. These small colonial buildings, often better constructed and more carefully finished than their English counterparts, create for the town the special charm that any place takes on when structures have evolved from limitations imposed by a handful of restorations—restrictions such as building height limits, climatic conditions, and available materials. As frequently happens in the absence of a monumental architecture, the prototype becomes the humbler form, and a body of builders, restless for a better type, develops an excellent vernacular building for the model. This happened often in colonial America, particularly in Virginia, and specifically at Williamsburg. This study considers the pattern from every angle, but particularly from the stance of the builders themselves, men whose ties to England were sometimes two, three, or even four generations removed and whose knowledge was thus more dependent on local tradition and (to a lesser degree) handbooks.

The story was told here for the first time in an admirably comprehensive way, and nothing has appeared since which even attempts a production of this scope. Building materials and early manufactury are cataloged. Craftsmen's works are traced through their apprenticeships to the collection of their tools and books. Designs are studied and analyzed, and the variants established. Above all, building construction is discussed with commendable thoroughness. This new edition necessarily makes certain corrections and provides updatings. More significant is the addition of several house analyses, notably one of Carter's Grove plantation which became part of the Colonial Williamsburg properties shortly after the publication of the first edition. That famous building was acquired with a large tract of land for the purpose of expanding the Williamsburg interpretation with an example of one of the plantation units which had surrounded the colonial town and in fact formed the economic and social system which had caused it and supported it. The Carter's Grove mansion offers a most notable example of the Georgian goal in Virginia, a stylish and comparatively sophisticated building to which the modest town structures would have played a subsidiary role in the eyes of their conceivers and builders. But Mr. Whiffen settled this affair once and for all, bringing to print the vital importance of vernacular buildings and the uniqueness of Williamsburg as the setting for an entire architectural group which rarely survives the passage of time, a type which we must continue to research if we expect to truly understand the environmental arts of our pre-industrial past.

ROY EUGENE GRAHAM, AIA
*Architect of the Texas State*
*Capitol, Austin, Texas, and*
*former Resident Architect*
*The Colonial Williamsburg Foundation*
*1973–1981*

# *Preface*

THE Introduction to the first edition of this book explained the choice of what could be described as a cumulative treatment of its subject in preference to the chronological one of its predecessor in the series, *The Public Buildings of Williamsburg:* that is to say, why it is a *study* and not a *history.* The reasons given were three. First, there was the impossibility of assigning exact dates, necessary for a chronological treatment, to many of the buildings under review. (In this connection the destruction at the close of the Civil War of two irreplaceable resources, the James City County and General Court records, was a factor that might have been mentioned.) The second consideration was that a chronological treatment would have tended to overemphasize change in an architecture that was remarkable for its traditionalism, its long-continued reliance on practices and procedures handed down by precept and example through the system of apprenticeship. Thirdly, the cumulative method permitted the fullest use of the great store of documentation, architectural, archaeological, and archival, that had been collected by the architects and research workers of Colonial Williamsburg and that it was the prime purpose of the Williamsburg Architectural Studies to publish.

That was more than twenty years ago. Today I would mention another advantage of the cumulative method as employed in Part II of the book: such a building-by-building account may include information about such matters as changes of ownership, alterations, and demolitions that would not find its way into an architectural history in the strict sense of the term but may constitute valuable evidence for social and economic historians. Practically, the treatment facilitates the incorporation of corrections and additions in a new edition with a minimum of disturbance to the original text.

This edition takes into account the discoveries made at Williamsburg during the last twenty years, describes the acquisitions and restoration activity of the same period, and contains an entirely new section on a building of the very first importance which came into the possession of the Colonial Williamsburg Foundation in 1969. Most of the changes are updatings and minor corrections, but two houses have been renamed, and one of them radically redated, since the book first appeared. What then was called the Allen-Byrd House is now known as the Lightfoot House, research having revealed that it was owned by the Lightfoot family, probably from the early years of the eighteenth century, until Philip Lightfoot III sold it in 1783. It also appears that it was built as a tenement and converted into a single-family dwelling around the middle of the century, thus helping to explain certain structural peculiarities.

If the Lightfoot House is the most atypical of the brick houses of Williamsburg, the other renamed house, the George Reid House, might fairly be described as the most typical wooden one—a story and one-half structure with a hall-passage-parlor plan and end chimneys, such as was built in Virginia from the seventeenth century until well into the nineteenth. When it was called Captain Orr's Dwelling and believed to have been built before 1730 the character of its detail and the asymmetry of its fenestration could be pointed to as evidence of an early date. We know now that Hugh Orr's house on the lot was a larger one with a square plan—doubtless a fitter setting for the "6 Views with gilt frames," the "21 large prints and maps," the two oval dining tables of walnut, and the twelve walnut chairs that were among his possessions when he died—and that the present house was built around 1790.

Occupying a considerable stretch of Duke of Gloucester Street frontage near the George Reid House stands Wetherburn's Tavern, Colonial Williamsburg's most important acquisition of the last twenty years within the limits of the colonial city. In the restoration of this building in 1966–1967 some notable carpentry and a number of original features of interest were found; the naming of certain of its rooms and the purposes for which they were evidently used provide additional corroboration of the Reverend Hugh Jones's statement that "the habits, life, customs, computations, etc. of the Virginians are much the same as about London."

Bassett Hall, which stands just outside the original city limits, was discussed in the first edition of this book as one of the privately owned eighteenth-century houses of Williamsburg. It has now been bequeathed by its owners to Colonial Williamsburg, and preliminary architectural research has already yielded additional facts to illuminate its structural history. As a plantation house of medium size it very neatly fills the gap between the townhouses in the restored area and the most spectacular of Colonial Williamsburg's recent acquisitions—and arguably the most important of all the buildings in its care—which stands some six miles from the city on the north bank of the James River: the great plantation house of Carter's Grove.

Mentioned only incidentally in the first edition of this book, Carter's Grove has a section to itself, which, besides relating its history and describing its construction, structure, and finishing, places it deftly in the context of Virginia plantation architecture. Seen in the context of American colonial architecture as a whole, Carter's Grove has the special interest of having been built at that moment in history when tradition was about to give way to book-learned taste as the chief determinant of style, and while its exterior is purely traditional, a fine product of the brick vernacular that came from southeastern England, both its plan and its interior woodwork exemplify, very splendidly, the ascendancy of taste. The name of the carver responsible for much of that woodwork, Richard Baylis, whom Carter Burwell brought over from England, may now be added to the roll of craftsmen who figure in Chapter 2. (Was he, one wonders, the Richard Baylis who advertised his skill in stone and wood carving on May 19, 1739, in the *South Carolina Gazette*, adding that he would instruct servants or Negroes "in the Art of Cutting and Curing Tobacco after the same Manner as in *England*"? [italics mine] And if he was, when and why did he return to England?) Carter's Grove also affords another instance of the use of geometry in house design, a subject discussed in the last section of Chapter 4, for its length is twice the altitude of an equilateral triangle constructed on its width; the height from grade of its eaves cornice is the altitude of an equilateral triangle constructed on one-half of its length, and the height of its roof ridge (altered in 1928–1931) was determined, as in the Archibald Blair and George Wythe houses (*Figures 15 and 16*), by a circle drawn from the center of the front at grade to pass through the extremities of the eaves.

Enough has been said to call the reader's attention to the major changes and additions he will find in the following pages. The text is basically that of the fourth reprinting (1969), which, as noted at the time, had been revised by Thomas K. Ford of the Publications Department of Colonial Williamsburg in consultation with other members of the Colonial Williamsburg staff. The work of revision for this edition was carried out by present members of the staff of the Colonial Williamsburg Foundation, and the credit for improvements is theirs.

M. W.
*Tempe, Arizona*

# Author's Acknowledgment

THIS book, like *The Public Buildings of Williamsburg*, owes what value it may be found to have to the labors of many people, and especially those—architects and archaeologists, antiquaries and historians—who over the past thirty years have collected, arranged, and (very often) interpreted that mass of source material which is embodied in the research reports in the files of Colonial Williamsburg. Without them it could not have been begun.

Without the personal interest and help of certain of those same people it could hardly have been finished. Foremost among them was Singleton P. Moorehead, who was my mentor, constantly resorted to, in the niceties of colonial design and construction. Not only did he read the manuscript and make many valuable suggestions, but his knowledge, supplemented by that of another colleague learned in the matters there discussed, Paul Buchanan, supplied the substance of the greater part of Chapter V—which because of the scarcity of published information about eighteenth-century building construction I think may be regarded as the most valuable in the book.

Other members of the Architect's Office of Colonial Williamsburg who gave the manuscript, or parts of it, the benefit of their perusal were Ernest M. Frank, John Henderson, and A. Edwin Kendrew. All made suggestions that I was glad to follow. Albert M. Koch, maintaining the high standard set by Mr. Moorehead in *The Public Buildings of Williamsburg*, has illustrated the book with drawings such as any author would be proud to see on his pages.

In Colonial Williamsburg's Department of Research, Mrs. T. Ruther-foord Goodwin and Miss Mary A. Stephenson gave freely of their time and knowledge, and Mr. Mills Brown directed my attention to several matters concerning craftsmen and their tools which otherwise would have escaped me. Professor Frederick D. Nichols of the University of Virginia, who read the manuscript for the publisher, is a fellow worker in the field of architectural history whom I am happy to have to thank. And it gives me pleasure to record a debt of gratitude to Alonzo T. Dill, Jr., who generously presented me with a typescript copy of his "Documentary History of the Governor's House at New Bern, N. C.," prepared in connection with the reconstruction of that monument; this was my source for most, if not all, of the references to building in North Carolina that appear in these pages.

Lastly, but not least, I wish to thank Mrs. John A. Marion, who typed, with an accuracy that never ceased to astonish me, both the final copy of the manuscript and more drafts than she probably cares to remember.

MARCUS WHIFFEN
*September, 1959*

# Part I

# 1

# *Building Materials and "Necessaries"*

TIMBER was the main building material throughout the colonial period in Virginia. By the beginning of the seventeenth century, a serious shortage of timber had developed in England,[1] where rural building was still predominantly carpenter's work in many areas, including the populous southeast. The first colonists therefore considered the forests of the new land as being among its most promising assets. The composition of forests in Virginia in the seventeenth century was quite different from those of today.[2] There were many more hardwoods then, and the common softwoods were the longleaf pine (*Pinus palustris*) in the Peninsula and the coastal plain to the south of it, and the loblolly (*P. taeda*) and the shortleaf pine (*P. echinata*) in the lower Piedmont and in the Tidewater north of the York River. Today there is little longleaf pine, and the other pines growing in Virginia cannot be compared with it for building purposes. In general, the timber standing in Virginia when the colonists arrived was of better quality than later growths. The more competitive conditions that prevailed in the virgin forests assured the survival of only the most resistant stocks, thereby resulting in slow growth that insured closeness of grain.

The authorities in England lost no time in trying to exploit this asset of apparently unlimited timber. On no fewer than three occasions before

---

[1] Although the shortage was not yet as serious as it became at the end of the century. See Anthony N. B. Garvan, *Architecture and Town Planning in Colonial Connecticut* (New Haven, 1951), pp. 85–86.

[2] James B. Hubbard of the North Carolina Forestry Department was good enough to cast his eye over the first draft of the remainder of this paragraph. If any mistakes have crept in since, the fault is not his.

the revocation of its charter in 1624, the London Company sent over workmen—Dutch, Polish, and German—skilled in building sawmills driven by water power.[3] The workmen had to be foreigners, since there was no sawmill in England until 1663.[4] How many sawmills were actually built in Virginia during the first quarter-century of settlement is unknown, but some were certainly working by 1632.[5] Owing to the lack of fast running streams, they never became as common in Virginia as they did in New England.

The circular saw was not introduced into America until the second decade of the nineteenth century. The cutting part of the first sawmills, therefore, was essentially a framed pitsaw[6] moved up and down by a crank-driven connecting rod, power being transmitted from the shaft of the water wheel to the crankshaft through gearing. The log or balk to be cut into boards or scantlings was moved against the saw—or saws, because two or three might be mounted side-by-side in the frame— either by a carriage with a rack-and-pinion device or, in a type of the machine described and illustrated by Edward Williams in 1650, by weights and pulleys.[7] In 1685 William Byrd I wrote to the London merchants Perry and Lane to order those parts for such a sawmill that could not be made in Virginia:

> I have inclosed Sent for the iron worke of a Saw Mill, w:ʰ I desire may bee Sent by the first Ship, & that the Cranke may bee made exactly according to the inclosed patterne. If it is cast (without flaws) it may doe best; the Racke & Nutt must fitt; I am told it may bee best & cheapest had out of Holland, but I thinke wrought iron is prohibited, therefore must leave it to you, onely earnestly desire that great care may be taken (in the Cranke especially) that the iron worke bee well & Exactly according to the dimensions inclosed, for I hope my timber worke will bee finished before the End of 7be [September] next.[8]

---

[3] Philip Alexander Bruce, *Economic History of Virginia in the Seventeenth Century,* II (New York, 1907), pp. 429–430.

[4] James Elliott Defebaugh, *History of the Lumber Industry of America* (Chicago, 1907), II, p. 9.

[5] Bruce, *Economic History of Virginia,* II, p. 431. In 1637 Hugh Bullock conveyed to his son William his "Corne Mills Sawmills Plantations" in York County. York County Records, Deeds, Orders, Wills, I, 1633–1694, p. 135.

[6] For information about the pitsaw, see p. 49.

[7] Williams offered the weight-and-pulley device as an improvement, but there is nothing to show that it was actually used in Virginia. Edward Williams, *Virginia: more especially the South part thereof . . .* (London, 1650).

[8] William G. Stanard, ed., "Letters of William Byrd, First," *Virginia Magazine of History and Biography,* XXIV (June 1916), p. 233.

The proportion of mill-sawed to pit-sawed timber used for building in seventeenth-century Virginia cannot be determined, although payments to sawyers were an important item in the accounts of the largest building project of that century, the erection of the main building at the College of William and Mary in 1695–1698.[9] In the first quarter of the eighteenth century, Hugh Jones wrote that although sawmills were among the few useful inventions to which Virginians had been "persuaded," and "the great benefit of them" was well known, there were not as many as there might have been.[10] "I am certain," he argued, "that if more sawing-mills were set up there, it would bring great profit to the owners, employ more people there, and make timber for ships and houses come at a much cheaper rate in England, than it now does, without any loss to the English landed gentlemen or timber merchants."[11]

From the first, sawmills had been proposed as an adjunct to shipbuilding. By preparing timber for export to the mother country, sawmills played an increasingly important part in the economic life of Virginia. Toward the end of the colonial period, advertisements of sawmills became common in the *Virginia Gazette* as the first of them, which appeared over the name of Samuel Hargrove in 1769, indicated:

> I HAVE built a saw-mill at the falls of *Pamunkey* river, where any person may be supplied on reasonable terms with any quantity of the best pine plank and scantling; or I will deliver it at any landing on said river as low as *Newcastle* town. My view is to serve the public as well as myself; and give this notice to all persons who have obstructed a free passage of the river, from the falls to *Newcastle*, by mills, stem stops, hedges, trees, &c. as soon as possible to remove the same, or I shall be under the necessity of making use of the act of Assembly.[12]

Sometimes the announcements specified the kinds of wood that could be supplied, as did the advertisement of William Aylett of King William County, which appeared in 1774:

> PLANK and SCANTLING to be sold by the Subscriber at his Saw Mill near *Aylett's* Warehouse, *Mattapony* River, upon the most

---

[9] Marcus Whiffen, *The Public Buildings of Williamsburg: Colonial Capital of Virginia* (Williamsburg, Va., 1958), p. 21.

[10] Hugh Jones, *The Present State of Virginia,* ed. Richard L. Morton (Chapel Hill, N. C., 1956), p. 81.

[11] *Ibid.,* p. 142.

[12] *Virginia Gazette* (Rind), Apr. 27, 1769.

reasonable Terms, and of the following Kinds, *viz.* White Oak, Black Walnut, Sweet Gum, Ash, Poplar, Birch (which makes elegant Furniture) best Yellow Heart Pine for Flooring, and clear of Heart and Sap if required, common high Land and Slash Pine for other Uses. A reasonable Credit will be allowed, and *European* or *West India* Goods received in Payment. I shall prepare several Sets of Plank and Scantling for executing *Hobday's* Wheat Machines, which, or any other kind of Plank or Scantling, I can send to *Norfolk,* or any part of *York* River.[13]

In the nine years following 1769, more than seventy references to sawmills appeared in the advertisement columns of the *Virginia Gazette.* Yet as those same columns show, manpower had not been completely superseded. In 1771 Benjamin Chapman of Brunswick County, "having Half a Dozen Pair of SAWERS," announced that he "would be glad to undertake, from the Stump, or otherwise, any considerable Job of sawing, within sixty or seventy Miles of Home, upon reasonable Terms."[14] In 1772 Samuel Long, "at the Halfway House betwen *York* and *Hampton,*" sought to "hire by the Month or Year, a Pair of good SAWERS," and "sawers" were among the workmen advertised for by master builder Robert Du Val of Richmond the same year.[15] When Du Val died early in 1773, his "sixteen valuable Slaves" included four sawyers, and it seems likely that in Virginia most of what Hugh Jones called "the stupid slavish work of sawing" was in fact done by slaves.[16]

In Williamsburg and its neighborhood, the woods most frequently used for house frames were yellow pine, poplar, and oak, with gum

---

[13] *Ibid.* (Purdie and Dixon), Apr. 7, 1774.

[14] *Ibid.,* Feb. 14, 1771.

[15] *Ibid.,* July 2, Sept. 3, 1772.

[16] *Ibid.,* May 13, 1773; Jones, *Present State of Virginia,* p. 142. Some interesting information about sawmills in North Carolina toward the end of the colonial period is in letters written by Gov. William Tryon to the Board of Trade. On Jan. 30, 1767, Tryon wrote: "On this river of Cape Fear and on its branches and creeks there are fifty erected and more constructing; chiefly with two saws. Upon a medium each mill is supposed to saw annually one hundred and fifty thousand feet of Board and scantling . . . These mills are constructed to saw planks only of 25 to 30 feet in length." He continued on Feb. 22: "Tho' the present mills will not allow of plank or scantling exceeding thirty feet and few above twenty five owing to the difficulty of raising a greater length of timber upon the stages of the mills; yet the pine trees will allow planks forty to fifty feet in length which could be sawed by hand in this country in any quantity." William L. Saunders, ed., *The Colonial Records of North Carolina,* VII (Raleigh, N. C., 1890), pp. 430, 440–441. When it was for shipbuilding, however, it was an obvious disadvantage, as Tryon indicated in his second letter.

as a rare fourth.[17] The many species of oaks growing in Virginia must have greatly impressed the first colonists, who had come from a country where oak was the time-honored building timber, but the Virginia oaks were found to be less lasting than the English.[18] Weatherboards and exterior trim were of yellow pine or poplar, while the thin boards some- times used for covering roofs were of oak.[19] For shingles, which were exported from Virginia to Madeira and the West Indies in quantities sufficient to necessitate an act of Assembly regulating their size,[20] cypress was the favorite wood in Williamsburg, as it was throughout the colony, although yellow pine[21] and white cedar were also used. No shingles of oak, which tended to warp and rot around the nails, or of chestnut have been found in Williamsburg, although undoubtedly they were used here as they certainly were elsewhere.[22] Window and door frames were of yellow pine, poplar, or oak, and window sashes, which were custom- arily fabricated and kept in stock by carpenters for any job that might come along,[23] could be of yellow pine, poplar, walnut, or cherry. Yellow

---

[17] Paul Buchanan, Architects' Office, Colonial Williamsburg Foundation, supplied the information about the different woods found in Williamsburg buildings in this para- graph.

[18] Jones, *Present State of Virginia*, pp. 76–77.

[19] Such boards were found in place in Williamsburg at the Brush-Everard, Archibald Blair, Peyton Randolph, and Chiswell-Bucktrout houses, and at the John Blair House as exterior facing.

[20] "An Act for regulating the size and dimensions of Staves, Heading, and Shingles, intended for exportation to Madeira, and the West Indies," 1752, in William Waller Hening, ed., *The Statutes at Large; Being A Collection of All the Laws of Virginia, From The First Session of the Legislature* (New York, Philadelphia, and Richmond, 1819–1823), VI, p. 233. All such shingles were to be 18½ inches long, 5 inches broad, and ⅝ inch thick. Cypress shingles specified for St. Peter's Church, New Kent County, in 1700 were to be "18 inches in length and none to be more than 5 inches in breadth or narrower than 3 inches and not to be Lesser than ½ an inch or more than ¾ of an inch thick." C. G. Chamberlayne, ed., *The Vestry Book and Register of St. Peter's Parish, New Kent and James City Counties, Virginia, 1684–1786* (Richmond, 1937), p. 80. The shingles for Stratton Major Church, King and Queen County, 1760, were to be 20 inches long and ¾ inch thick. C. G. Chamberlayne, ed., *The Vestry Book of Stratton Major Parish, King and Queen County, Virginia, 1729–1783* (Richmond, 1931), p. 132. On June 18, 1737, the sloop *Molly* cleared the Upper District of James River for Barbados with a cargo that included 4,000 shingles. *Virginia Gazette,* June 17, 1737.

[21] In 1772 Edward Hughes of Gloucester County advertised "good Pine Heart Shin- gles" that he would "warrant to be as good as any Cypress." *Virginia Gazette* (Purdie and Dixon), Feb. 27, 1772.

[22] In 1767 the roof of Stratton Major poorhouse was to be "cover'd with Cypress or Chestnut Shingles, 18 inches long to shew six inches." Chamberlayne, ed., *Vestry Book of Stratton Major Parish,* p. 159.

[23] Inventories that listed sashes included those of James Morris, 1718, "6 Sash Win- dows" appraised at £1 15s., Papers of the Jones Family of Northumberland County,

pine, poplar, oak, and walnut were used for doors. The same four woods and also white pine were used in paneling, with yellow pine, poplar, and walnut being used for internal trim (cornices, chair rails, baseboards) and for handrails and balusters. Floorboards and stair treads were invariably of yellow pine; the nosings of brick steps were oak. Cedar and locust were the preferred woods for fence posts; fence rails were usually of poplar.

## BRICKS, MORTAR, AND PLASTER

Two bricklayers were among the first settlers at Jamestown. Six more, along with four brickmakers, were included among the tradesmen who accompanied Sir Thomas Gates to Virginia in 1610, and bricks continued to be made in the colony throughout the colonial period. The bricks for a brick house of any size might be made on or near the site.[24]

Sometimes they were specially made if only the chimneys, or the chimneys and the cellar, were to be of brick, but it is reasonable to suppose that in such cases it would generally have been cheaper to buy bricks ready made. During the period 1740–1744, planter James Bray of Littleton plantation on the James River sold 83,350 bricks to twenty-five purchasers in and around Williamsburg including tradesmen, professional men, the College of William and Mary, other planters, and a bricklayer.[25] Bray undoubtedly had built his kilns initially to burn bricks for his own use. Forty years later, brickmason Humphrey Harwood, as his surviving ledger shows,[26] was supplying bricks for the numerous small jobs that he undertook in Williamsburg; that he also made them is indicated by items in the 1789 inventory of his property:

> 300 bushels of lime, a kiln of burnt brick about 25,000. A kiln of raw brick about 15,000.[27]

In England proclamations and statutes regulated the dimensions of bricks from time to time. Nathaniel Lloyd, the historian of English brick-

---

Virginia, 1649–1889, Manuscript Division, Library of Congress; James Wray, 1750, "2 pr. sashes" appraised with "1 oyl jar, 1 white lead mill" at £3 10s., York Co. Recs., Wills and Inventories, XX, 1745–1759, p. 206; Thomas Cobbs, 1774, "14 sashes" appraised at £1 5s., *ibid.*, XXII, 1771–1783, p. 246; and Mary Goodson, 1782, "20 *pr* Sashes and 3 Doors" appraised at £9, *ibid.*, p. 524.

[24] Remains or traces of brick kilns have been found in six or seven places in Williamsburg.

[25] Ledger of James Bray, 1736–1746, Burwell Papers, CWF.

[26] See p. 41.

[27] York Co. Recs., Wills and Inventories, XXIII, 1783–1811, p. 220.

work, cited an instance from the fifteenth century of an official brick mold being kept in the moot hall, like other official measures.[28] There is no evidence that any special regulations of this kind existed in Virginia. Some records indicate that the English standards may have been followed in the building trades in theory if not in practice. For instance, a Virginia statute of 1662 set the price of "bricks being statute bricks and well burned" at 150 pounds of tobacco per thousand.[29] In 1719 the agreement for the churchyard wall at St. Peter's, New Kent County, specified "Bricks to be according to the Statute something less than Nine Inches in Length, two Inches and one quarter thick, and four Inches and one quarter Wide."[30] An examination of colonial buildings in Virginia, however, reveals variations in brick sizes not only from one building to another but even in one wall. This was no local peculiarity, since similar variations are to be found in England.[31] In inferior work it may have been caused by failure to fill the molds to capacity, and sometimes it must have been due to variations in the size of the molds, but most often it was the result of uneven shrinkage in burning. If such variations seem unusual, it is because the twentieth century tends to equate efficiency with standardization, a habit of mind not shared by our ancestors who lived before the industrial revolution.[32] Early attempts to regulate the sizes of bricks were prompted simply by the desire to prevent fraud.

Many antiquaries have believed that it might be possible to date buildings by the size and shape of the bricks used in them. No such method would be accurate enough to be useful in dating the colonial buildings of Williamsburg and its neighborhood. Nevertheless, a general development in the shape of bricks can be detected. J. C. Harrington, the author of the most thorough study of brickmaking in the tidewater area yet published, which was based on excavations at Jamestown, has written:

> Study of the bricks from all structures excavated at Jamestown suggests that the bricks made during the first half of the [seventeenth] century were slightly longer and thinner than those made during the latter part of the century. Similarly, there is a marked

---

[28] Nathaniel Lloyd, *A History of English Brickwork* (London, 1928), p. 45.
[29] Hening, ed., *Statutes*, II, p. 173.
[30] Chamberlayne, ed., *Vestry Book and Register of St. Peter's Parish*, p. 174.
[31] Lloyd, *History of English Brickwork*, pp. 98–100.
[32] Analogous to the variation in size of bricks before the nineteenth century is the often amazing variation in the size of the aggregate in Roman concrete.

trend toward shorter, narrower, and thicker bricks during the next century.[33]

Variations in the colors of bricks are more noticeable to the casual observer than are variations in their sizes. Generally speaking, the trend was from light to dark and corresponded to an improvement in the quality of the bricks that was due to increased technical skill and a more thorough knowledge of the properties of the local clays. The difference in quality is most marked in the bricks used, not for facing walls, but inside them. In the earliest part of Bruton Church, for instance, and in the President's House at the College of William and Mary, Colonial Williamsburg architects found some of the bricks to be very poor indeed.[34] The use of glazed bricks for headers in walls laid in Flemish bond, an attractive device inherited from English practice, proves that hardwoods such as oak or hickory were used for burning the bricks because when bricks were made by the old process for the purposes of restoration, it was found that pine would not produce the desired glaze, even on the bricks nearest to the fire in the kiln.[35]

The story that such and such a colonial house "was built of bricks brought from England" is one that should always be treated with suspicion. This is not to say that bricks were not imported into Virginia: records show that they were, and frequently.[36] Their importation was encouraged by laws that forbade the dumping of ballast in rivers. Ballast was a necessity in the lightly laden ships that came to fetch the tobacco crop, and bricks were a reasonably handy kind of ballast—and one that could be sold. But the little ships of the eighteenth century could not hold a large number of bricks, and the most recorded in the *Virginia Gazette* as having arrived in one vessel was 80,000.[37] When it is remembered that 600,000 bricks were ordered for the Capitol,[38] it is obvious that one shipload of ballast did not contain a great many. Presumably the imported bricks were used somewhere, although there is not a single

---

[33] J. C. Harrington, "Seventeenth Century Brickmaking and Tilemaking at Jamestown, Virginia," *VMHB*, LVIII (January 1950), p. 35.

[34] This information was provided by A. Edwin Kendrew, Architects' Office, CWF.

[35] H. R. Shurtleff, "The Restoration Brick Kiln," research report, 1933, Architects' Office, CWF.

[36] In the *Virginia Gazette* alone, the importation of bricks was recorded in 1737, 1739, 1745, 1753, and 1768.

[37] "Enter'd in York District, June 6. Ship Braxton, of London, Thomas Reynolds, Master, from New-England, with 80,000 Bricks, 10 Barrels of Train Oyl, some Wooden Ware, and 400 Weight of Hops." *Ibid.*, June 10, 1737. Whether the bricks were made in England or in New England was not indicated.

[38] Whiffen, *Public Buildings*, p. 41.

building in Williamsburg, or for that matter within fifty miles of Williamsburg, of which it can assuredly be said that it was built of imported bricks.[39]

In tidewater Virginia, as in all the other early settled parts of British America except Rhode Island, there was no limestone to burn for lime to make mortar, so the colonists turned to oyster shells for a supply of that necessity. Practically limitless quantities of oyster shells were available in Virginia, as John Clayton informed the Royal Society in 1688:

> In some Places, for several Miles together, the Earth is so inter-mix'd with Oyster-shells, that there may seem as many Shells as Earth; and how deep they lie thus intermingled, I think, is not yet known. . . . In several Places these Shells are much closer, and being petrified, seem to make a Vein of Rock. Of these Rocks of Oyster-shells that are not so much petrified, they burn and make all their Lime; whereof they have that store, that no Generation will consume.[40]

Was shell lime mortar known in England before 1607, or was it invented in the New World? The available evidence indicates that the latter was the case. Oyster shells were used in building in England in the fifteenth and sixteenth centuries, but the records show they were not burned for lime but were embedded in mortar to adjust courses of stonework when there was some irregularity in the shapes or sizes of the stones.[41] The argument for a New World origin is strengthened by the fact that the use and merits of shell lime in mortar were known in the mother country by the end of the seventeenth century.

This is not the place to describe lime burning processes in detail, and a note on local methods will suffice.[42] In the eighteenth century, the field kiln, which had built-up brick walls and a brick floor, was the type of kiln most used in Virginia, and lime was no doubt often burned

---

[39] Imported clinkers, or Dutch bricks, were used in cellar floors at Jamestown and at Green Spring, Gov. William Berkeley's house in James City County.

[40] John Clayton, *A Letter from Mr. John Clayton . . . to the Royal Society, May 12, 1688,* in Peter Force, ed., *Tracts and Other Papers, . . . Relating Principally to the Origin, Settlement and Progress of the Colonies in North America, From the Discovery of the Country to the Year 1776,* III (Washington, D. C., 1844), no. 12, p. 14, quoted in Worth Bailey, "Lime Preparation at Jamestown in the Seventeenth Century," *William and Mary Quarterly,* 2nd Ser., XVIII (January 1938), pp. 1–12.

[41] See *Dictionary of Architecture,* VII, s.v. "shell," and L. F. Salzman, *Building in England down to 1540* (Oxford, 1952), p. 89.

[42] The following is based on Bailey, "Lime Preparation at Jamestown," pp. 1–12.

at the same time and in the same place as bricks. Sometimes, as the discovery in 1933 of an eighteenth-century brick kiln near Yorktown that had a foot-thick layer of oyster shell lime above the top brick portion revealed, it was burned in the same kiln. At Jamestown in the seventeenth century, coal was sometimes employed in the kiln. It must have been imported coal from England, and whether Virginia coal was used after its discovery in 1701 is unknown. Lime was sometimes burned by another method that did not necessitate the construction of a kiln and that was used to produce it for agricultural purposes until recently.[43] An open crib of pine logs, the successive layers crossing each other at right angles and the structure being about twelve feet square on plan, was built up to a height of five feet; on it was laid a floor of parallel contiguous logs to hold a layer of oyster shells, and on that the whole structure was repeated two or three times so as to form a square tower.

Shell lime was used in plaster as well as in mortar for rendering walls. John Harrower, tutor at Belvedere plantation near Fredericksburg, noted in his journal on October 31, 1774, "This morning two Carpenters was put to new weather board my house on the outside with featherage plank, and to new plaster it on the Inside with shell lime."[44] It was a far cry from that little schoolhouse to the great cathedral in which shells also played a part as described by its architect: "The vaulting of St. Paul's is a rendering as hard as Stone; it is composed of Cockle-shell-lime well beaten with Sand; the more Labour in the beating, the better and stronger the Mortar."[45] Many a slave in Virginia must have known as much about shell lime as Sir Christopher Wren did.

## STONE

There was no freestone to be quarried anywhere near Williamsburg. The little that was used in building for floors and steps was brought to the town wharves by water, and most of it, even after the Aquia Creek quarries on the Potomac opened, seems to have come from Brit-

---

[43] This information was supplied by Singleton P. Moorehead, Architects' Office, CWF.

[44] Edward Miles Riley, ed., *The Journal of John Harrower, An Indentured Servant in the Colony of Virginia, 1773–1776* (Williamsburg, Va., 1963), p. 68.

[45] "Letter to the Commissioners for Building Fifty New Churches in London and the Suburbs thereof," in *Life and Works of Sir Christopher Wren From the 'Parentalia' or memoirs by his son, Christopher* (orig. publ., 1750; reprinted, London, 1903, ed. Ernest J. Enthoven), p. 195.

ain. Much of this imported stone must have been precut, and there could hardly have been enough work to support a stonemason in the Williamsburg area, although in diary entries for 1709 and 1712, William Byrd II mentioned "the stonecutter."[46]

The stones most used were Purbeck and Portland.[47] Purbeck stone, quarried in the Isle of Purbeck in Dorset, was commonly employed in Williamsburg in flags of eighteen or twenty inches square and about four inches thick for paving interiors and porches. Portland stone from the Isle of Portland, also in Dorset, was used for steps. Another stone commonly used for steps has been identified as blue Yorkshire stone, which was and is quarried in the Leeds area and presumably was shipped to Virginia from the port of Hull. Also found here are Red Wilderness stone from Mitcheldean in Gloucestershire, and Forest of Dean blue stone from the same part of England, both of which must have been shipped from Bristol. More surprising, because the quarries were so much farther inland, was the use of Horderley stone from Shropshire. When it was needed for the construction of the second Capitol in 1755, it was described as "blue Shrosberry [i.e., Shrewsbury] Stone,"[48] and it too probably came via Bristol. From Scotland came Corsehill red stone, quarried near the Solway Firth at Annan, Dumfriesshire, a reddish sandstone that was used in Williamsburg for simple steps and paving. It crossed the Atlantic in larger quantities in the nineteenth century and was used in many important buildings from Baltimore to Toronto.

Italian marbles, carved in England and shipped in knockdown form, reached Virginia as chimneypieces. William Byrd's references to "the stonecutter" in 1712 related to the installation of a marble chimneypiece in the library at Westover. Such chimneypieces were expensive items and were more likely to be purchased for the plantation house than for the townhouse, which was generally regarded by wealthy planters as a secondary establishment. So it is not really surprising that a mere half-dozen should have survived in Williamsburg, where joiners were capable of producing very passable wooden substitutes. Even when money was of limited concern, the acquisition of a chimneypiece from

---

[46] Louis B. Wright and Marion Tinling, eds., *The Secret Diary of William Byrd of Westover 1709–1712* (Richmond, 1941), pp. 52–53, 539–540. Since the first entry noted a report that "the stonecutter" had died, Byrd may have been referring to two men.

[47] This paragraph is largely based on a report by B. W. L. Gallannaugh on samples of stone from eighteenth-century buildings and excavations in Williamsburg sent to him by A. Edwin Kendrew in June 1945, Architects' Office, CWF.

[48] Whiffen, *Public Buildings*, p. 138.

England was apt to be a hit-or-miss affair, as a letter from William Nelson to Samuel Athawes in 1771 showed:

> I send you enclosed, at the Request of Nat Burwell, a Draught of Chimney Pieces & Steps which he wants. If you understand it, or the statuary, it's more than I do. If you do, you will send them to him, observing to insure them.[49]

## LEAD

Lead, which had to be imported, was not much used in building in eighteenth-century Virginia. As a roof covering it was not only expensive, and consequently confined for the most part to relatively grand buildings like the Governor's Palace and Rosewell, but it was also unreliable due to the wide range of temperatures to which the Virginia climate subjected it.[50] It says much for the skill of the colonial carpenter that he was able to make his roofs tight, even around the dormers, without lead flashing. Lead was, however, sometimes used over unprotected brickwork such as belt courses and doorway pediments.[51] Eaves gutters and rainwater pipes were rarely employed.[52]

Plumbing was evidently among the trades that Virginians thought were better understood in the mother country, a point of view that may be inferred from an advertisement in a May 1769 issue of the *Virginia Gazette:*

> The subscribers having engaged a person from *England,* well acquainted with the useful branches of PLUMBING, GLAZING,

---

[49] William Nelson to Samuel Athawes, Nov. 19, 1771, Nelson Letter Book (1766–1775), CWF.

[50] See Whiffen, *Public Buildings,* pp. 58 and 214, n. 30. Another instance of lead proving an unsatisfactory roofing material in the southern colonies was supplied by the history of the Governor's Palace at New Bern, N. C. An entry in the Journals of the State Council dated Nov. 18, 1779—only nine years after the completion of the building— referred to "the daily damage the Palace sustains by reason of the lead in several places of the roof being cracked and otherways so much out of repair that every shower of rain runs through, which if not timely prevented will soon destroy the ceiling and otherways considerably damage the rest of the building." Walter Clark, ed., *The State Records of North Carolina,* XXII (Goldsboro, N. C., 1907), p. 961.

[51] In 1722/3 James Skelton, the builder of Poplar Spring Church in Gloucester County, agreed with the vestry of Petsworth Parish "to Civer the pediments over the dors with Lead." C. G. Chamberlayne, ed., *The Vestry Book of Petsworth Parish, Gloucester County, Virginia, 1677–1793* (Richmond, 1933), p. 166. Belt courses were covered with lead on the main buildings at William and Mary, on the Lightfoot House, and at Rosewell in Gloucester County.

[52] See pp. 105–107.

and PAINTING, hereby inform all Gentlemen who please to employ them that they may depend upon having their work executed in such a manner as cannot fail of giving satisfaction, and upon most reasonable terms.

KIDD & KENDALL[53]

Five months later, Joseph Kidd advertised again, specifying some of the uses to which lead was put:

At the LEAD MANUFACTORY, behind the church, may be had all sorts of sheat lead, pipes for conveying water from the tops of houses, cisterns, milkpans (which will keep milk in the height of summer) . . . and every other article in the plumbing business . . . [performed] in the neatest manner,

JOSEPH KIDD[54]

A postscript stated that gilding, painting, and glazing would be undertaken as usual, and it seems unlikely that plumbing alone could have supported a man in eighteenth-century Williamsburg. Both of the partners were occupied in other lines, Joseph Kidd as an upholsterer and Joshua Kendall as a carpenter, joiner, and wood-carver.[55]

## HARDWARE

That a certain amount of building hardware was made in Virginia is known from the advertisements of smiths. David and William Geddy of Williamsburg announced in 1751 that besides smithery they carried on the "Cutler's and Founder's Trade" and could supply "Hinges, Squares, Nails and Bullions, curious Brass Fenders and Fire Dogs, House Bells of all Sizes."[56] John Bell, blacksmith, advertised his impending departure in 1766 from Williamsburg to Portsmouth, "where he will carry on his business in all its branches, make locks, hinges, jacks, etc."[57] Nevertheless, it is safe to say that throughout the colonial period, most of the building hardware used in Virginia was imported from England. Many orders to English merchants for hardware are extant. A letter from lawyer George Wythe, dated July 18, 1771, to one of those mer-

[53] *Virginia Gazette* (Purdie and Dixon), May 4, 1769.
[54] *Ibid.*, Sept. 28, 1769. The advertisement also appeared *ibid.* (Rind), Oct. 5, 1769.
[55] *Ibid.* (Purdie and Dixon), Dec. 28, 1769; *ibid.* (Rind), Jan. 18, 1770.
[56] *Ibid.* (Hunter), Aug. 8, 1751.
[57] *Ibid.* (Purdie and Dixon), Mar. 14, 1766.

chants included a telltale phrase. "I am about building a small house," wrote Wythe, "and must be obliged to you for the english materials."[58] Wythe's letter indicates that certain things needed in building a house— even a small one—customarily came from England. The invoice enclosed with his letter showed what they were apt to be. It began with tools—"A chest of Nice joiner's and other tools, to cost six or seven guineas, or even eight to be complete"—and went on to list paint and brushes, window glass, and all the manufactured hardware that would be needed, concluding with a cask of nails.[59]

Nails were the most essential of all items of hardware. In building a house of timber, they were needed for fastening nearly everything except the principal members of the frame, which were secured with wooden pegs. Throughout the colonial period, nails were made by hand from iron rods. In Virginia in the early days they evidently were a scarce commodity because a 1645 act of the Assembly prohibited people who deserted their plantations from burning their houses in order to recover the nails. Instead, they were to be given as many nails as had been used in building the structures.[60] The manufacture of nails on a commercial scale was never successfully established in the American colonies.[61]

There were many special types of nails, and they were called by a wide variety of names. In the inventory of the property of Williamsburg carpenter James Wray, who died in 1750, were listed flooring brads, which were nails with narrow heads that could be sunk into the wood to allow the passage of a plane over their surfaces; clout nails, which had flat heads and were used for nailing on ironwork; dog nails, which had the same function as clout nails but differed from them in shape because their heads were raised; round-head nails, whose name was self-explanatory; and bullins, nails with short shanks and convex heads that were used for fastening hangings and upholstery. The clout nails were divided into "2d clout nails," "3d d[itt]o," and "4d do," while the round-head nails were described as "2nd round head nails"; "3d

---

[58] Frances Norton Mason, ed., *John Norton & Sons, Merchants of London and Virginia* (Richmond, 1937), p. 169.

[59] *Ibid.*

[60] Hening, ed., *Statutes*, I, p. 291.

[61] Gov. Francis Bernard of Massachusetts reported to the Lords of Trade in 1768: "There has been an attempt to make nails [in Massachusetts]; it is found that they cannot be brought within a saleable price." King's MS 206, fol. 22, British Museum, transcript, Manuscript Division, Library of Congress. This is the only report of such an attempt from any of the colonies, but unsanctioned nail manufacture in Virginia may have far exceeded the Board of Trade's knowledge from official reports.

nails," "6d do," and "8d do," were also itemized.[62] As had been the case in England for three hundred years or more, this was the usual way of specifying the size of nails. When they were introduced, twopenny nails were nails that cost twopence, or 2d., per hundred, threepenny nails cost 3d. per hundred, and so on. In time the price of nails fell, but the names of the various sizes had become so familiar that they survived the loss of their literal meaning.[63] So Wray's threepenny nails were appraised, not at 3d. per hundred or 2s. 6d. per thousand, but at 1s. 6d. per thousand.

Other sizes of nails mentioned in the records were 4d., 10d., 20d., "double 10d," and "thirty peny."[64] Brads too were classified as 4d., and 20d., while one of John Norton's customers ordered "2000 small brads the size of a 3d Nail."[65] In 1773 Lord Dunmore sent for 6,000 tacks.[66]

Screws were sometimes used instead of nails for attaching hardware. John Robinson, who sent for the brads, ordered at the same time "1 doz bolts for fastning shutters with the Necessary Screws for putting them on," while Dunmore ordered "1000 Screws of different Sizes from 2 Inches to a ½ do."[67] They would have been blunt-ended screws, since the pointed wood screw was not introduced until 1846.[68]

After nails, hinges were the most important item of hardware. Before the Revolution they were made of wrought iron, or, rarely, of brass, but never of cast iron. In Williamsburg there were brass hinges in the central section of the Peyton Randolph House (circa 1730) and in Tazewell Hall (circa 1770),[69] in each case on walnut doors. In 1777 an adver-

---

[62] York Co. Recs., Wills and Inventories, XX, pp. 206–208.

[63] It appears that this way of naming nails was introduced in the fourteenth century and became common in the fifteenth, and that the price had already fallen by the middle of the fifteenth century. Salzman, *Building in England*, p. 315.

[64] "4000 4d nails," Inventory of Mathew Tuell, 1775, York Co. Recs., Wills and Inventories, XXII, p. 253; "50 M 10d [nails]," invoice of goods for Mann Page, 1771, in Mason, ed., *John Norton & Sons*, p. 124; "20 M 20d [nails]," *ibid.; Virginia Gazette* (Rind), June 7, 1770; *ibid.* (Purdie and Dixon), Aug. 20, 1772.

[65] "2,000 4d [brads]," invoice of goods for the Earl of Dunmore, 1773, in Mason, ed., *John Norton & Sons*, p. 330; "6,000 20d Brads," *ibid.;* invoice of goods for John Robinson, 1770, *ibid.*, p. 120.

[66] *Ibid.*, p. 330.

[67] *Ibid.*, pp. 120, 330.

[68] Henry C. Mercer, "The Dating of Old Houses," *Collection of Papers Read before the Bucks County Historical Society*, V (1923), pp. 536–549.

[69] Tazewell Hall was removed from Williamsburg in 1954. See S. P. Moorehead, "Tazewell Hall: a Report on its Eighteenth-Century Appearance," *Journal of the Society of Architectural Historians*, XIV (March 1955), pp. 14–17.

tiser in the *Virginia Gazette* offered "a few Pair large Brass Hinges, fit
for large Doors."[70] Although known in the eighteenth century, the kind
of hinge that is most familiar today, the butt hinge fixed on the edge
of the door, was little used in building until a cast-iron version was
patented in England in 1775,[71] and no wrought-iron colonial examples
have been found in Williamsburg buildings.

Of the various types of hinges fixed on the face of the door, the
simplest was the strap hinge, consisting of a long, horizontal strap with
an eye that turned on a hook or gudgeon or pintle that might be spiked
into the doorpost or set on a plate. Most strap hinges were probably
made locally. Derived from the strap hinge by substituting a "knuckle"
with a pin inserted to connect the two plates in place of the hook-
and-eye was the T hinge or—as it was usually termed both in England
and in Virginia—the cross garnet. When James Wray died, his stock
included "9 pr. x garnetts wt. 41 lbs.," which were appraised (at £1
14s. per hundredweight) at 12s. 6d., and "12 small x garnetts," valued
at 6d. each.[72] Cross garnets needed to be made more accurately than
the simpler strap hinges, and most of them were probably imported.
In 1770 John Robinson ordered "6 pr large X-Garnets for barn doors"
and "6 pr smaller do for 4 Pannel do" from Norton and Sons in London,
while the following year James Carter sent to the same merchants for
"1 doz pr. large X-garnet Hinges at about 30/-."[73]

H hinges and HL hinges—the terms were self-explanatory—were
mentioned in the records perhaps less frequently than cross garnets,
but surviving examples are rather commoner. Wray had six pairs of
H hinges, which evidently were small ones since they were appraised
at 3d. per pair.[74] HL hinges were listed in John Robinson's order with
the cross garnets: he needed "4 pr large HL for out Doors," "6 pr
do for 4 pannel do," and "12 pr do for window shutters."[75] George
Wythe ordered "48 pr. HL rising joint for shutters," which were to
cost £4, together with "48 pr. side hinges [for] do."[76] Rising joint hinges
are those in which the bearing surfaces of the knuckles are finished
diagonally so that the door is lifted when it is opened. A door so hung
has a self-closing tendency, and rising joint hinges were sometimes

---

[70] *Virginia Gazette* (Dixon and Hunter), Dec. 19, 1777.
[71] Mercer, "Dating of Old Houses."
[72] York Co. Recs., Wills and Inventories, XX, p. 206.
[73] Mason, ed., *John Norton & Sons*, pp. 120, 152.
[74] York Co. Recs., Wills and Inventories, XX, p. 206.
[75] Mason, ed., *John Norton & Sons*, p. 120.
[76] *Ibid.*, p. 169.

fitted for that reason, but their chief advantage was that they allowed the door to fit snug to the floor when shut and yet rise to clear a carpet when opened. The reference to side hinges indicates that Wythe was going to use the rising joint HL hinges on the folding leaves of inside shutters.

Finally there was the hinge now sometimes called the butterfly, but known in the eighteenth century as the dovetail. Wray had "2 10/12 doz. dove tails sorted," which were appraised at 8s. 6d., and Wythe required "6 pr. 4 inch dovetail hinges" priced at £1 4s. and "3 pr. smaller do."[77] Dovetail hinges were not suitable for doors of any weight, and in building were chiefly used for cupboards. In the George Wythe House, they are employed on the folding leaves of the shutters. The best place in Williamsburg to see the other main types of hinges is the Brush-Everard House, where there are cross garnets and H and HL hinges, mostly with floriated ends, indoors, and strap and HL hinges on the outside shutters.[78]

Door fastenings included three kinds, latches, bolts, and locks. During the first half of the eighteenth century, the thumb latch was doubtless the type most often used in the average Williamsburg house because its manufacture was well within the capabilities of any local smith. By the middle of the century, the knob latch was beginning to supersede it, especially where appearance was a consideration. In 1750 James Wray's stock included "1 brass knob latch," value two shillings.[79] It was probably a bow latch with a spring that had a plate or open box fixed to the stile of the door so that the works were visible. Old examples may be seen on the upper floor of the Brush-Everard House. The "6 strong Catches with brass Nobs to them fit for Chamber doors" ordered from Norton and Sons by John Robinson in 1770[80] must have been latches of the same type.

Little need be said about bolts. Robinson's order for "1 doz bolts for fastening shutters" describes their commonest function.[81] A stout

---

[77] York Co. Recs., Wills and Inventories, XX, p. 206; Mason, ed., *John Norton & Sons*, p. 169.

[78] The shutters for the window in the south gable were hung on the old strap hinges. The rest of the shutter hinges were reproductions made from a design based on marks found on the original frames and shutter. The cross garnets were on the back door, and the H and HL hinges were on room and closet doors throughout the house.

[79] York Co. Recs., Wills and Inventories, XX, p. 206.

[80] Mason, ed., *John Norton & Sons*, p. 120.

[81] Listed in Wray's inventory was "1 pr. shutter bolts." York Co. Recs., Wills and Inventories, XX, p. 206.

wooden bar running in iron staples was much used on doors.

Locks were generally of the type known today as the rim lock, called in the eighteenth century the stock lock—that is to say, a lock that had a case of iron, brass, or wood fixed to the surface of the stile on the inside of the door. In 1750 Wray had "1—10 inch stock lock" appraised at 2s. 6d. and twenty-seven smaller ones whose value ranged from 7d. to 2s. 3d.[82] Mann Page ordered "6 large stock Locks" from John Norton and Sons in 1770.[83] No eighteenth-century mortise locks have survived at Williamsburg, and they were probably not common in the colonial period; however, the house that George Wythe was planning to build in Hampton in 1771 was to have had them throughout. His order to merchants in England included "2 Mortis locks large costing £1 13s.," clearly for the outer doors, and "4 ditto smaller" that were priced at £2 12s. for room doors.[84]

Nails, screws, hinges, and door fastenings, then, were the main kinds of hardware needed for building a house, and more often than not they were imported into Virginia from England. Of course, other things had to be sent for from time to time, three of which appeared in the invoice of goods ordered by Wythe in 1771: "40 2/2 wainscot pullies for sashes," "48 brass jointed rings for shutter," and "10 pieces flywire 3 feet 1 inch square."[85] These last, which would be called insect screens today, were expensive. They cost £10 15s., or more than half as much as the four hundred panes of window glass ordered for the house. When Lord Botetourt died in 1770, the inventory of his effects at the Palace included "100 feet fly lattice" in one of the storerooms.[86] Most people troubled with mosquitoes could only resort to the "easie Remedy" described by Robert Beverley: "Whoever is persecuted with them in his House . . . let him but set open his Windows at Sun-set, and shut them again before the Twilight be quite shut in, and all the Musketaes in the Room, will go out at the Windows, and leave the Room clear."[87]

## GLASS

Glassmaking was one of the first industries to be introduced into

---

[82] *Ibid.*

[83] Mason, ed., *John Norton & Sons*, p. 124.

[84] *Ibid.*, p. 169.

[85] *Ibid.*

[86] "Inventory of the Personal Estate of his Excellency Lord Botetourt . . . ," Oct. 30, 1770, Botetourt Papers, Virginia State Archives, Richmond.

[87] Robert Beverley, *The History and Present State of Virginia*, ed. Louis B. Wright (Chapel Hill, N. C., 1947), p. 302.

British America; glass was made at Jamestown in 1608–1609 and again in 1621–1624. But it failed to take root, and all the window glass used in Williamsburg in the colonial period was imported from Britain. London and Bristol were the chief sources of supply of this "necessary," as they were of others. In 1752, however, the *Virginia Gazette* contained the following news item:

> *May* 5. They write from Glasgow, that they have begun a new Branch of Manufacture, the making of the best Crown Window Glass, which is already brought to great Perfection.[88]

Since Glasgow was in the process of becoming the leading tobacco port, this information was of special interest to Virginians.

Glass was frequently listed as part of the cargo of newly arrived ships. In 1768, for instance, the *Virginia Gazette* noted a series of arrivals at Accomack with glass on board—on May 13, *Anne* with "2 box of glass," on July 7, *Peggy* with "three half boxes of glass," and on December 8, *Old Plantation* with "1 box of window glass."[89] These three ships had called at New York, Boston, and Philadelphia, respectively, and the relatively small quantities of glass they brought may have represented what had not been sold in those cities or perhaps were individual orders for Virginia planters or tradesmen. A much larger importation of glass was recorded in a news item that appeared in the *Virginia Gazette* on January 18, 1770:

> BOSTON, *Dec.* 4 [1769]
> THE price of nails and window glass having been lately greatly advanced here, the publick are now informed that between four and five hundred casks of nails, and between three and four hundred boxes of glass, have been imported into this port, in the Captains Ware and Capesthorn, who arrived here a few days ago from Bristol.[90]

It is remarkable that it should have been considered worthwhile to advertise these commodities so far from Boston, their port of arrival.

In 1772 Robert Adam and Company of Alexandria announced that it had "Just Imported, in the Ship *Martha* . . . from *London* . . . Common Window Glass. *London* Crown Ditto."[91] These two main kinds and

---

[88] *Virginia Gazette*, Aug. 7, 1752.
[89] *Ibid.* (Purdie and Dixon), June 23, Sept. 8, Dec. 22, 1768.
[90] *Ibid.*, Jan. 18, 1770.
[91] *Ibid.*, Aug. 20, 1772.

qualities of glass used in windows were manufactured in different ways. Window glass, often called cylinder or broad glass, was blown in cylindrical tubes that were slit down one side so as to fall outward into flat sheets, while the better quality crown glass was blown into globes that were twirled around by the glass blower and thus were flattened into circular pieces by centrifugal action. Plate glass, which is cast and then polished rather than being blown, was used for mirrors in the eighteenth century, although windows were not made from it until the nineteenth.

The size of the "400 panes of crown glass" costing twenty pounds that were ordered by Wythe in 1771 was not specified.[92] Panes of eight inches by ten inches are perhaps the commonest in surviving buildings, and references to that size occurred frequently in the records. In 1768 an advertiser in the *Virginia Gazette,* James Lang, gave notice that in his warehouse at Tappahannock was "a box marked TR in a piece, No. 1, containing 100 feet of 8 by 10 WINDOW GLASS, imported last summer from *Bristol,* which the owner may have on paying charges."[93] In 1779 cabinetmaker Benjamin Bucktrout of Williamsburg, selling off his stock in trade before leaving Virginia, offered "window glass 8 by 10."[94] John Lewis, on moving to Williamsburg from New Kent County in 1770, advertised two sizes of window glass, "8 by 10 and 10 by 12."[95] A third size appeared in the goods ordered from John Norton and Sons by Thomas Everard in 1773: "100 feet window Glass—11 Inches by 9½."[96]

The interruption of trade with England caused by the Revolution necessitated finding other sources of supply, and in 1779–1780 the *Virginia Gazette* contained advertisements for window glass imported from France, Holland, and the West Indies.[97] It was not until 1792 that the manufacture of glass was established on a commercial basis at Boston.

## PAINT AND TAR

Paint colors were another import of which it seemed that the colonists could never have enough. Advertisements of colors for sale in the *Virginia Gazette,* many of which began with the words "Just imported," were

---

[92] Mason, ed., *John Norton & Sons,* p. 169.
[93] *Virginia Gazette* (Purdie and Dixon), Mar. 3, 1768.
[94] *Ibid.* (Dixon and Hunter), Aug. 28, 1779.
[95] *Ibid.* (Purdie and Dixon), Feb. 15, 1770.
[96] Mason, ed., *John Norton & Sons,* p. 355.
[97] *Virginia Gazette* (Dixon and Hunter), July 24, 1779; *ibid.* (Clarkson and Davis), Nov. 13, 1779, Feb. 19, 1780.

legion. Most paint colors were imported and sold in dry form, to be ground and mixed with oil by their users, although white lead was more often than not described in invoices as ground in oil and other colors were ordered ready mixed from time to time. For instance, in 1739 William Beverley sent to England for "As much paint of a deep olive col[o]r ready ground with linseed oyl as will paint 200 yds wainscot,"[98] and in 1771 Dr. James Carter of Williamsburg ordered from John Norton and Sons of London:

> 100 lb. White Lead Grd in Oil in 2 Cags
> 200 lb. Spanish Brown grd in Oil in 2 Do.
> 2 lbs. Lamp Black—56 lb. Yellow Okar grd in Oil[99]

Almost every familiar color, and a number whose names are unknown today, occurred in the records, although every color mentioned was not used in house painting.

Paints were among the items included in the nonimportation agreements, and consequently they were in short supply during the period immediately preceding the Revolution. "The White Lead is not to be had for Love or money," wrote Falmouth merchant William Allason to his brother-in-law in 1775. "What you have make go as far as you can."[100] There were those who took advantage of the shortage, if we are to believe the allegations of a correspondent in Pinkney's *Virginia Gazette* in 1775:

> I would recommend it to this committee to take cognizance of a certain John GREENHOW in this city. . . . It can be proved by many that he sells a number of articles at an advanced price, of at least 200 *per cent* . . . yellow oker at 15d. per pound, which cost 3d. sterling, and lake at 6 1. per pound, which cost about 40s. &c.[101]

At the same time, the need for Virginia-grown flax for linen resulted in a shortage of linseed oil. A contemporary reference to the shortage appeared in another letter by Allason, also written in 1775:

> By the bearer I send you 4 Casks Linseed Oil in place of 2 which Mr. Williamson directed. My reason for it is, that you need not

---

[98] July 24, 1739, William Beverley Letterbook, 1737–1744, Manuscript Division, New York Public Library, New York, N. Y.

[99] Mason, ed., *John Norton & Sons*, p. 152.

[100] William Allason to Gerard Hooe, Aug. 27, 1775, Letter Book of William Allason, Virginia State Archives.

[101] *Virginia Gazette* (Pinkney), Sept. 14, 1775.

expect any, or very little more this Season, occasioned by the Flax seed being chiefly bought up by those who intended Sowing it for the purpose of making Flax. You will also observe its dearer than formerly for the same reason.[102]

In June 1776 the prudent Mr. Greenhow still had linseed oil for sale "in casks of 11, 16, and 27 gallons."[103]

There was never any shortage of tar, which was used on shingled roofs and to a lesser extent on weatherboarded walls. In this instance, the flow of the commodity was in the other direction, since the production in Virginia of tar from pines growing on land unfit for tobacco was encouraged by law,[104] the object being to supply the British navy. By the second decade of the eighteenth century, as many as 3,500 barrels, each of which held thirty to thirty-two gallons, were exported from Virginia in one year.[105]

## MATERIALS AND DESIGN

With few exceptions, most of the raw materials used in the houses of Williamsburg were products of the colony, while most of the manufactured "necessaries" were imported. Without materials there can be no building, yet the effect on architectural design of the materials available was not so great as it might have been in an age less given to thinking of design in purely formal terms. In the eighteenth century, the notion that design should develop out of the nature of the materials was unheard of. According to Isaac Ware, as representative a spokesman for the period as can be found, it was "the honour of the architect that the form triumph over the materials." Virginia architecture inevitably was modified by the ready availability of some building materials and the absence or scarcity of others, but the basic assumptions and aims of the Virginia architect were not.

---

[102] Allason to Archibald Ritchie, May 16, 1775, Allason Letter Book.

[103] *Virginia Gazette* (Purdie), June 14, 1776.

[104] "An Act for encouraging the making of Tar and Hemp," passed in 1722 and reenacted in 1748, offered a reward of two shillings for every barrel of tar made according to directions given in the act. Hening, ed., *Statutes*, IV, pp. 96–99, VI, pp. 144–146.

[105] *WMQ*, 1st Ser., XXVI (January 1918), p. 214.

# 2

# *Building Crafts and Craftsmen*

A man may stand in one or more of several relationships to a house that is being built—that of the owner who will pay for it, of the architect who has designed it and who supervises its erection, of the contractor who has undertaken to build it according to the architect's plans, or that of a laborer or a craftsman employed in the work. Today he is unlikely to be more than one of those things, yet sometimes in the eighteenth century, especially if the house was a small one, he could be said to be all of them at once. More often, it happened that he combined two of them, so that the historian finds it convenient to use such composite terms as owner-designer, builder-architect, and craftsman-contractor.

The building owner who did not design his own house, essential though he was in the scheme of things, concerns the historian of architecture only insofar as his individual needs, personal or professional, found direct expression in its design. Some instances of this will be noted in the second part of this book. The present chapter will examine the men whose connections with building were more permanent and more specific. At no time will "architects," as the term is understood today, be discussed, for the architectural profession had not yet come into being in America. "Architect" had a much broader meaning in the colonial period. When in 1771 Thomas Jefferson wrote to a business correspondent "I desired the favor of you to procure me an architect," it was a master builder to execute his own designs that he wanted.[1] In

---

[1] Fiske Kimball, *Thomas Jefferson, Architect* (Boston, 1916), p. 29.

25

the eighteenth century, almost anyone who could draw might produce
the design for a building, and in Virginia the superintendence of building
works was sometimes committed to men who must have been recom-
mended by a reputation for honesty rather than technical knowledge.
Even the general contractor, or "undertaker," might lack training in
any of the building trades, making up for it in the possession of slaves,
the means to hire skilled workmen, and the equivalent of a good credit
rating.[2] Nevertheless, it was on the competence of the trained craftsman
that the building industry in eighteenth-century Virginia rested. It is
to his skill and taste that we owe most of what we admire in the buildings
that have survived. To him, therefore, the largest share of attention
must be given.

## APPRENTICESHIP

In Virginia as in England, training in the building crafts was effected
through the system of apprenticeship. In the Middle Ages, apprenticeship in England was regulated by the guilds until 1562, when it was
made a national system by the Statute of Artificers. Since this statute
was never enacted in the colonies, the system here owed its general
form to custom rather than to law, although custom was modified from
time to time by colonial legislation bearing on one or more of its aspects.
The letter of the law was beginning to be less strictly observed in England itself by the time Williamsburg was founded.

When an apprenticed orphan entered a master's service in Virginia,
an indenture was drawn up and recorded by the county clerk. Because
of the destruction of the James City County records during the Civil
War, knowledge of apprenticeship in Williamsburg and its neighborhood depends on the York County records. The following indenture,
which dates from 1762, is typical:

> This Indenture Witnesseth that John Webb an Orphan hath put
> himself, and by these Presents doth voluntarily and of his own
> free Will and Accord, put himself apprentice to William Phillips
> of Williamsburg Bricklayer to learn his Art, Trade and Mystery;
> and after the Manner of an Apprentice to serve the said William
> Phillips from the day of the date hereof for and during and unto
> the full end and Term of five Years next ensuing during all which

---

[2] Richard Taliaferro (d. 1779) was a local example of the type. See Whiffen, *Public
Buildings*, p. 141.

Term, the said Apprentice, his said Master faithfully shall serve, his Secrets keep, his lawful commands at all Times readily obey; He shall do no damage to his said Master, nor see it to be done by others, without giving Notice thereof to his said Master. He shall not waste his said Master's Goods nor lend them unlawfully to any. He shall not committ Fornication, nor contract Matrimony within the said Term. At Cards, Dice or any other unlawful Game he shall not play whereby his said Master may have damage. With his own Goods, nor the Goods of others without Licence from his Master, he shall not buy nor sell. He shall not absent himself day or night from his said Master's Service, without his Leave, nor haunt Alehouses, Taverns, or Play Houses, but in all Things behave himself as a faithful Apprentice ought to do during the said Term, And the said Master shall use the utmost of his Endeavours to teach, or cause to be taught or instructed the said Apprentice in the Trade or Mystery of a Bricklayer and procure or provide for him sufficient Meat Drink Cloaths, Washing and Lodging fitting for an Apprentice during the said Term of five Years and for the true Performance of all and singular the Covenants and Agreements aforesaid the Parties bind themselves, each unto the other firmly by these Presents. In Witness whereof the said Parties have interchangeably set their Hands and Seals hereunto dated the 21$^{st}$ day of June in the Second year of the Reign of our Sovereign Lord George the third King of Great Britain Annoque Domini one thousand seven hundred and sixty two.

John Webb
William Phillips[3]

The things enjoined on and forbidden to the apprentice varied hardly at all, whatever the master's trade, although the words might vary. Henry Johnson of Elizabeth City County, binding himself in 1709 to Nathaniel Hook of York County, carpenter, undertook not to "keep Company with any Lewd Woman," while Henry Burradall, binding himself to Matthew Burradall of the same county and trade in 1750, was not to "haunt bad Suspected Houses."[4] In rare instances, the prohibition of matrimony might have been dropped because the apprentice was already married—as perhaps was Moses Armes, "lately an Inhabitant of the Province of Maryland," whose master, house carpenter John Moss of York County, promised in 1766 "to pay him for the first four Years

---

[3] York Co. Recs., Deeds, VI, 1755–1763, pp. 463–464.
[4] *Ibid.*, Deeds, Orders, Wills Etc., XIII, 1706–1710, p. 242; *ibid.*, Deeds, V, 1741–1754, p. 385.

Service Yearly the Sum of six Pounds Cash the Year and one pair of Shoes and Stockings Yearly and every Year and the fifth or last Year to pay him the Sum of ten Pounds Cash with one pair of Shoes and Stockings as before."[5]

An annual payment such as that made by Moss to Armes was quite exceptional. It was usual, however, for a gift to be given to the apprentice at the end of his term. No such gift is mentioned in the Webb-Phillips indenture transcribed above because in 1753 the Assembly of the colony had passed "An Act for the Better Government of Servants and Slaves" in which it was directed "that every servant, male or female (except convicts) not having wages, shall, at the expiration of his, or her time of service, have and receive three pounds ten shillings current money, for freedom dues, to be paid by his or her master or owner."[6] With the matter thus regulated by law, there was in theory no need to commit it to paper, although some apprentices (or more often, their parents or guardians) chose to play safe by writing into the indenture that they should be given "such Freedom Dues as the Law directs."[7]

Before the act of 1753, the gift to be made to the apprentice at his freedom was often specified in the indenture. It always took the form of clothes or tools or both, although Daniel Pegram, apprenticed to Thomas Whitby of James City County, carpenter, in 1703/4, could have money instead of tools—"a Gentile Suite of Clothes & Carpenters Tools to the worth of five pounds or five pounds Sterling money."[8] Daniel's brother George, apprenticed five months later to Daniel Duvalle of Gloucester County, joiner, was to receive "a broad Cloth Suit of Apparell, two Dowlass Shirts one pair of Shoes one pair of Stockins & a Hatt."[9] When Owen Morris was bound to the same Thomas Whitby in 1711, the value of the tools to be given him was set at six pounds.[10] In the indenture of 1709 by which Henry Johnson abjured the company of lewd women, the tools that Nathaniel Hook was required to give him were actually named—"One Broad Ax, one Hand Saw, three Au-

---

[5] Indenture dated Apr. 20, 1766, *ibid.*, Deeds, VII, 1763–1769, pp. 182–183.

[6] Hening, ed., *Statutes*, VI, p. 359.

[7] Charles Moss to John Howlett of Gloucester County, carpenter, May 16, 1774, York Co. Recs., Deeds, VIII, 1769–1777, p. 413. An exception to the general rule that an apprentice was given no more than the legal dues at his freedom after the act of 1753 was in the indenture by which James May bound himself to William Garrow of Warwick County, bricklayer, in 1765. May was to receive "a new Suit of Cloaths and Tools fit for such an Apprentice." *Ibid.*, VII, dated Aug. 19, 1765, pp. 131–132.

[8] *Ibid.*, Deeds, Orders, Wills Etc., XII, 1702–1706, p. 165.

[9] *Ibid.*, p. 214.

[10] *Ibid.*, Orders, Wills Etc., XIV, 1709–1716, p. 112.

gurs, one Gouge Three Chissells & three Planes all New Tools."[11] The later indentures in the York County records are less specific. In 1746/47 John Harvey, carpenter, agreed to give John Garron "one suite of Cloaths befitting such Apprentice & as many Carpenters tooles as will build a common Clabboard House."[12] In 1750/51 William Langston of Warwick County, carpenter, promised to give his brother Enos at the expiration of his five-year term "four Pounds Current Money or the Value thereof in such Goods as the said Apprentice shall think fit to have likewise as many tools as shall be thought Sufficient to build a Clapboard House."[13]

The Statute of Artificers had laid down a minimum term of seven years for apprentices in England. This was longer than was needed to learn most trades, and the seven-year term was never uniformly adopted in the colonies.[14] In Virginia—to judge by the York County records— the commonest arrangement was for the apprentice to serve until he reached the age of twenty-one. In some cases this in fact meant seven years; in others—as when in 1753 a mulatto woman bound her seven-year-old son to Yorktown carpenter John Richardson[15] —it could mean twice as many; but as a rule it probably meant less. Specified terms of service for apprentices entering the building trades in York County varied between three and eight years.

The payment of premiums to masters for taking apprentices was certainly not unknown in Virginia, although it is hard to determine how common the practice was because such payments were private transactions between the master and the parent or guardian and did not have to be entered in the indentures. Occasionally in the York County records there were instances when at least a part of what might be considered a premium was paid over a period of years and so formed an item in the bargain between the parties concerned. When Frederick Bryan, an orphan, was bound for eight years to carpenter Benjamin Powell in 1756, "the Guardian of the said Frederick" agreed "to pay the said Powell forty Shillings per Year and also his Levies out of the Profits of his Estates."[16] Ellyson Armistead, binding his son James Bray Armi-

---

[11] *Ibid.*, Deeds, Orders, Wills Etc., XIII, p. 242.

[12] *Ibid.*, Deeds, V, p. 208.

[13] *Ibid.*, p. 426.

[14] For apprenticeship in the colonies in general, see Richard B. Morris, *Government and Labor in Early America* (New York, 1946), pp. 363–389.

[15] The boy's name was Gabriel Muray. York Co. Recs., Deeds, V, p. 550. Another mulatto apprentice of the same master was John Whitlock Surlock, who bound himself at the age of eighteen for six years. *Ibid.*, pp. 558–559.

[16] *Ibid.*, VI, pp. 57–58.

stead in 1757 to John Brown of Bruton Parish, carpenter, for five years, promised to "find & provide for the said James during his Term aforesaid good and sufficient Cloathing &c and to pay his Levies and that he the said James shall Claim no Freedom dues."[17] In 1765 James Taylor of Williamsburg, carpenter, taking Thomas Robinson as an apprentice for a five-year term, agreed to provide "sufficient Meat, Drink, Cloaths, Washing, and Lodging fitting for an Apprentice" on the condition that Robinson's guardian, Thomas Chisman, pay "annually two Pounds Seventeen Shillings towards the same."[18]

Besides being instructed "in the Trade or Mystery" or "Art and Mystery" or "Science or Trade" of his master—the exact phrasing varied from one indenture to another even when the master was one and the same person—the apprentice might be taught to read and write. The earliest building craft indenture in the York County records that contains such a clause dated only from 1752.[19] The apprentice was eighteen. A 1748 act of Assembly required that orphan servants and apprentices be taught to read and write.[20] Such a stipulation appeared in twelve indentures out of fifteen in the 1760s and 1770s. In only one instance was there any mention of the third "R." John Howlett of Gloucester County, carpenter, agreed that Charles Moss should be taught "to Read Write and Cypher."[21]

There is no reliable way to determine how apprentices were generally treated in Virginia. Now and again the *Virginia Gazette* contained an advertisement for an apprentice who had run away, which of course does not necessarily mean that he had been ill treated. Occasionally more than one made off at once, as occurred in 1767 when James Geddy and Francis Smith advertised from King William Court House that two apprentice carpenters and an apprentice bricklayer had left them.[22] It was a master's duty to try and recover a runaway apprentice, although he might feel that the youth was more trouble than he was worth, and he might show it too. When William Bolton ran away in 1773, Williamsburg carpenter and joiner James Gardner's advertisement stated, "He ran away once before, when a Handful of Shavings were offered as a Reward for any Person who would apprehend him."[23]

---

[17] *Ibid.*, p. 79.

[18] Dated June 17, 1765, *ibid.*, VII, p. 106.

[19] Hugh Campbell to John Richardson, *ibid.*, V, p. 486.

[20] "An Act for the better management and security of Orphans, and their estates," in Hening, ed., *Statutes*, V, p. 453.

[21] Dated May 16, 1774, York Co. Recs., Deeds, VIII, p. 413.

[22] *Virginia Gazette* (Purdie and Dixon), Apr. 2, 1767.

[23] *Ibid.*, Aug. 19, 1773.

By far the greatest number of apprenticeship indentures in the York County records related to the building trades. A statistical analysis of them probably gives a fair idea of the relative numbers of men employed in the different trades, although of course it does not provide anything approaching the actual number employed in any trade. Of forty-eight indentures dating from the period 1700–1780, thirty-six recorded the binding of apprentices to carpenters, "house carpenters," or "carpenters and joiners," seven to bricklayers, and five to joiners. Of the thirty masters concerned, twenty-one were carpenters, six were bricklayers, and three were joiners. The ratio of carpenters to bricklayers is about what one would expect considering the ratio of carpentry to brickwork in the building of the period; the small number of joiners may be explained by the fact that many carpenters undertook what was, strictly speaking, the joinery in the houses they built.

## CARPENTERS AND JOINERS

Building craftsmen were still scarce in the colony when Williamsburg was founded. Three carpenters and three bricklayers arrived from England to work on the Capitol in 1700,[24] just as a few years previously "several" workmen (trades unspecified) had come from the mother country to build the College of William and Mary.[25] Many—if not most— of the skilled men in the colony had been born and perhaps also trained in England. Among them was James Morris, carpenter, who in 1712– 1714 built the nave and chancel of Bruton Parish Church under contract.[26] One of his grandsons wrote that he was "Cheif workman in the City of Williamsburg," who "came in Virginia with Coll. Ludwell Gent . . . and was an Englishman Born." No doubt some allowance should be made for family pride. Nevertheless, with his large holdings of land that amounted in 1704 to 1,150 acres,[27] Morris was clearly a person of consequence. He lived outside the city limits on the north side of Queen's Creek,[28] the creek referred to in the following document,

---

[24] Whiffen, *Public Buildings*, p. 41.

[25] *Ibid.*, pp. 21–22.

[26] *Ibid.*, p. 79.

[27] Morris owned 100 acres in York County, 800 in James City County, and 250 in Gloucester County—assuming that he was the James Morris in the Quit Rent Rolls in each case. *VMHB*, XXXI (January 1923), p. 73; *ibid.*, (April 1923), p. 158; *ibid.*, XXXII (October 1924), p. 339.

[28] In 1708 he paid £200 for "two messuages or tenements and tracts of land" on the north side of the upper end of Queen's Creek, containing by estimation 200 acres. York Co. Recs., Deeds, Bonds, II, 1701–1713, p. 293.

which described a transaction of a type that must have been common enough in colonial Virginia where ready money was always in short supply:

> This Bill shall obleige me James Morris my Heirs &c. to pay to Christo. Jackson or Order the sume of Twenty Shill. of Curr. Money of Virga. or 6 Days Worke of a good Carpenter (to be at the Choice of the sd. Morris which he will do) when the sd. Jackson shall demd. the Same also the frame of a Sixteen foot Square house and the sd. Morris to bring the sd. frame upon a Lott in the Citty of Williamsburgh where the sd. Jackson shall Direct the sd. Jackson bringing the sd. frame over the Creek and to find Morris's Team Corn whilst they are about bringing in the sd. frame and the workmen Dyet whilst they are at work about it as Wittness my hand this 8th day of Augt. 1714.[29]

After Morris's death in 1717/18, his personal estate was appraised at about £100.[30]

James Morris's own house has disappeared, and Bruton Church is the only building in Williamsburg to which he can definitely be connected. Even less surviving work is attributable to Morris's contemporary, Richard King, although his own house, known later as Green Hill, stood until early in the twentieth century.[31] King's will indicated that he was the son of Mark King of South Mimms, Middlesex, husbandman.[32] In 1716 Richard King purchased nine lots—nearly the whole of the block bounded by Prince George, Henry, Scotland, and Nassau streets— from the trustees of the city of Williamsburg for the sum of £6 15s.[33] A master builder who bought four and one-half acres of land in what was at least nominally a city might have done so with a view to building on them and then reselling, but speculative building, which was responsible for the development of so much of London in the eighteenth century, was never much practiced in Williamsburg. Whatever King's original intentions may have been, when he died in 1727/28 his own house, valued at £20, and his outbuildings were all that stood on the property. King's landholdings were not comparable to Morris's, but the value

---

[29] Jones Family Papers, fol. 26.
[30] *Ibid.*, fol. 77.
[31] It was known in King's lifetime and for many years after his death simply as "King's."
[32] Dated Jan. 3, 1727/8, proved Feb. 19, York Co. Recs., Orders, Wills, XVI, 1720–1724, p. 504.
[33] *Ibid.*, Deeds and Bonds, III, 1713–1729, pp. 217–218.

placed on his personal estate, a little over £206, was more than twice that of Morris's.[34]

Although nothing approaching a trade precinct system in the true sense of the term can be detected in the distribution of tradesmen in Williamsburg, there was a natural tendency for property to pass from one owner to another within the same group of trades. Thus in 1736 James Wray, carpenter, bought two lots on the north side of Prince George Street west of Henry Street owned by David Minitree, bricklayer, for £86.[35] Nine years later, in 1745, he bought the lot on the same side of Prince George Street immediately to the west of Nassau Street from the widow of William Pegram, bricklayer, for £60.[36] It was the only one of the ten lots in the block that had not already been purchased by Richard King.

James Wray was a man of means. When he died in 1750, he owned eighteen slaves and household goods and tools of trade worth more than £650.[37] The inventory of his personal estate gave an impression of solid middle-class comfort and culture. Among his pictures, of which he had twenty-six on the walls in addition to "a parcel of old prints," were "2 greenwich hospitols." Wray was involved with at least two of the most important buildings in the colonial capital, since he carried out repairs at the College in 1739 and surveyed the Governor's Palace ten years later to determine what work was necessary.[38]

Another carpenter of prominence at mid-century was John Wheatley, who leased the house that then occupied the site of the present Custis-Maupin House on Duke of Gloucester Street opposite Bruton Church from 1746 until some date prior to 1757.[39] In 1751 he did carpentry, including sash work, for the new Capitol, and in September of that year he entered into a contract for repairs to the Palace.[40] At the same time in 1751–1752, he was carrying out the structural carpentry for Carter Burwell at Carter's Grove under contract.[41] The accounts show that Wheatley was paid £200 in four equal installments and that four

---

[34] *Ibid.*, Orders, Wills, XVI, p. 588.

[35] *Ibid.*, Deeds, IV, 1729–1740, p. 432.

[36] *Ibid.*, V, p. 134.

[37] *Ibid.*, Wills and Inventories, XX, pp. 206–208.

[38] Whiffen, *Public Buildings*, p. 141.

[39] *Ibid.*, p. 136.

[40] *Ibid.*, p. 142.

[41] Ledger of Carter Burwell, 1738–1756, with accounts for the building of Carter's Grove, Burwell Papers.

men, Edward Hansford, Jenkins Watkins, Hollywood, and Thomas Wade, worked for him. The accounts contain a separate entry for work valued at £21 done in Wheatley's shop in Williamsburg, which indicates the great preponderance of work done on site when a large plantation house like Carter's Grove was under construction. Smaller houses and houses in town undoubtedly contained more shopwork.

As the century advanced, building tradesmen advertised their services more frequently in the newspaper. As a rule, the announcements were brief. For example, in Dixon and Hunter's *Virginia Gazette*, April 1, 1775, John Lamb, house carpenter and joiner of Williamsburg, "BEGS Leave to inform the Public that he carries on the said Business on his own Account, and that it shall be his constant Study in prosecuting the different Branches of the same to give Satisfaction to all who may please to employ him."[42] Sometimes the advertiser mentioned one or more of his specialties. In 1771 James Gardner, carpenter and joiner, announced that he had opened a shop behind the church where he made window sashes.[43] House carpenter and joiner Joshua Kendall in 1770 begged "leave to inform the publick that he has removed to a house nearly opposite to Doctor *James Carter's*, in the back street . . . all Gentlemen who shall honour him with their commands . . . may depend on their being faithfully and expeditiously executed, upon the most reasonable terms."

> He also makes and carves CHIMNEY PIECES of wood, as ornaments to any Gentleman's apartments; and likewise makes the best and newest invented *Venetian* SUN BLINDS for windows, that move to any position so as to give different lights, they screen from the scorching rays of the sun, draw up as a curtain, prevent being overlooked, give a cool refreshing air in hot weather, and are the greatest preservatives of furniture of any thing of the kind ever invented.[44]

Lamb's, Gardner's, and Kendall's announcements show a determination to succeed, but the building trades in Williamsburg, as elsewhere, had their failures, too.

> BY great severity, and many misfortunes, the subscriber is rendered incapable of carrying on the CARPENTER business in

---

[42] *Virginia Gazette* (Dixon and Hunter), Apr. 1, 1775.
[43] *Ibid.* (Purdie and Dixon), Jan. 3, 1771.
[44] *Ibid.* (Rind), Jan. 18, 1770.

the manner he has done for several years past: He therefore would be glad to engage with any Gentleman by the year, either in *Virginia, Carolina, Florida,* or the *West Indies.*—He has tools for eight or ten hands.

JAMES ATHERTON[45]

Benjamin Powell, the most successful carpenter in Williamsburg during the third quarter of the century, never found it necessary to advertise his services. He was first recorded as a Williamsburg resident in 1753 when his daughter Hannah was baptized in Bruton Church.[46] Powell bought lot number 30 on the north side of York Road for £10 in the same year.[47] He was described in the conveyance of the lot as a wheelwright, although in subsequent documents he was called a carpenter or a house joiner. After the Revolution, in 1782, he became "Gent."[48]

For nearly a decade and a half, the only information about Powell related to his real estate transactions. In 1755 he obtained a patent for two more lots, numbers 35 and 36,[49] whose former owner had died before being able to build on either of them the "one good dwelling house, containing 20 feet in length and 16 feet in width at the least with a brick chimney thereto" that was requisite for saving a lot in that section of the town. Powell sold one of the lots in 1757 for £150,[50] a sum which, together with the reference in the conveyance to "all buildings, yards, gardens," indicates that he had built a house on it. He conveyed the other to John Brown, carpenter, for £10 in 1758.[51]

Meanwhile, in 1756 and 1757, Powell added lots 34 and 31 to his holdings. He evidently improved number 34 to some extent, because when he sold it within a year, he received £50. He combined lot 31 with lot 32, which he bought in 1758, and in the course of time built on the double lot that resulted. In 1764 he sold part of lot 32 to Simon Whitaker, bricklayer, for £35; ten years later, carpenter John Lamb bought the remainder of the two lots for £140.[52]

Benjamin Powell presumably lived on this double lot for a time, since

---

[45] *Ibid.* (Purdie and Dixon), June 18, 1767.

[46] W. A. R. Goodwin, *Historical Sketch of Bruton Church, Williamsburg, Virginia* (Williamsburg, Va., 1903), p. 125.

[47] York Co. Recs., Deeds, V, p. 565. The house he built for himself there now stands on Tyler Street. See p. 255.

[48] *Ibid.*, VI, p. 118.

[49] The patents are referred to *ibid.*, pp. 73, 133.

[50] *Ibid.*, p. 73.

[51] *Ibid.*, p. 133.

[52] *Ibid.*, pp. 70, 95, 135, 171, VII, p. 79, VIII, p. 439.

between the sale of lot 30 for £150 to his brother Seymour in 1760 and his purchase of lots 19 and 43 in 1763,[53] it constituted, so far as the records show, his only property in town. Lots 19 and 43, on the east side of Waller Street near the end of Nicholson Street, are the site of the present-day Powell-Waller House. Since Powell paid as much as £75 for the two lots, evidently there was a house on them when he took possession; however, it is reasonable to attribute to Powell himself the form to which the Powell-Waller House is restored today.

In 1764–1765 Powell did more than £388 worth of work at the Public Gaol.[54] He was chosen to fill one of five vacancies on the Williamsburg city council in 1767, and in 1769 he undertook the addition of a steeple, evidently of his own design, to Bruton Church and was paid nearly £80 for repairs at the Capitol. In 1771 Powell was awarded the contract for building the Public Hospital after the design of Robert Smith of Philadelphia, an undertaking that he completed in 1773.[55] The fact that the three jobs overlapped suggests that he had a considerable shop, although it is important to remember that because he was a carpenter, he sublet the brickwork—a large item in both the steeple and the hospital—to others.[56] By 1774 Powell was well enough established as a public figure to be made a member of the Williamsburg committee for the enforcement of the Continental Association.[57] In 1776 he furnished tents valued at £63 to the army, received £590 "for sundry work for the Troops in W'msburg," directed the employment of "six slaves now in the public jail, the property of certain Tories . . . upon the prison lot for the use of the public," and appraised furniture in the Palace and blankets and "other effects" taken in a prize ship.[58] As marshal of the Court of Admiralty, he signed a 1779 notice in the *Virginia Gazette* advertising the contents of a captured privateer brig and sloop.[59] His first wife, Annabella, died in January 1782,[60] and in June he sold his house on Waller Street for £340.[61] He had purchased 220 acres costing

---

[53] *Ibid.*, VI, p. 299, VII, p. 4.

[54] Whiffen, *Public Buildings*, p. 150.

[55] *Virginia Gazette* (Purdie and Dixon), Dec. 3, 1767; Whiffen, *Public Buildings*, pp. 150–152, 164.

[56] The master bricklayer at the Hospital was Samuel Spurr. See p. 40.

[57] *Virginia Gazette* (Purdie and Dixon), Dec. 22, 1774.

[58] *VMHB*, XXVI (October 1918), p. 398; *Calendar of Virginia State Papers*, VIII (Richmond, 1890), pp. 149, 150, 173, 226.

[59] *Virginia Gazette* (Dixon and Hunter), Aug. 7, 1779.

[60] Her tombstone is in Bruton Parish churchyard.

[61] York Co. Recs., Deeds, VI, p. 118.

£840 on the south side of Queen's Creek in 1774 where he lived during his last years. In 1784 he was appointed a justice of the peace in York County.[62] He died in 1791, leaving to his second wife, Fanny, two-thirds of his "Household and Kitchen furniture (excepting Plate) half a Box of Sugar now in the House, fifteen Gallons of Wine and all the old Rum," and desiring his executors to "inclose the lot in Williamsburg whereon John Bryan now lives and remove the Kitchen thereon to such part of the Lot as my said Wife may chuse and to refit the same . . . in a frugal and comfortable manner.[63]

Benjamin Powell's career shows to what prominence a master craftsman could attain in Virginia. Unfortunately, little is known of the building works—apart from the public undertakings—from which the wealth that raised him up presumably derived.

## BRICKLAYERS

Bricklayers were less numerous than carpenters, and the evidence suggests that they were less apt to enter into general contracts. David Minitree, presumably the son of the smith of the same name who worked at the Capitol and the Gaol in 1710, bought lot 317 from Henry Cary for £10 in 1723, and purchased the neighboring lot, no. 316, for £15 from the trustees of the city in 1725.[64] He then rented the two lots to carpenter James Wray, who was occupying them when he purchased them for the sum of £86 in July 1736. The location of the house in which Minitree lived is unknown. Perhaps it was located in that part of Williamsburg which lay in James City County, whose records are lost, or perhaps he already owned the plantation that was offered for sale after his death thirty-eight years later.

The earliest of the buildings attributable to Minitree, Mattapony Church in King and Queen County where his name appears on a brick over one of the doorways, dates from the early 1730s.[65] In 1746 he worked on Marlborough, the house of John Mercer in Stafford County, where he made and burned 104,604 bricks at 4s. 6d. per thousand, stacked and burned 11,200 more at 1s. 6d., and built part of the house,

---

[62] *Ibid.,* VIII, pp. 391, 394, 400; W. G. Stanard, "Abstracts of Virginia Land Patents," *VMHB*, I (October 1893), p. 192.

[63] His will is in York Co. Recs., Wills and Inventories, XXIII, pp. 222–225.

[64] H. R. McIlwaine, ed., *Legislative Journals of the Council of Colonial Virginia* (Richmond, 1918–1919), I, p. 493; York Co. Recs., Deeds, Bonds, III, pp. 415, 447.

[65] George Carrington Mason, *Colonial Churches of Tidewater Virginia* (Richmond, 1945), p. 304.

which has disappeared, for £45 10s. 4d.[66] Minitree undertook the brick-work of Carter's Grove in James City County for Carter Burwell in 1751.[67] The bricks for the house were evidently made by Burwell's own servants or slaves although Minitree burned them. The contract price, which was for brickwork only, was £115, and Burwell was pleased enough with the result to make Minitree a present of £25. Minitree was also responsible for glazing the 540 window panes of the house at 2½d. per square.

The Carter's Grove accounts indicate that Minitree had a son. That his family affairs did not always run smoothly is evident from the following notice in Joseph Royle's *Virginia Gazette*, February 12, 1762:

> Whereas my Wife *Elizabeth (Minnetree)* hath eloped from me, with-out any reasonable Cause, I do therefore forewarn all Persons from crediting her on my Account, as I will not pay any Debts she may contract.
>
> *David Minnetree*[68]

David Minitree died before December 1774, for on the first of that month Purdie and Dixon's *Virginia Gazette* contained an announcement of the sale of his James City County property:

> *To be* SOLD *on* Tuesday *the 20th Instant on the Premises,* the Tract of Land whereon *David Minitree,* deceased, lately lived, containing 163 Acres, within five Miles of *Williamsburg,* adjoining *Greenspring* and *Powhatan* Swamp, chiefly Wood Land, and some excellent Swamp already drained, and now fit for a Meadow. The Terms will be made known on the Day of Sale.
>
> JOHN BROWNE, Sheriff[69]

Bricklayer Samuel Spurr must have been David Minitree's junior by a few years. The first mention of Spurr dates from 1749, when he bought lot 27 on the north side of York Road from Benjamin Waller for the sum of £10.[70] In 1753 he added lot 28 to his holding, and in 1755 lot 29.[71] In 1752 he undertook the building of the wall around Bruton

---

[66] John Mercer Account Book, Feinstone Collection, American Philosophical Society, Philadelphia.

[67] Burwell Ledger.

[68] *Virginia Gazette,* Feb. 12, 1741.

[69] *Ibid.* (Purdie and Dixon), Dec. 1, 1774.

[70] York Co. Recs., Deeds, V, p. 340.

[71] *Ibid.,* p. 568, VI, p. 37.

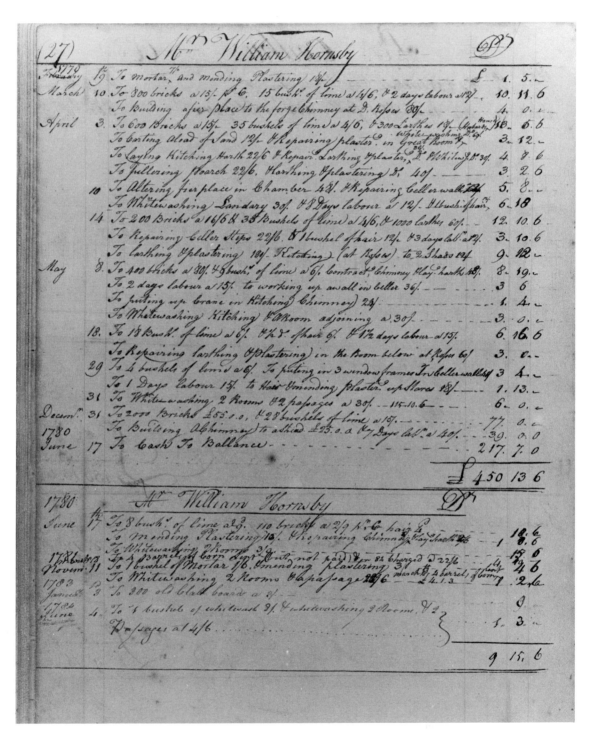

*Figure 1*   Page from Account Book (1776–1794) of Humphrey Harwood, Williamsburg bricklayer.

churchyard after another bricklayer had failed to perform his contract.[72] Spurr's advertisement for bricklayers in the *Virginia Gazette* in October 1771 indicates that he was subcontractor under Benjamin Powell for the brickwork of the Public Hospital.[73] Another advertisement for bricklayers or plasterers in July 1773 may or may not have been occasioned by the same undertaking.[74] In October 1779 Dixon and Nicolson's *Virginia Gazette* contained Spurr's announcement that he was going out of business because of ill health:

> This is to acquaint those Gentlemen that have any demands against me, to apply to Mr. *William Goodson* at his store, who has money lodged in his hands to satisfy any demands against me, and should be glad they would immediately apply as I do not expect to pay any interest from the date hereof, as my infirmity has induced me to decline carrying on business any longer. I should be glad to have my concerns settled as soon as possible.
> SAMUEL SPURR
> I have about 15 or 20,000 bricks, which I will barter for corn.[75]

After Spurr's retirement, the "cheif workman in the City of Williamsburg" in the bricklaying trade was Humphrey Harwood. He first appeared in the columns of the *Virginia Gazette* just ten years before, in 1769, when he offered forty shillings for the return of an indentured servant, Arthur Kating, a bricklayer who had run away.[76] Three months before, Harwood had taken the fifteen-year-old Richard Hobday as an apprentice "to learn his Art, Trade and Mystery," and also to be taught to read and write.[77] Young Hobday was to serve until the age of twenty-one, but he evidently decided that he could not stay the course, because two or three weeks before the second anniversary of Hobday's entry into Harwood's service—in September 1771—he too ran away. Harwood put his price at twenty shillings.[78] The previous June, Harwood had announced in the *Gazette* that journeymen bricklayers would meet with good encouragement by applying to him.[79] In 1774 he became a comember with Benjamin Powell of the Williamsburg committee for the en-

---

[72] Whiffen, *Public Buildings*, p. 145.
[73] *Ibid.*, p. 164.
[74] *Virginia Gazette* (Purdie and Dixon), July 8, 1773.
[75] *Ibid.* (Dixon and Hunter), Oct. 16, 1779.
[76] *Ibid.* (Purdie and Dixon), Dec. 21, 1769.
[77] York Co. Recs., Deeds, VIII, p. 23.
[78] *Virginia Gazette* (Purdie and Dixon), Sept. 5, 1771.
[79] *Ibid.*, June 6, 1771.

forcement of the Continental Association, and, like Powell, he purchased a plantation during the Revolutionary period that lay in James City County east of Williamsburg on the north side of the old road to Yorktown.[80] Harwood's townhouse was on the north side of Duke of Gloucester Street.[81] In 1782 his "family" consisted of seven whites and seven blacks.[82] He died in 1789, leaving his plantation to his son William, who succeeded him in the bricklaying business and was responsible for the brickwork of the St. George Tucker House, and his Williamsburg property to his other son, Humphrey. At his death he owned fourteen blacks, nine men and five women, and livestock that included forty-six head of cattle and two beefs.[83] Harwood's most valuable bequest to posterity was unintentional. An account book for the years 1776–1794 was discovered in 1930 by Singleton Moorehead in the attic of a modern outbuilding behind the George Reid House.[84] It shows that Harwood worked at the College, the Courthouse of 1770, the Capitol, and for many private residents. Most of the period covered by the account book falls after the seat of government was removed to Richmond when there was little new building in Williamsburg. For that reason, it is a precious document of itemized repairs to earlier buildings. A specimen page is reproduced here as *Figure 1,* and other entries are transcribed in the Appendix.

### PLANS AND PROCEDURES

Besides the carpenters, joiners, and bricklayers, there were also members of the secondary trades—painters and plasterers, paper hangers and plumbers—and men like James Wilson, *"Carver, from* LONDON," who announced in the *Virginia Gazette* on June 20, 1755, that he "MAKES all Kinds of Ornaments in Stuco, human Figures and Flowers, *&c &c* Stuco Cornishes in Plaster, carved or plain, after the best Manner: likewise Stone finishing on Walls; he likewise carves in Wood, cuts Seals in Gold or Silver; and is to be spoken with at Mr. *Anthony Hay's,* Cabinet-maker, in *Williamsburg.* "[85] Only the carpenters, joiners, and bricklayers,

---

[80] *Ibid.,* Dec. 22, 1774; York Co. Recs., Deeds, VI, p. 121.

[81] York Co. Recs., Deeds, VI, p. 138.

[82] List of Heads of Families in Williamsburg in 1782, Virginia State Archives.

[83] Harwood's will, dated Aug. 25, 1788, and proved Apr. 20, 1789, is in York Co. Recs., Wills and Inventories, XXIII, pp. 176, 220.

[84] It comprises three ledgers, B, 1776–1791, C, 1784–1796, and D, 1793–1794. Ledger D contains the accounts of the estate of Humphrey Harwood, Sr., as settled by his son William.

[85] *Virginia Gazette,* June 20, 1755.

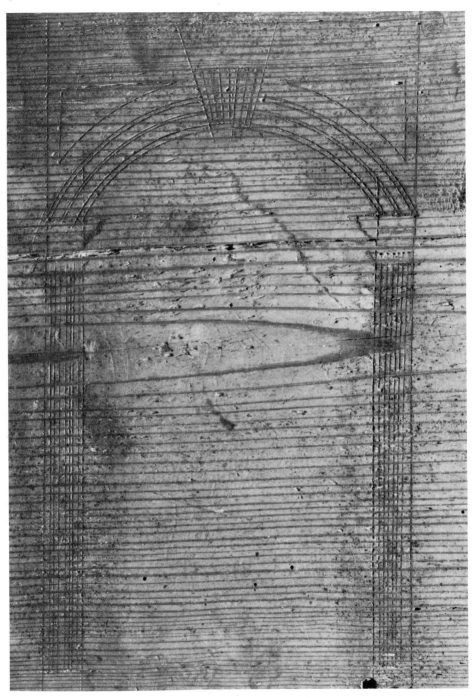

*Figure 2*    Design for archway incised on board. Belle Farm, Gloucester County, Virginia.

however, had any claim to the term master builder in its proper sense.

These men, often in close collaboration with the building owner, designed as well as built most of the houses of eighteenth-century Williamsburg. No plan from which a Williamsburg house was built has been identified. Most of the colonial plans that have survived elsewhere are of a diagrammatic nature,[86] and it may be assumed that those from which the Williamsburg master builders worked were no exception to

[86] See, for instance, the plans of the Ninyon Challoner House (1735), the Daniel Ayrault House (1739), and the James Gordon Farm (1733), at Newport, R. I., reproduced

*Figure 3*    Mantel design on board. Belle Farm, Gloucester County, Virginia.

the rule. On the other hand, working drawings for the individual craftsman to follow might have been as detailed and precise as the designs
for an archway and a mantel found on boards incorporated in Belle
Farm, Gloucester County, well demonstrate (*Figures 2 and 3*). Both features were executed substantially as designed.

Like a public building, a house might have been built under a general
contract; only infrequently, however, were tenders invited through announcements in the press.[87] There are as few building contracts relating
to Williamsburg houses as there are plans for them. In the case of a
general contract, if the "undertaker" were a carpenter, he would sublet
the brickwork, and if he were a bricklayer, he would sublet the carpentry.
In other instances, the building owner, instead of agreeing with a single
master builder for the whole work at a fixed price, might choose to
contract with members of each of the necessary trades separately. Carter
Burwell followed this procedure at Carter's Grove in the 1750s, as did
St. George Tucker when he built his house on Nicholson Street forty
years later. Such a procedure may well have been more common than
the general contract in domestic building, but without more evidence
we cannot be sure.

---

in Antoinette F. Downing and Vincent J. Scully, Jr., *The Architectural Heritage of Newport
Rhode Island 1640–1915* (Cambridge, Mass., 1952), plates 71 and 72.

[87] One such announcement read *"Pursuant to the will of* Samuel Hargrove, *deceased,
will be exposed to publick sale,* on Monday *the 17th* of November, *at his late dwelling-house.*
. . . Also to be let, on the same day, the building of a house 20 feet by 26, with a
stone or brick chimney. One half of the consideration to be paid on the raising, and
the other half when the house is finished in a good and workmanlike manner . . .
The EXECUTORS." *Virginia Gazette* (Purdie), Oct. 24, 1777.

# 3

# *Craftsmen's Tools and Books*

The tools used in building have changed little over the centuries, and the craftsman of today would be able to recognize nearly all of the tools employed by his predecessors two hundred years ago. He would, however, call some of them by different names, since the terminology of a practical craft is less static than is the evolution of its forms, methods, and instruments. It is to documentary manuscript and printed records that we owe much of our knowledge about the tools used in eighteenth-century Williamsburg. The most informative records are the inventories of the personal estates of deceased craftsmen, orders for tools placed with English merchants, and advertisements in the *Virginia Gazette*. A letter from John Blair, acting governor of the colony, to the Board of Trade in London in 1768 indicated that very few tools were made in Virginia.

> Our pig-iron and some bar-iron is chiefly shipped to Britain. We do not make a saw, augur, gimlet, file or nails, nor steel; and most tools in the country are imported from Britain.[1]

The actual tools once used in Williamsburg, unearthed during archaeological excavations at various Williamsburg sites, confirm the print and manuscript sources. These artifact tools comprise a rich study collection for insight into the colonial builder's craft. It should be remembered, however, that tools—a craftsman's means of livelihood—were

---

[1] King's MS. 206, fol. 26.

45

regarded as valuable possessions and were often handed down from one generation to the next.

## WOODWORKERS' TOOLS

The one tool without which there could have been little building in Virginia was the woodsman's felling ax. To appreciate its importance, it must be noted that felling trees with a saw was a development of the late nineteenth century; in colonial times, all trees were felled with axes. The English felling ax of the seventeenth and eighteenth centuries had a blade, or bit, much longer than it was broad, and the handle, or helve, was straight. The American ax, with its much shorter, nearly square blade and heavy poll, as that part of the head on the side of the helve opposite from the bit is called, made its appearance in New England and the Middle Colonies before 1750, according to Henry Mercer.[2] All of the old felling axes that have been found at Williamsburg, however, were English or approximated the type. This is not surprising in view of the general dependence of Virginians on Great Britain for tools.[3] An order from Mann Page of Rosewell plantation to merchant John Norton in London in 1770 for "4 Dozn. Felling Axes" gave an idea of the numbers in which this essential tool must have been imported into the colony.[4]

The broad ax, a heavy, short-handled tool held with two hands, was used to dress the vertical faces of timbers that had been rough-squared with the felling ax. In the older type of broad ax, the bit was ground to a basil or beveled like a chisel from right to left so that the surface to be dressed had to be against the carpenter's left side as he worked right-handed. Mann Page ordered "6 Broad Axes" at the same time he did the forty-eight felling axes.[5] Half a century earlier, an appraisal of the effects of carpenter James Morris, contractor for the nave of Bruton Church, included "2 Old Broad Axes" valued at five shillings.[6]

---

[2] Henry C. Mercer, *Ancient Carpenters' Tools* (Doylestown, Pa., 1929), p. 4. See also n. 3.

[3] In a letter dated June 1957, W. L. Goodman suggested another reason: "It is not surprising that the American wedge axe does not figure in your collections, as it is treated as quite a novelty in the earliest tool catalogue I have so far encountered, that of William Marpels & Sons, Sheffield, dated 1864. In spite of Mercer, I would personally put its introduction in its present form to about 1820."

[4] Mason, ed., *John Norton & Sons*, p. 124.

[5] *Ibid.*

[6] Dated Mar. 26, 1718, Jones Family Papers.

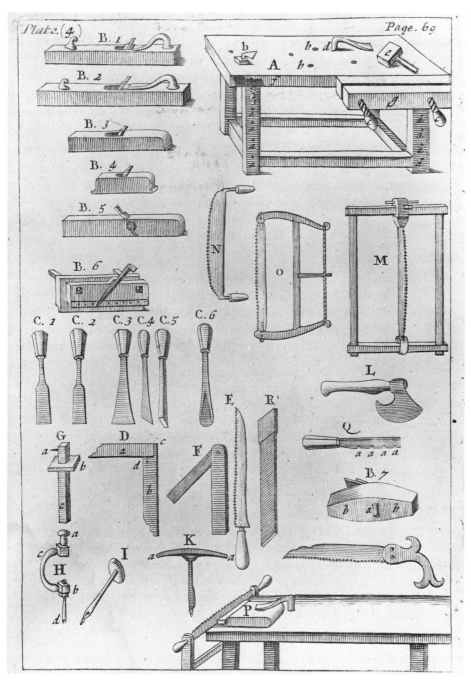

*Figure 4* Joiner's tools from Joseph Moxon, *Mechanick Exercises* (London, 1703),
Plate 4. A. work bench, B. planes, C. chisels, D. square, E. compass saw, F.
bevel, G. gauge, H. piercer, I. gimlet, J. hand saw, K. auger, L. hatchet, M.
pit saw, N. whip saw, O. frame or bow saw, P. whetting block, Q. saw wrest,
R. miter square.

James Morris also owned "2 narrow Axes," which with "1 old hammer 1 old Ads & 2 old Spades" were appraised at 4s. 6d. In 1770 "two broad axes, one narrow ditto" were taken from a certain George Churn, who evidently had stolen them together with other tools from Edward Stubblefield of Charles City County.[7] What these narrow axes were is uncertain, since none of the standard reference works, old or new, gives the term. Two axheads resembling those illustrated by Mercer as mortising axes are in the Colonial Williamsburg archaeological collections,[8] and it seems likely that they are examples of the narrow ax of the Virginia records, which was in fact a mortising ax.

Smaller cousins of these axes were the short-handled hatchets. The inventory of Williamsburg carpenter James Wray, who died in 1750, included one hatchet valued at two shillings.[9] Like the axes, hatchets came in broad and narrow varieties, as an order from Lord Dunmore to John Norton and Sons in 1773 for a half-dozen of each indicated.[10] A special kind of broad hatchet, of which old examples have been found at Williamsburg,[11] was the shingling hatchet, which had a hammerlike poll for driving nails in and a notch in the bit for pulling them out. The lathing hatchet shared both features with the shingling hatchet, but it was narrower in the bit and had a flat top to facilitate nailing laths just under the ceiling. Again, examples have been found at Williamsburg,[12] although, as in the case of the shingling hatchet as well, the lathing hatchet was not listed under its full name in any of the eighteenth-century records.

The best description of the adz and its uses, as of so many other tools, was in that paragon of handbooks, Joseph Moxon's *Mechanick Exercises:*

> As the Ax hath its edge parallel to its Handle, so the *Adz* hath its edge athwart the Handle, and is ground to a Basil on its inside to its outer edge. . . . Its general Use is to take thin Chips off Timber or Boards, and to take off those Irregularities that the Ax by reason of its Form cannot well come at; and that a Plane (though rank set) will not make riddance enough with.[13]

---

[7] *Virginia Gazette* (Rind), June 7, 1770.

[8] Colonial Williamsburg Archaeological Collections, 7140–28.A, 7142–9.L.

[9] York Co. Recs., Wills and Inventories, XX, p. 207.

[10] Mason, ed., *John Norton & Sons*, p. 330.

[11] Colonial Williamsburg Archaeological Collections, 7148–9.A, 7141–18.D.

[12] *Ibid.*, 7147–8.C, 7144–10.B, 7143–11.B.

[13] Joseph Moxon, *Mechanick Exercises: or the Doctrine of Handy-Works*, 3rd ed. (London, 1703), p. 119.

An adz was among the tools found in George Churn's possession.[14]

Several of the many kinds of saws were mentioned in the records. The largest was the pitsaw used to saw timber into boards, so called because the balk to be sawed is laid over a pit or trench in which one of the two sawyers stands. Moxon described the pitsaw as "a great Saw fitted into a square frame" and illustrated it (*Figure 4*).[15] A pitsaw was advertised for sale in the *Virginia Gazette* by Lawrence Howse in Sussex County in 1777.[16] In 1773 Lord Dunmore ordered from John Norton and Sons "1 Frame Saw," doubtless a pitsaw, together with "3 Dozen files for do," which were triangular files for sharpening the saw.[17] On his death in 1778, "1 large framed saw" that had belonged to Edmund Dickinson was appraised at five pounds.[18]

"Open" or unframed two-handed saws that had a handle at each end included the whipsaw and the crosscut saw. The former performed the same function as the pitsaw. In 1718 James Morris left "an Old Steel Whip Saw" valued at one pound; sixty years later Edmund Dickinson's whipsaw was appraised at three pounds.[19] The crosscut saw was not used for making boards but, as its name implies, for cross cutting the trunks of ax-felled trees, and it was distinguished from other saws in that its teeth were shaped and sharpened so the effort was divided equally between the two sawyers. When James Whaley died in 1701, he owned "2 cross cut saws with wrest and file," a wrest being an instrument for setting the teeth of a saw.[20] Lawrence Howse in 1777 offered a crosscut saw for sale in the *Virginia Gazette*.[21] The announcement that an "iron plate cross-cut saw" had been taken from the delinquent George Churn shows that steel had not altogether superseded hammer-hardened iron for saws even in 1770.[22]

References to handsaws were numerous. The inventory of James Morris's personal property in 1718 included "1 Old hand Saw" that was

[14] *Virginia Gazette* (Rind), June 7, 1770.
[15] Moxon, *Mechanick Exercises.* See also Mercer, *Ancient Carpenters' Tools*, figs. 21–24.
[16] *Virginia Gazette* (Dixon and Hunter), Dec. 19, 1777.
[17] Mason, ed., *John Norton & Sons*, p. 330.
[18] York Co. Recs., Wills and Inventories, XXII, p. 401.
[19] Jones Family Papers; York Co. Recs., Wills and Inventories, XXII, p. 401.
[20] York Co. Recs., Deeds, Orders, Wills, XI, 1698–1702, p. 506. The back of the blade, or plate, of a saw is thicker than its cutting edge. In order that the slit, or kerf, in the wood being sawed may be wide enough for the whole plate to follow through, the teeth are turned outward by putting the wrest, or saw-set, between each pair of teeth and giving it a wrench.
[21] *Virginia Gazette* (Dixon and Hunter), Dec. 19, 1777.
[22] *Ibid.* (Rind), June 7, 1770.

valued at one shilling.[23] When James Wray died in 1750, his handsaws were included in "a parcel carpenters and joiners tools" and were not itemized, although the inventory shows that he possessed forty-four handsaw files that were valued at 1s. 9d. a dozen.[24] A distinct type of handsaw was the tenon saw or, as it was generally called in Virginia, tenant saw, whose blade, or plate, was stiffened by a metal rib along the upper edge. The inventories of John Lewellin (1733), James Wray (1750), and Thomas Cobbs (1774) mentioned tenant saws, while that of Edmund Dickinson (1778) listed a tenant saw and also "3 dove tailed . . . and 1 Sash saw," varieties of the same tool.[25] The Matthew Tuell inventory of 1775 included "1 cross cut tenent saw,"[26] perhaps a larger version of the tool.

Quite different in character and purpose from the tenon saw was the compass saw, "a very narrow saw, without a back . . . used to divide boards into pieces of curved outline."[27] In 1770 John Robinson ordered "½ doz Compass saws sized from largest to keyhole saw" from John Norton and Sons.[28] At the same time, he sent for a panel saw, stipulating that it should have a steel plate. A panel saw was among the tools owned by Edmund Dickinson at his death in 1778.[29] Dickinson also owned an example of the bow saw, that interesting and useful tool in which a thin blade that could be turned on its long axis to any angle desired was strained between the lower ends of an H-shaped frame by means of a twisted cord between the upper ends.[30]

The froe (or frow) was a splitting tool. It had a narrow, heavy blade about a foot long with a wooden handle at right angles to it. The handle was held in the left hand while the workman, holding a froe club in his right hand, drove the blade into the wood to be split, which was held upright in a froe horse.[31] The froe was used most often for making shingles, and to a lesser extent for splitting boards. It was frequently

---

[23] Jones Family Papers.

[24] York Co. Recs., Wills and Inventories, XX, p. 207.

[25] *Ibid.*, XVIII, p. 59, XX, p. 207, XXII, pp. 246, 401; Mercer, *Ancient Carpenters' Tools*, p. 139.

[26] York Co. Recs., Wills and Inventories, XXII, p. 253.

[27] *Dictionary of Architecture*, II, p. 119.

[28] Mason, ed., *John Norton & Sons*, p. 120.

[29] York Co. Recs., Wills and Inventories, XXII, p. 401.

[30] Mercer, *Ancient Carpenters' Tools*, pp. 149–150.

[31] For descriptions and illustrations of the froe, froe club, and froe horse, see *ibid.*, pp. 11–15.

mentioned in documentary records such as the James Morris inventory of 1718, where both spellings occurred:

> To 1 frow ..........—,, 1 ,, 3
>  . . . .
> To 1 1 froe ..........—,, 1 ,, 3.[32]

There are many examples of froes in the archaeological collections at Williamsburg.

The plane family included many types, and cabinetmaker Edmund Dickinson owned "81 Planes of different sorts."[33] The first plane to be used for dressing wood after the ax or saw was the jack plane or fore plane. Moxon said that the former was the carpenter's, and the latter the joiner's, name for the same tool.[34] This plane was from sixteen to eighteen inches long, and the iron or cutting bit was ground to a convex curve to take off coarse shavings. The John Lewellin inventory of 1733 itemized, among the planes, "3 jacks,"[35] while the Wray inventory of 1750 included two fore planes valued at 1s. 7d. each. John Robinson's 1770 order to John Norton and Sons specified two fore planes.[36]

Moxon wrote that long plane or jointer were two names for one tool used by the carpenter and the joiner respectively. This presumably was correct in Moxon's day, although the fact that Robinson sent to England for "One Jointer, one long Plane"[37] suggests that a distinction between them came to be made. Moxon described the tool and its function:

> The *Joynter* is made somewhat longer than the *Fore-plane,* and hath its *Sole* perfectly straight from end to end. Its Office is to follow the *Fore-plane,* and to *shoot* an edge perfectly straight, and not only an edge, but also a Board of any thickness; especially when a *Joynt* is to be *shot.*[38]

---

[32] Jones Family Papers.

[33] York Co. Recs., Wills and Inventories, XXII, p. 401.

[34] Mills Brown, Research Dept., CWF, found a few eighteenth-century inventories that listed both jack planes and fore planes; the distinction was implied in nineteenth-century American tool catalogs, which listed the fore plane as a slightly longer tool than the jack, corresponding to the English trying plane.

[35] York Co. Recs., Wills and Inventories, XVIII, p. 59, XX, p. 206.

[36] Mason, ed., *John Norton & Sons,* p. 120.

[37] *Ibid.*

[38] Moxon, *Mechanick Exercises,* p. 69.

James Morris owned "2 Joynters" that were appraised at four shillings after his death in 1718, and in 1755 "long Planes" were advertised for sale in the *Virginia Gazette* by Christopher Ford, Jr., and Anthony Hay.[39]

A much shorter plane was the smoothing plane. Only six or seven inches long, it was used to put the finishing touches on joints. In 1733 John Lewellin owned two smoothing planes, and in 1750 James Wray had three that were valued at 1s. 6d. each.[40]

The jack plane, long plane, and smoothing plane were designed to produce a flat surface and could be moved freely across the wood in any direction. They belonged to the group known as bench planes. The fitting planes differed in that they were designed to produce rabbets and grooves in the edges of boards to be joined together, and were equipped with a fence—that is, a downward projection of, or attachment to, the stock. Pressed against the side of the board, the fence guided the plane as it moved along the edge. Perhaps the most frequently used fitting plane was the plow, whose "office," wrote Moxon, was "to plow a narrow square *Groove* on the edge of a Board."[41] Morris had two plows valued at 2s. 6d., while Robinson ordered "One best plated plow with set of Irons" from John Norton and Sons.[42]

The fence was an integral part of the stock of the plow and therefore was immovable. The mysterious sounding moving fillister had a separate fence that was attached by screws working in slots and so could be adjusted in order to vary the width of the cut. "One moving philister" was among the tools taken from George Churn in 1770; St. George Tucker paid Robert Greenhow twelve shillings for "1 movg phillester" in 1791.[43]

Different from the fitting planes were the molding planes, described by Mercer as a "variety of decorative instruments, which in make, adjustment and blade contour, seem to have no end."[44] They were of great importance to the colonial builder, who depended on them for most of his decorative effects both indoors and out. Christopher Ford and Anthony Hay advertised "Moulding Planes of all Sorts" in the *Virginia*

---

[39] Jones Family Papers; *Virginia Gazette,* Mar. 21, 1755.

[40] York Co. Recs., Wills and Inventories, XVIII, p. 59, XX, p. 206.

[41] Moxon, *Mechanick Exercises,* p. 72.

[42] Jones Family Papers; Mason, ed., *John Norton & Sons,* p. 120.

[43] Memorandum by William Harwood, Box 90, Tucker-Coleman MSS, Swem Library, College of William and Mary, Williamsburg, Va.

[44] Mercer, *Ancient Carpenters' Tools,* p. 130.

*Gazette* in 1755.[45] One can be sure that they included the sash plane, a double plane that cut the molding and the glass-holding rabbet of a window sash simultaneously. John Robinson's order for tools in 1770 included this vital tool—"2 Sash planes"—together with other molding planes whose names are more or less self-explanatory: "One set of Cornish [cornice] planes for Carpenter & House Joiner," a set of "Surbase plains for chair boards," another set of surbase planes "for hand rails to staircases," and a set of "Sash & door planes."[46] "One bead plane" was taken from Churn in 1770.[47] It was a plane in which both the iron and the sole of the stock were concave. Finally, the tooth plane scored the surface of wood to be veneered in order to give a key for glue. Ford and Hay had tooth planes for sale in 1755.[48]

The draw knife or drawing knife was a shaping tool that was pulled toward the user instead of being pushed away from him as was the plane. Consisting of a narrow blade basiled on its upper side and a wooden handle at right angles at either end, it was used for thinning the tops of shingles and for taking off shavings generally. It appeared in the inventories of John Dickeson (1676) and Armistead Lightfoot (1772), in both of which it was called a drawing knife. John Robinson ordered "2 best drawing knives" from England in 1770.[49] There are three examples in the Colonial Williamsburg archaeological collections.

Gouges were chisels with concave blades. In 1718 carpenter James Morris had "19 Chisells & Gouges" appraised at 9s. 6d.[50] When cabinet-maker Edmund Dickinson died in 1778, he owned "47 Carving Chissels & Gouges" worth £4 14s.[51] In 1770 John Robinson sent to England for "2 doz Chissels sorted from framing to small tinners."[52] Used with a mallet for forming large mortises, the framing chisel par excellence was the firmer or former. It was advertised for sale under the second name by Ford and Hay in the *Virginia Gazette* in 1755.[53] The mortise chisel was employed for smaller mortises such as those in windows and doors. Edmund Dickinson's "6 Morticeing Chissels" were appraised

[45] *Virginia Gazette*, Mar. 21, 1755.
[46] Mason, ed., *John Norton & Sons*, p. 120.
[47] *Virginia Gazette* (Rind), June 7, 1770.
[48] *Ibid.*, Mar. 21, 1755.
[49] York Co. Recs., Deeds, Orders, Wills, V, p. 166; *ibid.*, Wills and Inventories, XXII, p. 124; Mason, ed., *John Norton & Sons*, p. 120.
[50] Jones Family Papers.
[51] York Co. Recs., Wills and Inventories, XXII, p. 401.
[52] Mason, ed., *John Norton & Sons*, p. 120.
[53] *Virginia Gazette*, Mar. 21, 1755.

at one pound.[54] The paring chisel, a sharper version of the firmer used without a mallet, did not appear in the records examined unless the "3 trimers chiswells" in the inventory of Thomas Barbar,[55] who died in 1727, can be identified as examples of this tool.

The most important tool for boring was the T-shaped auger. When he died, Morris had five augers valued at twelve shillings.[56] The blade, or bit, of the auger varied in form, but it always was derived from a section of hollow cylinder, straight or twisted, until the invention of the spiral auger late in the eighteenth century. Among the augers in the archaeological collections is one of the spiral kind, of uncertain date.

A miniature one-handed tool for boring that followed much the same development as the auger was the gimlet. At his death in 1750, James Wray owned no fewer than 116 "gimblets" worth threepence each.[57] In 1770 Mann Page ordered "1 Dozn. Gimblets sorted" from John Norton and Sons, and John Robinson sent for "3 doz best box handle double bit Gimblets."[58] Another boring tool specified by Robinson in the same order was the stock—"One stock & set of bits to fit it"— while Edmund Dickinson had "1 Stock and 20 Bitts" valued at three pounds.[59] A tool with a U-shaped handle that was turned with the right hand while pressure was applied by the left hand or the shoulder to a button at the top, the stock today is usually called a brace.

Used after the actual boring had been done with the auger, the hook pin is a less familiar tool today. It was an iron pin six inches or more long with a hooked or "figure four" top. Moxon described the hook pin:

> Its Office is to pin the Frame of a Floor, or Frame of a Roof together, whilst it is framing, or whilst it is fitting into its Position. They [i.e., carpenters] have many of these *Hook-Pins* to drive into the several Angles of the Frame. These drive into the Pin-holes through the Mortesses and Tennants, and being made Taper, do with a Hammer striking on the bottom of it knock it out again; or they most commonly strike under the Hook, and

---

[54] York Co. Recs., Wills and Inventories, XXII, p. 401.
[55] *Ibid.*, Orders, Wills, XVI, p. 475.
[56] Jones Family Papers.
[57] York Co. Recs., Wills and Inventories, XX, p. 207.
[58] Mason, ed., *John Norton & Sons,* pp. 120, 124.
[59] York Co. Recs., Wills and Inventories, XXII, p. 401.

so knock it out. Then if the Frame lie in its place, they pin it up with wooden Pins.[60]

The inventory of James Wray's property (1750) listed "6 carpenters hookpins," evidently large ones of the best quality because they were appraised at two shillings each.[61]

The hammer has changed in no essential respect and hardly in detail since Roman times. Two hammers among James Morris's tools in 1718 were appraised at 3s. 6d.[62] Whether they were claw hammers with heads adapted to drawing nails was not indicated, although the claw hammer was probably the usual kind of the tool employed by carpenters in the eighteenth century. The James Wray inventory of 1750 listed three "clew hammers" valued at 1s. 3d. each.[63] The spelling is of interest because the earliest mention of the tool by an English name, which dates from 1473, called it a "clouehamer."[64] In 1771 James Carter ordered "6 large claw Hammers" from John Norton and Sons.[65]

The center of every carpenter's and joiner's operations was his bench. James Morris had two benches worth ten shillings, the same value set on Thomas Cobbs's single workbench in 1774.[66] The most important attachment to the bench for holding wood to be dressed was the vise, which was called a bench vise to distinguish it from the various kinds of clamps employed to hold pieces of wood to be fastened together. John Greenhow advertised "Pin vices, hand and bench vices" in 1766.[67] It seems reasonable to suppose that the pin vise, which is not to be found under that name in the standard reference books, was a clamp for holding pieces of wood to be pinned together, and that glue jointers, as advertised by Christopher Ford and Anthony Hay in 1755,[68] were for holding the glued pieces until the glue set. An alternative name for a clamp was cramp, and Edmund Dickinson's tools included "1 large cramp" and 1 small *Do,*" appraised at two pounds and one pound respectively.[69] Dickinson's bench vise was appraised at £1 10s. The workshop might also contain a lathe, which was used by house carpenters

---

[60] Moxon, *Mechanick Exercises*, p. 123.
[61] York Co. Recs., Wills and Inventories, XX, p. 207.
[62] Jones Family Papers.
[63] York Co. Recs., Wills and Inventories, XX, p. 206.
[64] Quoted by Salzman in *Building in England*, p. 344.
[65] Mason, ed., *John Norton & Sons*, p. 151.
[66] Jones Family Papers; York Co. Recs., Wills and Inventories, XXII, p. 246.
[67] *Virginia Gazette* (Purdie and Dixon), Apr. 11, 1766.
[68] *Ibid.*, Mar. 21, 1755.
[69] York Co. Recs., Wills and Inventories, XXII, p. 401.

chiefly for turning banisters. Thomas Cobbs had one, and in 1777 a *Virginia Gazette* advertisement announced the sale of "a Set Turners Tools, and the Bench with 2 Screws and Points, and a moving Steel Rest."[70]

Tools and instruments for measuring the drawing included the ten-foot measuring rod, which carpenters evidently made for themselves more often than not. It did not appear in any of the inventories examined, but surely it was used in Williamsburg.[71] For smaller dimensions, the two-foot rule was standard, and the Wray inventory (1750) listed seven valued at 7½ d. each.[72] Wray also had seven pencils at 3½ d. each; James Morris had "3 pencils & Ruler & brass Compasses" worth four shillings.[73] Wray owned eleven compasses appraised at fourpence apiece.[74] The square was another essential instrument, and in view of what Mercer said about the preponderance of wooden squares before 1800, it is interesting to note that in 1718 Morris had "a Small iron Square," and that John Lewellin had "1 iron Square" valued at one shilling in 1733.[75] Morris also had a chalk line appraised at 1s. 3d.,[76] which was a chalked string that was stretched tightly against a long plank or board and then twanged so as to leave a mark for the saw to follow. Wray owned "5 Brass Chaulk Roles,"[77] which must have been reels for holding chalk lines. The level, used to ascertain whether work is true, did not appear in the inventories, but artifact levels, or at least their more lasting parts, the bob and guard, have been found at Williamsburg. For drawing directly on the wood, the scratch awl or scriber was employed. In 1755 Ford and Hay advertised "Scribing Gouges," which may have been the same thing or may perhaps have been gauges, adjustable cruciform instruments for scratching lines parallel to the edge of a plank or board.[78] There were "Gages" as well as "Bevels," joined

---

[70] *Ibid.*, p. 246; *Virginia Gazette* (Dixon and Hunter), Dec. 12, 1777. The advertisement appears over the name of Maurice Evington. See n. 89.

[71] Information about carpenters who made their own measuring rods is in Mercer, *Ancient Carpenters' Tools*, p. 63.

[72] York Co. Recs., Wills and Inventories, XX, p. 206.

[73] *Ibid.;* Jones Family Papers.

[74] York Co. Recs., Wills and Inventories, XX, p. 206.

[75] Mercer, *Ancient Carpenters' Tools*, pp. 54–57; Jones Family Papers; York Co. Recs., Wills and Inventories, XVIII, p. 59. Wooden and iron squares in the Middle Ages are discussed in Salzman, *Building in England*, p. 339.

[76] Jones Family Papers.

[77] York Co. Recs., Wills and Inventories, XX, p. 207.

[78] *Virginia Gazette*, Mar. 21, 1755; the Lewellin inventory lists "gouges and squares." York Co. Recs., Wills and Inventories, XVIII, p. 59. It is tempting to read "gauges"

instruments for drawing angles, among the tools of cabinetmaker Edmund Dickinson in 1778.[79] All these things might have been found in any carpenter's shop. The "1 case drawing Instruments" valued at two pounds left by Dickinson probably corresponded to the drafting room equipment of our own day.

## TOOLS OF THE OTHER CRAFTS

Compared with a carpenter's, a bricklayer's tools were few. A trowel for spreading mortar was essential, and when the important Williamsburg bricklayer Humphrey Harwood died in 1788, he possessed "8 trowells."[80] He also had "Chisels for brick work," which undoubtedly included the double-bladed variety called the brick ax. Bricks for quoins and cut bricks for door and window arches were smoothed with a rubstone, which Moxon said was "round, and . . . about fourteen Inches Diameter, and sometimes more or less at pleasure."[81] James Morris in 1718 owned "1 Rubb Stone" appraised at one shilling.[82] The bricklayer would also have had a leveling device, string lines, brushes, a tool for lining mortar joints, buckets, hods, and shovels.

Painter's and glazier's tools were often listed together, since the two crafts were probably more often than not combined in practice. The appraisal of the estate of Robert Orchard, who died in 1756, provided a useful list of painter's tools:

> 1 Pallet Knife 2/-
> 1 large D*o* 2/6 . . . . . . . . 0 . 4 . 6
> 2 Paint Brushes 4/6
> 5 finer D*o* 2/6
> 5 broad D*o* 6/3 . . . . . . . . 0 . 13 . 3
> 29 old Paint Brushes 5/-. .
> 1 Painters stone, 1 D*o* larger
> 1 D*o* larger 1 D*o* larger 60/- 5 . 10 . -
> 1 Stone Mill
> 1 Wooden Mill 5/- . . . .[83]

---

for "gouges" here, too, because it would have been natural to group the drawing instruments together.

[79] York Co. Recs., Wills and Inventories, XXII, p. 401.

[80] *Ibid.*, XXIII, p. 220.

[81] Moxon, *Mechanick Exercises,* p. 245.

[82] Jones Family Papers.

[83] York Co. Recs., Wills and Inventories, XX, p. 391.

The mills and stones were for grinding the colors, which were less often bought ready mixed than they are today. Colors were ground on the stone with a muller, a conical stone with a flat base that was designed to be held in the hand. When James Wray died in 1750, he had "1 paint stone and muller."[84] Finer powder could be produced on the stone than in the mill. Wray also owned "1 Oyl Jar" and "1 wt Lead Mill."[85]

Both Orchard and Wray possessed glazier's tools as well as painter's and, in Wray's case, the tools of a carpenter since that was his principal trade. The glazier's diamond belonging to Orchard was appraised at twenty-six shillings. The glazier's tools owned by Wray included some for lead work, glazier's vises (of which he had two), and lead molds. Although sash windows had been used in Williamsburg from the founding of the town, older houses with leaded casements still remained in the neighborhood. In October 1733 Wray himself put in seventy-one diamond panes at "Mr. Wetherburns," and the following August an additional twenty.[86] The use of the mold and vise was described succinctly and with a touch of humor by Thomas Willsford:

> To fix the glass in panes, the Glasier hath a mould to cast the lead in, a foot in length, which he draws through a Vice, as some men their words through the nose, extending them wonderfully 4 times as long, and more.[87]

As the lead cames (also called caumes, or canes) passed through the vise, they were given grooves to receive the glass on either side by the two opposed wheels in the machine. Other glazier's tools that belonged to Wray included "pinchers" or pincers, a glazier's hammer, a light tool with a long, slender head, and a long claw for drawing nails, sometimes called a bradding-hammer.[88]

## BOOKS

In August 1777 a master craftsman by the name of Evington, Evengton, or Eventon[89] inserted an announcement about the availability of

---

[84] *Ibid.*, p. 206.

[85] *Ibid.*, p. 205.

[86] Jones Family Papers.

[87] Thomas Willsford, *Architectonice* (London, 1659), pp. 27–28.

[88] *Dictionary of Architecture*, IV, p. 13.

[89] In one of the *Virginia Gazette* announcements, his name was given as Mardum V. Evengton, and in the other, as Mardun V. Evington. His names first appeared in an

his services in each of the two rival editions of the *Virginia Gazette.* According to the longer of the two advertisements:

> Wants Employment, and is now at Leisure, a Master Workman in the various Branches of the Cabinet Business, chinese, gotick, carving, and turning; is well acquainted with the Theory and Practice in any of the grand Branches of the five ancient Orders; *viz.* Ornamental Architects, gothick, chinese, and modern Taste, &c. also Colonades, Porticoes, Frontispieces, &c. to Doors; compound, pick Pediment, and plain Tabernacle Chimney Pieces; chinese, ramp, and twist Pedestals; geometrical, circular, plain, and common Stair Cases, and sundry other Pieces of Architect too tedious mentioning. My chief Desire is to act in the Capacity of Superinter, or Supervisor, over any reasonable Number of Hands, either in public or private Buildings. I have an elegant Assortment of Tools, and Books of Architect, which I imported from *London* and *Liverpool.* [90]

The mere mention of "Books of Architect" in such a context is indicative of the importance that books had assumed for the master craftsman of the time, while the phraseology of the whole announcement is reminiscent of, and might well have been inspired by, the title pages of those very books.

A later advertisement inserted when Evington's books were up for sale indicated that there were "12 or 15" of them "by the latest and best authors in *Britain, viz. Swan, Pain, Langley, Halfpenny,* &c. &c."[91] All were authors that such a craftsman could have been expected to own, and it would be possible to supply some of the titles with at least a fair chance of being correct. But what were the books mentioned in the inventory of the personal estate of carpenter Richard King, which had been made all of fifty years before?

---

advertisement for journeymen cabinetmakers and mahogany planks in the *Maryland Gazette* (Annapolis), June 22, 1762, as Mardan Vaghn Eventon, while a walnut secretary in Burlington, King William County, Va., is inscribed "Made by Mardun V. Eventon." Helen Comstock, "Discoveries in southern furniture: Virginia and North Carolina," *Antiques,* LXV (February 1954), pp. 131–133, illus. on p. 122. Maurice Evington advertised his books for sale in 1777 and again in 1779. *Virginia Gazette* (Dixon and Hunter), Dec. 12, 1777; *ibid.* (Purdie), Dec. 12, 1777; *ibid.* (Dixon and Hunter), Dec. 11, 1779. Maurice Evington, the spelling of whose name did not vary, advertised for workmen in 1769 and in 1776. *Ibid.* (Rind), Feb. 23, 1769; *ibid.* (Dixon and Hunter), Sept. 21, 1776. What the relationship between the two Evingtons may have been is unknown. Mardun V. Evington died in Chesterfield County, Va., in 1778.

[90] *Virginia Gazette* (Dixon and Hunter), Aug. 15, 1777.

[91] *Ibid.,* Dec. 11, 1779.

1 umbrella 5/-, 1 case razors 1/6, 2 books of Architecture & 1
D⁹ Surveying . . . .   16s. 6d.[92]

One would like to know, because it appears that this was the earliest
contemporary record of architectural books in Williamsburg, although
it is certain that Governor Spotswood owned some.[93] Because it was
the earliest reference, there is little to go by in making a guess.

Books on architecture that were available in the eighteenth century
may be divided into four groups: the academic treatise dealing primarily
with the classical orders and the "grammar" of classical architecture
in general; the work of descriptive archaeology illustrating ancient buildings; the builder's handbook, in which the main emphasis was on technical and practical matters; and the book of designs that contained plans
and elevations, executed or unexecuted, of whole buildings, or patterns
for individual features such as ceilings or staircases. There was, however,
much overlapping—as witness two of the three volumes listed in the
first advertisement of architectural books to appear in the *Virginia Gazette*.
The year was 1751, nearly a quarter-century after King's death, and
the printer of the *Gazette* announced as "Just Imported, and to be Sold
reasonably, at the Printing-Office in Williamsburg, on early Application"
a long list of titles of all kinds in which architecture was represented
by "Ware's Palladio," "Salmon's Palladio," and "Harmonick Architecture."[94]

The first of the trio, Ware's Palladio, was the English translation of
the *Quattro Libri dell'Architettura* by the sixteenth-century Italian master
whose word was almost law in England between 1725 and 1760. It
was published in London by the architect Isaac Ware in 1738, and
the comprehensive work included a book on the orders and certain
matters of construction and proportion, a book of Palladio's own designs, and two books in which Roman buildings were illustrated and
described.

"Salmon's Palladio" was not, as might be supposed, another edition
of the revered work but a builder's handbook that contained some geometry, detailed instructions for drawing the inevitable orders, a few en-

---

[92] York Co. Recs., Orders, Wills, XVI, p. 588.

[93] On his death in 1749, Spotswood's books went to the College of William and
Mary. The only one that survives in the college library is one volume of a description
of Versailles, Trianon, and Marly, published in Amsterdam in 1715. When it was cataloged in 1695, Gov. Francis Nicholson's library contained no architectural books. Arthur
Foley, *The Early English Colonies* (London, 1908), pp. 39–44.

[94] *Virginia Gazette*, May 24, 1751.

graved designs for doorways, windows, and chimneypieces, and a quantity of useful information about practical business matters such as measuring and pricing, and about practical structural ones such as building staircases and framing roofs. Its author, William Salmon, was a Colchester carpenter, its complete title was *Palladio Londinensis: or, The London Art of Building,* and it went through six editions in the eighteenth century, three (1734, 1743, and 1748) before the advertisement appeared and three more (1752, 1755, 1762) afterward.

The third book, "Harmonick Architecture," must have been *Harmonic Architecture, exemplified in a Plan etc. of a Building, with four different fronts, upon an Harmonic Form of Cube, now made Octangular, Being designed for a Museum, in a retired situation of a Park or Garden.* The author of this very slim volume—it contains eight plates and two pages of text—published in 1741 by the "Society of Booksellers for promoting learning" was J. Shortess, Gentleman, to whom H. M. Colvin tentatively attributed a design in the Bodleian Library at Oxford University for an apiary.[95] It is difficult to explain its export to Virginia except as an instance of dumping stock that was hard to sell in England in a book hungry colony.

Subsequent advertisements of books for sale by the printers of the *Virginia Gazette* do not add to the knowledge of architectural books in Virginia as much as this promising beginning leads one to hope. Books on gardening, for example, tended to outnumber those on architecture throughout the period during which both were advertised. In July 1771 "Swan's Designs in Carpentry, containing Domes, trussed Roofs, Flooring, trussing of Beams, Angle Brackets, and Cornices" was advertised. Presumably it was Abraham Swan's *The Carpenter's Complete Instructor in Several Hundred Designs, consisting of Domes, Trussed Roofs, and various Cupolas,* of which there were editions of 1759 and 1768. The title was still offered for sale two years later, in June 1773.[96] Does this mean that it did not sell, or does it mean that Purdie and Dixon had laid in several copies? Perhaps it was among the books owned by Evington, although if he told the truth when he said that he had imported his books from London and Liverpool, he did not acquire his copy in Williamsburg. Or perhaps Evington owned one or more of Swan's other works, the *Designs for Chimnies,* the two-volume *Collection of Designs in Architecture,* or *The British Architect,* the last of which, first published in England in

[95] H. M. Colvin, *A Biographical Dictionary of English Architects 1660–1840* (London, 1954), p. 541.
[96] *Virginia Gazette* (Purdie and Dixon), July 18, 1771; *ibid.,* June 10, 1773.

1745, had the distinction thirty years later of being the first book on architecture to be printed in America.[97]

Books by William Pain that Evington could have owned were *The Builder's Companion* (1758), *The Builder's Pocket Treasure* (1763), and *The Practical Builder* (1774). At least the first of them reached pre-Revolutionary Virginia, if Fiske Kimball was correct in thinking that he found evidence of its use by William Buckland at Gunston Hall.[98] In the case of Batty Langley, the range of possibilities is much greater, since before his death in 1751, Langley had been responsible for a score or more of publications. One whose presence in Virginia can be established from the records was *The Builder's Treasury of Designs for Piers, Gates, etc.*, recorded by Philip Vickers Fithian (as "Builders Treasure of Designs") as being in Robert Carter's library at Nomini Hall.[99] The only other architectural book listed by Fithian was Salmon's *Palladio Londinensis*. William Halfpenny, whose works appeared during the same period, was as prolific an author as Langley. The Byrd family library at Westover, as indicated in the sale catalog of 1777, contained two of them, the folio volume *The Art of Sound Building* and the duodecimo *Practical Architecture.*[100] Both were published in the 1720s, and William Byrd II may have acquired them then when he was preparing to build his new house. Listed in the sale catalog as "Richard's Palladio," *The First Book of Architecture . . . by A[ndrea] P[alladio] . . . Translated out of French by G[odfrey] R[ichards]* may also have been acquired then. The last of the many editions of the book, first published in 1668, appeared in 1733.

It is worth noting that the Byrd library did not contain Salmon's *Palladio Londinensis* despite the fact that the designs of the north and south doorways of Westover came line for line from plates in that book.[101] Since the doorways are of Portland stone and must have been imported ready-made from England, there was no need for Byrd to have owned a copy. Nor did it contain that other mainstay of the colonial designer, James Gibbs's *Book of Architecture* (1728), although one of the Westover mantelpieces seems to have been derived from it.[102] However,

---

[97] It was printed in Philadelphia in 1775 by R. Bell for J. Norman. See Henry Russell Hitchcock, *American Architectural Books*, 3rd ed. (Minneapolis, 1946), p. 103.

[98] Fiske Kimball, "Gunston Hall," *Journal of the Society of Architectural Historians*, XIII (May 1954), pp. 7–8.

[99] Hunter Dickinson Farish, ed., *The Journal & Letters of Philip Vickers Fithian, 1773–1774, A Plantation Tutor of the Old Dominion*, 2nd ed. (Williamsburg, Va., 1957), p. 222.

[100] *Virginia Gazette* (Dixon and Hunter), Dec. 19, 1777.

[101] Thomas Tileston Waterman, *The Mansions of Virginia 1706–1776* (Chapel Hill, N. C., 1946), pp. 150–153.

[102] *Ibid.*, p. 156.

the mantelpiece, which is of marble, must also have been imported. Although Thomas Jefferson's architectural library will not be discussed here, it is interesting that he bought a copy of Gibbs's work together with William Kent's *Designs of Inigo Jones* (1727) in Williamsburg in 1778, paying John Dixon, printer of the *Virginia Gazette,* ten pounds for each.[103]

There were two copies of "Palladio's Architecture" at Westover, one quarto and one folio. In the case of an author so frequently republished, a positive identification of the editions is impossible, but since the title was given in English and there apparently was only one volume, it seems more likely than not that the folio was Ware's translation. The book entered in the sale catalog as "Architecture di Scamozi" can only have been *L'Idea della Architettura Universale* by Palladio's fellow townsman and follower, Vincenzo Scamozzi. Perhaps, since it was a folio, it was a copy of the first edition of 1615. "Alberti's Architecture" in two volumes, folio, may be identified with some confidence as Leoni's English edition of 1726.[104] There were two French books among the architectural books at Westover, cataloged as "Principes L'Architecture" and "Traite d'Architecture." These must have been André Félibien's *Des Principes de l'Architecture, de la Sculpture, de la Peinture, et des autres Arts qui en Dependent,* first published in 1676, and Sebastien Le Clerc's *Traité d'Architecture* of 1714. Neither could have been of much practical use to a building owner dependent on workmen trained in the English tradition. The three volumes of Colen Campbell's *Vitruvius Britannicus* (1715–1725), also in the library, illustrated buildings that were nearly all too grand to be imitated in Virginia.

Among the books that Robert Carter ordered from England in 1771–1773—either it went to his Williamsburg house or it arrived too late to be cataloged by Fithian—was "Chambers on Architecture."[105] *A Treatise on Civil Architecture* by Sir William Chambers was first published in 1759, and a second edition appeared in 1768. Representing contemporary academicism at its best, it long remained a standard textbook on the classical proprieties. Very different was the book listed in the inventory of the estate of cabinetmaker Edmund Dickinson in 1778 and appraised at six pounds, "Chippendales Designs."[106] This must have been

---

[103] Almanac Account Book, 1778, p. 69, Massachusetts Historical Society, Boston.

[104] This is often listed as a three-volume work, but volume III, entitled *Some Designs for Buildings . . . by James Leoni,* is not always found with the other two.

[105] K. M. Rowland, "Robert Carter of Virginia," *Magazine of American History* (September 1893), pp. 115–136.

[106] York Co. Recs., Wills and Inventories, XXII, p. 401.

*A Collection of Ornamental Designs, Applicable to Furniture, Frames, and the Decoration of Rooms* by Thomas Chippendale, which contains "Chinese," "Gothick," and rocaille motifs.

The taste that Chippendale's book represented was hardly the latest, because the first volume of the *Works in Architecture of Robert and James Adam,* which did so much to consolidate the victory of neoclassicism over the rococo in England, had appeared in 1773. There seems to be no record that the volumes of the Adam brothers reached Virginia in the period under discussion, and nothing in the design of any surviving building suggests that they did so. Williamsburg did have an opportunity to learn of the change in taste even before the Revolution, however. In 1774 George Hamilton, "Carver and Gilder, just from *Britain,* and now in this City," informed the public through the *Virginia Gazette* that he would execute "Ornaments and Decorations for Gentlemens Houses, Chimney Pieces, Door and Window Cornices, Mouldings and Enrichments," together with a variety of articles of a more portable nature, "after the new *Palmyrian* Taste."[107] Was Mr. Hamilton, who with metropolitan sophistication offered to furnish gentlemen with "Designs," the proud possessor of a copy of Robert Wood's great folio, *The Ruins of Palmyra?* It is not impossible, but it seems more likely that he found his inspiration in a more modest work, namely *A Book of Ornaments in the Palmyrene Taste* by N. Wallis, published in 1771.

Books influenced architecture in two ways: individually, by supplying designs for whole buildings or for details that could be taken straight from the printed page; and cumulatively, by establishing standards and trends of taste. In Williamsburg there is no instance of the plan and elevations of a whole building being taken from a book that is as obvious and striking as that of Mount Airy in Richmond County, Virginia, for which Gibbs's *Book of Architecture* supplied so much more than inspiration. Nor can the design of any considerable extent of interior work in the town be traced to a literary source as certainly as can that of the woodwork in the hall and west parlor at Carter's Grove, James City County, which was executed after plates in *Palladio Londinensis* within two years of its owner's purchase of a copy of that book.[108] Nevertheless, one may be sure that but for books the design of moldings and other small but telling details in Williamsburg houses would be less correct,

---

[107] *Virginia Gazette* (Purdie and Dixon), July 28, 1774.

[108] Carter Burwell paid ten shillings for the book on Dec. 12, 1751. Virginia Gazette Day Books, 1751–1752, Alderman Library, University of Virginia, Charlottesville. I would like to thank Miss Mary Stephenson for bringing this to my notice.

by classical criteria, than they generally are. And there are a number of features—the "Chinese" stair in the Coke-Garrett House, for instance, and the enrichment of the mantelpiece in the west room of the Semple House—which quite clearly must owe their character to their designers' having had some acquaintance with books propagating the stylistic trends that they exemplify.

# 4

## *Houses of Williamsburg: General Design*

WHEN the first colonists arrived in Virginia, the basic element of the English rural dwelling was, as it had been for hundreds of years, the hall, a rectangular room entered near one end through either of its longer sides. The simplest houses consisted of nothing more than this one room and a garret above, reached by a ladder, and such no doubt were the first framed houses built at Jamestown. All of the more complex types of houses had evolved as the result of adding rooms for special purposes to the originally all-purpose hall.[1] The nature and the arrangement of the additions varied with the needs and social status of the building's owner. The manor house early acquired two extra rooms—the solar or parlor was added at the "upper" end of the hall (that is, at the end farther from the entrance), and the kitchen was placed at the lower end with its door opening into the passage formed by a wooden screen that ran from one side of the hall to the other. In the house of the yeoman, who was lower on the social and economic scale, the cooking was still done in the hall and the sole addition might have been a parlor at the lower end of the hall where the kitchen was located in the manor house.

It was from this kind of yeoman house that the characteristic story and one-half house of colonial Virginia, which was entered in the center of the front and has two rooms on the ground floor, developed (*Figures 5 and 6*). Nothing shows this more clearly than the survival in eighteenth-

---

[1] In the account of domestic planning that follows, there are necessarily generalizations to which exceptions may be found. It seemed better to treat the subject broadly than to weary the reader with qualifications. To fill in details—and to discover exceptions—he may turn to Part II of this book.

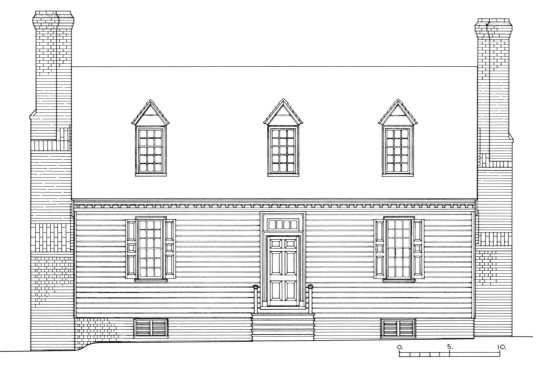

*Figure* 5    Bracken House. North elevation.

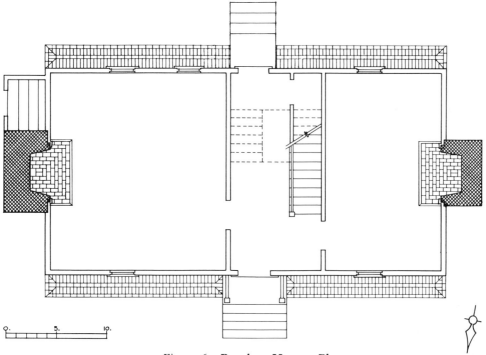

*Figure* 6    Bracken House. Plan.

century inventories of the old names for the three parts into which
the first floor was divided: hall, parlor, and passage. The present custom
of referring to the central passage of an eighteenth-century house as
the hall is not in accordance with eighteenth-century usage. There was,
however, one significant difference between the English room nomencla-
ture and that used in Virginia. According to the "Builder's Dictionary"
appended to the 1748 edition of Salmon's *Palladio Londinensis*, "Chambers,
in a House or Building are the Rooms between the Ground Story and
Garrets," that is, the upstairs rooms. The naming of the rooms in the
Samuel Timson inventory of 1704/5 agreed with this definition, since
they were described as "Hall, Palar, chamber over the Palar, Porch
Chamber, Hall Chamber, Garret over the Hall, Garret over the Palar."[2]
Often there was a room called a chamber on the first floor in Virginia
houses such as Matthew Pierce's dwelling, whose rooms were named
by the 1738 inventory as the chamber over the chamber, the chamber
over the hall, the hall, and the chamber below stairs.[3] In a story and
one-half house, the only chamber so called might be on the first floor.
Robert Davidson's house was described in the 1739 inventory as com-
prising a hall, a chamber, and "upstairs"; Thomas Hornsby's house
in 1772 had a chamber, hall, passage, and "upstairs."[4] The explanation,
borne out by the contents of the rooms as listed in the inventories, is
that in Virginia a chamber was a bedchamber. As for the parlor, it
was defined by the *Builder's Dictionary* as "a fair lower Room designed
for the Entertainment of Company," and parlors, in Virginia as in England, were invariably on the lower floor.

A factor that helped to insure the survival of the hall-passage-parlor
type of one and one-half story house in Virginia was the use of the
outhouse kitchen. In the seventeenth century, the larger houses sometimes had cellar kitchens, and the feature was not unknown in
Williamsburg.[5] By the beginning of the eighteenth century, the smaller
planter and the tradesman had attained to a standard of living that
made them unwilling to tolerate the fuss and smells of cooking in the
hall. Their social equals in England would have added a kitchen to
the house itself. But in Virginia the possession of slaves facilitated,
and perhaps even necessitated, the adoption of an alternative that the

---

[2] York Co. Recs., Deeds, Orders, Wills, XII, p. 211.
[3] *Ibid.*, Wills and Inventories, XVII, p. 416.
[4] *Ibid.*, pp. 587–588.
[5] For example, the Blue Bell and the Red Lion. See also Whiffen, *Public Buildings*,
p. 103.

heat of summer alone would have made desirable. The removal of the kitchen to a separate building was a domestic ideal in eighteenth-century England too, but it was achieved there only in great country houses, while in Virginia it was a commonplace of middle-class living arrangements.

Nor was only the kitchen removed from the house. Robert Beverley wrote, "All their Drudgeries of Cookery, Washing, Daries, &c. are perform'd in Offices detacht from the Dwelling-Houses, which by this means are kept more cool and Sweet."[6] Moreover, the story and one-half house itself tended to be superior to its English equivalent. As early as 1656, John Hammond remarked that Virginia houses were "pleasant in their building, which although for the most part they are but one story besides the loft, and built of wood, yet contrived so delightfully that your ordinary houses in England are not so handsome, for usually the rooms are large, daubed and whitelimed, glazed and flowered [floored], and if not glazed windows, shutters which are made very pr[e]tty and convenient."[7] The testimony of Hugh Jones stated that "the common planters live in pretty timber houses, neater than the farm houses are generally in England."[8] The physical evidence supports the literary testimony. In Williamsburg, most of the frame houses are similar to English village types, but have a generousness of scale and a sophistication of detail hardly to be found in their English counterparts (*Figures 7–10*).

When the hall-passage-parlor nucleus proved too small, even after the building of the separate kitchen, there were three ways in which accommodations could be increased. The first was simply to build onto one end, as was done at Williamsburg in the John Blair House. The second was to build a lean-to along the back of the house with a roof that continued the slope of the main roof; the John Blair House and the Moody House illustrate this type. The third was to build a wing or wings at right angles to the long axis of the original house. One wing resulted in an L plan like that of the Benjamin Waller House. When two wings were added, the result was the U-shape, which is exemplified by the Brush-Everard House. The half-H had been a favorite plan in Elizabethan and Jacobean England, where the wings normally projected forward to form a forecourt. At the Brush-Everard House, however, they are at the back. Eighteenth-century taste had little use

---

[6] Beverley, *History and Present State*, p. 290.

[7] *A Perfect Description of Virginia* (1649), quoted in Thomas Jefferson Wertenbaker, *The First Americans 1607–1690* (New York, 1927), p. 286.

[8] Jones, *Present State of Virginia*, p. 74.

*Figure 7*  John Blair House before restoration.

*Figure 8*  House at Tillingham, Essex, England.

*Figure 9*  Powell-Hallam House before restoration.

*Figure 10*  Gambrel-roofed house at Tillingham, Essex, England.

for the effects of projection and recession that had delighted an earlier age, preferring a unified facade. Aesthetic predilection also accounted for the disappearance of the two-story porch with its "porch chamber,"[9] which was evidently a common feature of Virginia houses in the seventeenth century.

All of the house types discussed so far have one thing in common: the principal rooms extended from front to back. The house with partition walls along its longer axis making it two rooms deep was introduced in England early in the seventeenth century. In Virginia, the first double-pile dwelling seems to have been the Governor's Palace, begun in 1706; another early example was the first part of the Peyton Randolph House, which was built about 1715. Both of these houses differ somewhat from later examples in Virginia, the first in the placement of the stairs, the second in its possession of a massive central chimney as well as a two-story porch chamber. In the classic type of Virginia double-pile house, the stairs retained their traditional position in the central passage, which was often considerably widened, and there were four rooms to a floor (*Figures 11 and 12*). The position of the chimneystacks varied. Sometimes they were at the ends of the house, and sometimes they rose from the center of the partition between each pair of rooms. Their placement did not depend, as might be supposed, on the main structural material of the building. The George Wythe House, which is of brick, has interior chimneys, but so does the Robert Carter House, which is of wood. The Archibald Blair House, which is of wood, has terminal chimneys, as does the Ludwell-Paradise House, which is of brick. The all-purpose hall had no place in the double-pile house. On the first floor were parlors, perhaps a dining room, a parlor in which one of the functions of all parlors had been developed to the exclusion of the others, and a drawing room, while the bedchambers were above. Studies and nurseries were other specialized rooms sometimes named in inventories.

In origin and by use, the double-pile was a rural type that could be built in the "green country towne" of Williamsburg only because there was plenty of space. The other types that have been distinguished, which had their long fronts to the street, had been crowded out of most towns in England before the seventeenth century. There the typical urban dwelling was what Sir John Summerson has called the unit house, "with a narrow frontage to the street, [and] rooms back and front on each

---

[9] Foundations of porch chambers at the Peyton Randolph and Orlando Jones houses substantiated the reconstruction of both.

*Figure 11*  George Wythe House. East elevation.

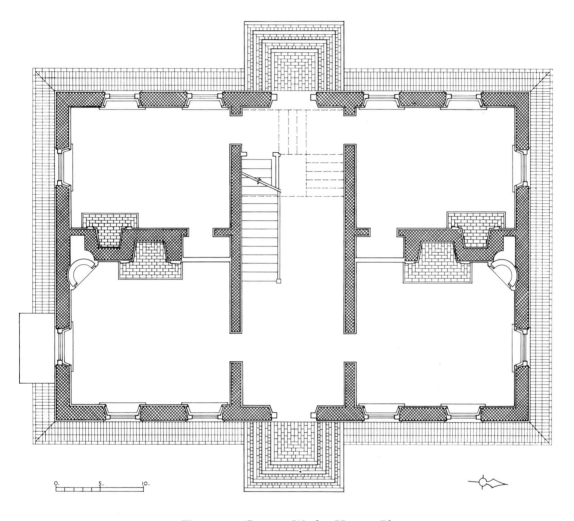

*Figure 12*  George Wythe House. Plan.

floor," the front room on the first floor often being a shop.[10] Such unit houses were built at Jamestown in the seventeenth century,[11] and, although they were built in Williamsburg throughout the eighteenth, the wide street frontages of the lots favored other types. The genre is most easily recognized in the shops or stores, such as Prentis Store and Nicolson Shop, which followed medieval practice in presenting gable ends to the street. But there are also dwelling houses that belong to it, such as the gambrel-roofed William Lightfoot (*Figures 13 and 14*), Powell-Hallam, Tayloe, and Orrell houses and the two-story brick Palmer House. With their lateral entries and paired back and front rooms, the plan of these houses was essentially that of the London

[10] Sir John Summerson, *Architecture in Britain 1530–1830* (London, 1954), p. 56.

[11] Henry Chandlee Forman, *Jamestown and St. Mary's: Buried Cities of Romance* (Baltimore, 1938), pp. 49–50, 104.

*Figure 13*    William Lightfoot House. North elevation.

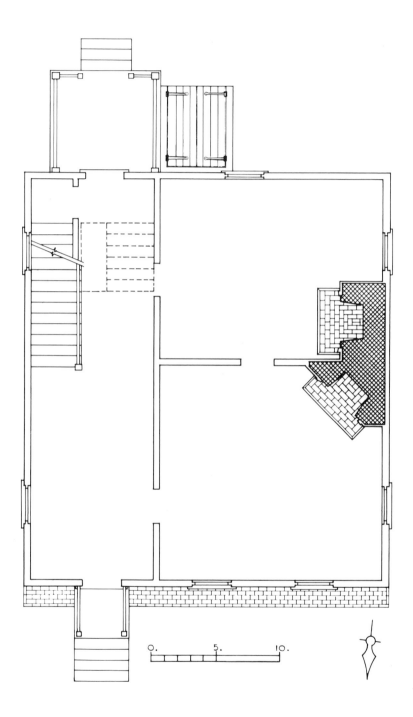

*Figure 14*  William Lightfoot House. Plan.

terrace house. Moreover, the gambrel roof that covers all but one of them lurks behind the parapets of many of the terraces of Georgian London, where it was called a curb roof. One can be confident that the resemblance is no mere coincidence. "The habits, life, customs, computations, etc. of the Virginians," wrote Hugh Jones, "are much the same as about London, which they esteem their home."[12] Of the power of those habits and customs to influence architecture, the isolated terrace house, so to call it, supplies a striking demonstration.[13]

## HOUSE DESIGN AND THE CLIMATE

The piazza, in the Charlestonian and West Indian sense of a porch of one or two stories stretching along the whole of one or more sides of the house, was not common in eighteenth-century Virginia. If one thinks of domestic warmth in terms of open fires rather than central heating, the reason becomes clear—Virginia is far enough north for winter sunshine to be welcome. Virginians thought that on the whole they were fortunate in the climate of their land. "The Country," wrote Robert Beverley, "is in a very happy Situation, between the extreams of Heat and Cold, but inclining rather-to the first."[14] It was true, he said, that the summers had a bad reputation, but that was because "many of the Merchants and others that go thither from *England,* make no distinction between a cold, and a hot Country: but wisely go sweltering about in their thick Cloaths all the Summer, because they used to do so in their *Northern* Climate; and then unfairly complain of the heat of the Country."[15] The truth was that their heat was "very seldom troublesome, and then only by the accident of a perfect Calm, which happens perhaps two or three times in a year, and lasts but a few Hours at a time; and even that Inconvenience is made easie by cool Shades, by open Airy rooms, Summer-Houses, Arbors, and Grottos."[16]

---

[12] Jones, *Present State of Virginia,* p. 43. According to Jones, the Virginians "for the most part have contemptible notions of England, and wrong sentiments of Bristol, and the other outports, which they entertain from seeing and hearing the common dealers, sailors, and servants that come from those towns, and the country places in England and Scotland, whose language and manners are strange to them."

[13] In western Pennsylvania, there are later rural examples of the type that presumably were Philadelphia-inspired. Charles Morse Stotz, *The Early Architecture of Western Pennsylvania* (New York, 1936), p. 44.

[14] Beverley, *History and Present State,* p. 296.

[15] *Ibid.,* p. 297.

[16] *Ibid.,* p. 299. Cf. William Byrd to Charles, Earl of Orrery, July 5, 1726, *VMHB,* XXXII (January 1924), p. 26: "I must own to Yr Ldship that we have about three

"Grottos," as Charles C. Wall has suggested, probably meant groves of trees. A few old summer houses have survived, and the gardens of Williamsburg contain a number of reconstructed examples as well as arbors. As for the airiness of the rooms, ceiling heights were generous even in the smaller eighteenth-century houses. Virginians understood very well that for comfort in summer, air should be kept circulating. Describing the houses of the colony in 1724, Hugh Jones affirmed that they were "cool in summer; especially if there be windows enough to draw the air." There was, he says, "a passage generally through the middle of the house for an airdraught in summer."[17] The central passage was not invented for this purpose since it was inherited from English tradition, but climatic considerations were a factor that favored its retention. In its widened form in larger houses, its function as a ventilator was analogous to that of the two-story *salone* in an Italian villa. One should be chary of describing the "four square" plan of such houses as Palladian, for in fact it could have developed without direct influence from the published works of Palladio.[18] Nevertheless, those free standing, cubical dwellings, with windows facing each of the four quarters from which a breeze might come, were as well adapted to the Virginia summers as were Palladio's villas to the similar summers of the Veneto— and through the application of just the same principles. Their internal planning was often of an uncompromising regularity and symmetry such as was found only in the more doctrinaire of their Palladian counterparts in England. Here again, one may assume that considerations of climate reinforced aesthetic preferences. The drafts which in England set the satirists against Italianate houses had their use in Virginia, and for at least part of the year there was no risk of catching cold at a Venetian door.

The climate also influenced the choice of building materials, although the choice made was in fact the result of a misunderstanding of a climatic phenomenon, the humidity of the atmosphere in the Tidewater. Thomas Jefferson, in his *Notes on the State of Virginia*, wrote that "the unhappy prejudice prevails that houses of brick or stone [are] less wholesome

---

months that impatient People call warm. . . . Yet there are not 10 days in the whole summer that Yr Ldsp would complain of, and they happen when the Breazes fail us and it is a dead Calme. But then the other nine Months are most charmingly delightfull, with a fine Air and a Serene Sky that keeps us in Good Health and Good Humour. Spleen and vapours are as absolute Rarities here as a Winter's Sun, or a Publick Spirit in England."

[17] Jones, *Present State of Virginia*, p. 71.

[18] Marcus Whiffen, "Some Virginian House Plans Reconsidered," *Journal of the Society of Architectural Historians*, XVI (May 1957), pp. 17–19.

than those of wood."[19] Because people did not know that the "dew
. . . on the walls of the former in rainy weather" was condensed moisture
from the air, they thought that it was rain that had penetrated the walls.
Not, Jefferson added, that rain never penetrated brick walls:

> But with us it is only through the northern and eastern walls
> of the house, after a north-easterly storm, these being the only
> ones which continue long enough to force through the walls.
> This however happens too rarely to give a just character of un-
> wholesomeness to such houses. In a house, the walls of which
> are of well-burnt brick and good mortar, I have seen the rain
> penetrate through but twice in a dozen or fifteen years. The
> inhabitants of Europe, who dwell chiefly in houses of stone or
> brick, are surely as healthy as those of Virginia. These houses
> have the advantage too of being warmer in winter and cooler
> in summer than those of wood; of being cheaper in their first
> construction, where lime is convenient, and infinitely more
> durable.[20]

He pointed out that even the "huts of logs" built by "the poore people"
were "warmer in winter, and cooler in summer, than the more expensive
constructions of scantling and plank."[21]

## HOUSE DESIGN AND THE LAW

While in Virginia as a whole the design of the commoner forms of
dwellings was thus the result of combining English traditions with special
social and climatic conditions, in Williamsburg it was affected by another
factor as well—the law. The founders of Williamsburg were determined
that the city should achieve a certain architectural dignity as befitted
the seat of government, and they incorporated in the "Act Directing
the Building the Capitoll and the City of Williamsburgh" certain provisions with that end in view.[22]

---

[19] Thomas Jefferson, *Notes on the State of Virginia*, ed. William Peden (Chapel Hill,
N. C., 1955), p. 153.

[20] *Ibid.*, p. 154. The vulnerability to weather of the northern and northeastern parts
of a house was touched on by Edmund Jenings in a June 9, 1754, letter to John Tayloe,
who was about to build Mount Airy in Richmond County: "It may be proper to observe
that Closets on the North or N. E. part of the House are Generally Damp without
Fires being near Them. Also on those aspects No windows (In Gable Ends & not
Fronts) should be made." Edmund Jenings Letter Book, Jenings Family Mementoes
and Papers, Virginia Historical Society, Richmond. I am indebted to John M. Hemphill
II for calling my attention to this letter.

[21] Jefferson, *Notes on Virginia*, p. 152.

[22] The act is printed, with the additions of 1705, in Hening, ed., *Statues*, III, pp.
419–432.

It was not the first time an act of Assembly had tried to give a Virginia capital worthy buildings. Thirty-seven years before, in 1662, an "Act for building a Towne" had tried to do the same for Jamestown.[23] The act provided for the erection of thirty-two houses, "each house to be built with brick, forty foot long, twenty foot wide, within the walls, to be eighteen foote high above the ground, the walls to be two brick thick to the water table, and a brick and a halfe thick above the water table to the roofe, the roofe to be fifteen foote pitch and to be covered with slate or tile . . . regularly placed one by another in a square or such other forme" as the Governor, Sir William Berkeley, should decide. "For the better expediteing this worke," each of the seventeen counties into which Virginia was then divided was to make itself responsible for the erection of one house, and was authorized to impress building tradesmen for the purpose. Prices and wages were fixed "for avoiding the exaction of workemen." Toward the end of the act, there was a clause that showed concern about the inflammability of timber construction: "And though in the infancy of this designe it might seem hard to demolish any wooden houses already built in the towne, yett it is hereby *provided and enacted* that noe wooden houses shall hereafter be built within the limitts of the towne, nor those now standing be hereafter repaired, but brick ones to be erected in theire steads."[24]

The practical results of the act of 1662 were negligible: only four or five brick houses were built.[25] The framers of the 1699 act for the building of Williamsburg began with the advantage that they were concerned with a new site. Whereas the chief inducement offered to a Jamestown building owner under the 1662 act was a grant of ground on which to build a store, in Williamsburg the building of a house within two years was made the condition of the saving of each of the half-acre lots into which the city land was divided. There was nothing new in this. In Maryland, for instance, an act of 1683 for the establishment of six towns had stipulated that each lot holder was to build "one sufficient twenty foot square house" by the end of August 1685 or forfeit his lot.[26] The act that brought Annapolis into being in 1694 required each lot holder to "build one Twenty foot Square Dwelling house att least within twelve months after takeing up the same unless such building be larger then herein Expressed."[27] Where the Virginia

[23] *Ibid.*, II, p. 172.
[24] *Ibid.*, p. 176.
[25] Forman, *Jamestown and St. Mary's*, p. 146.
[26] Frederic Emory, *Queen Anne's County, Maryland* (Baltimore, 1950), pp. 314–315.
[27] William Hand Browne et al., eds., *Archives of Maryland*, XIX (Baltimore, 1899), p. 112.

act of 1699 differed from other colonial acts for the founding of towns was in its attention to aspects of domestic architecture other than the dimensions on plan of the houses. On Duke of Gloucester Street, at least, an urban scale and regularity was insured by the requirement

> That whosoever shall build in the maine Street of the said city of *Williamsburg*, as laid out in the aforesaid draught or plot, shall not build a house less than ten foot pitch, and the front of each house shall come within six foot of the street, and not nearer; and that the houses in the several lots in the said main street shall front alike.[28]

As for superficial dimensions, the floor area of each house was to be half as much again as the twenty-foot-square minimum of the Maryland statutes—"twenty foot in width, and thirty foot in length."[29] The houses elsewhere than on Duke of Gloucester Street were to "be built in such manner, and according to such rules and orders as shall be given and made by the directors, by virtue of this act; hereafter appointed, or by the incorporation of the Mayor, Aldermen, and Commonalty of the City of Williamsburg."[30]

In October 1705 the act was reenacted with additions that provided for certain contingencies for which no special provision had been made in 1699. Under the act in its original form, anyone who bought two contiguous lots on Duke of Gloucester Street was required to build a twenty-by thirty-foot house on each. Not only was this inconvenient for the owner, but its effect ran counter to the clear intention of the framers of the act that the houses on the main street of the new town should be as large as possible. Thus in 1705 it was enacted that the purchaser of two lots on Duke of Gloucester Street might save them by building a single house with dimensions of fifty feet by twenty or, if it had two brick chimneys and a cellar, of forty feet by twenty. Furthermore, the house could stand on either or both of the two lots:

> If any Person shall hereafter take a Grant of two lots, or half acres of land, upon the great street of the said city, commonly called *Duke of Gloucester* street, and within the space of four and

---

[28] Hening, ed., *Statutes*, III, p. 423.

[29] *Ibid.*

[30] *Ibid.*, pp. 423–424. The city of Williamsburg was incorporated by royal charter in 1722.

twenty Months next ensuing such grant, upon the said lots or half acres, or either of them, shall build and finish one house fifty foot long and twenty foot broad, or within the space aforesaid upon the said lots, or half acres, or either of them, shall build and finish one brick house, or framed house, with two stacks of brick chimnies, and cellars under the whole house, bricked, forty foot long, and twenty foot broad, either of the said performances, shall be sufficient to save the grant of both the said lots.[31]

It was also made possible for the purchaser of two lots on Duke of Gloucester Street and one or more lots on a secondary street to save all of the lots by building on his Duke of Gloucester Street holding alone:

And if any person shall hereafter take a grant of two lots, or half acres of land, upon the great street of the said city, and one or more lots, or half acres backward, and within the space of four and twenty months next ensuing such grant, upon the lots or half acres contiguous to the great street, or either of them, shall build and finish in ordinary framed work, as much dwelling housing, as will make five hundred square feet superficial measure, on the ground plat, for every lot, or half acre taken up; or within the space aforesaid, upon the said two lots, or half acres, or either of them, shall build and finish, in brick work, or framed work, with brick cellars under the whole, and brick chimnies, as much dwelling housing, as will make four hundred square feet superficial measure on the ground plat, for every lot, or half acre taken up, either of the said performances shall be sufficient to save the grant of all and every of the said lots.[32]

The purchaser of two lots on Duke of Gloucester Street and one other lot on the street behind could thus fulfill the requirements of the law by building, for example, a sixty- by twenty-five-foot framed house or, if he preferred, one in brick of forty-eight by twenty-five feet on the Duke of Gloucester site. And he could, of course, look forward to his vacant lot increasing in value as the town grew.

Another clause in the act of 1705 stated that no house, "be the dimensions thereof never so large," could save more than two lots on Duke of Gloucester Street, the building up of which was the end to which the other additions to the act of 1699 were directed. Furthermore, "every

---

[31] *Ibid.,* p. 429.
[32] *Ibid.*

person having any lots, or half acres of land, contiguous to the great street, shall inclose the said lots, or half acres, with a wall, pails, or post and rails, within six months after the building, which the law requires to be erected thereupon, shall be finished."[33] The penalty for nonperformance was set at five shillings per month per lot. Since the height of the walls and fences was not specified, there is a question whether the four foot, six-inch minimum that the law had already laid down as the height of a "sufficient fence" around cleared ground[34] applied, because it would have made a considerable difference in the general appearance of the town. But lots in the city of Williamsburg were hardly in the same category as the cleared land with which the previous laws about fencing had been concerned. If they had been, there would have been no need for a new law; the old would have applied to lots on Duke of Gloucester Street as much as to those elsewhere in the town, of which the new law made no mention.

The 1699 "Act directing the building the Capitoll and the City of Williamsburgh" and the continuing act of 1705 constituted a very respectable achievement in the history of town planning legislation. Where housing was concerned, their requirements were clear and could be enforced easily. Nor did they attempt the impossible by forbidding the building of wooden houses as the Virginia "Act for building a Towne" of 1662 had done and as later colonial acts outside Virginia were to do.[35] The legislators' realism in this respect is the more noteworthy because the most famous and most successful legislative measure that had the control of housing among its objects was the act for rebuilding London after the Great Fire, passed in February 1667, which had banned wood for the exterior of houses except for certain limited purposes.[36] Virginians certainly would have been familiar with the Rebuilding Act and may have derived the idea of controlling the "pitch" of the houses

---

[33] *Ibid.*, p. 430.

[34] Acts that required the fencing of cleared ground were passed in 1631/2, 1642/3, 1657/8, 1661/2, and 1670. The act of 1657/8, titled "What fences shall be sufficient," ordered "that everie planter shall make a sufficient fence about his cleered ground at the least fower [four] foot and a halfe high." *Ibid.*, I, pp. 458, 176, 244, II, pp. 100–101, 279.

[35] In South Carolina, for instance, "in 1706 the building of wooden frame-houses in [Charleston] had been declared a common nuisance and prohibited, but . . . the act was repealed" in 1717. Edward McCrady, *The History of South Carolina under the Proprietary Government 1670–1719* (New York, 1897), pp. 573–574.

[36] For a discussion of the building provisions in this act, see Thomas Fiddian Reddaway, *The Rebuilding of London after the Great Fire* (London, 1940), pp. 80–81 and *passim*.

on Duke of Gloucester Street from it since a system of height control, with houses divided into classes according to the relative importance of the streets on which they fronted, was one of its great novelties.[37] Moreover, the specification of all measurements in multiples of ten shows that the Virginia legislators had London practice in mind, for ten feet was the length of the London carpenter's measuring rod.[38] The respect in which the London Rebuilding Act and the Williamsburg building acts were most similar was their workability and consequent effectiveness.

The act of 1705 was the last piece of legislation that directly affected building practices in Williamsburg. From the 1730s on, the colony's lawmakers attempted time and again to eradicate in other towns the notorious fire hazard of wooden chimneys, that is, chimneys with wooden frames that had an infilling of "cats" of clay and straw.[39] Thanks to its founders' foresight and to what one might term the metropolitan mentality of its inhabitants, it was a trouble from which Williamsburg never suffered.

## HOUSE DESIGN AND GEOMETRY

The architecture of eighteenth-century Williamsburg demonstrates the fascination with mathematical formulas that had played such an important role in the development of Western design. Geometrical pre-

---

[37] The requirements for the four classes of London houses are given in Moxon, *Mechanick Exercises,* pp. 262–264. Even the "first and least sort" had to have two stories and a cellar as well as a garret.

[38] Before and after the act, country buildings in Virginia were often built to measurements derived from the traditional "bay" system, which was based on a module of 16 feet, which was the width needed by two yokes of oxen in the stall. Thomas Tileston Waterman, "The Bay System in Colonial Virginia Building," *WMQ,* 2nd Ser., XV (April 1935), pp. 117–122. The minimum dimensions for the first houses at Savannah, Ga., were derived from the same system. In 1733/4, the trustees ordained that those who took up lots in the new town should erect "one House of Brick, or framed, square timber work, . . . containing at the least Twenty four feet in length, upon Sixteen in breadth, and eight feet in height." Frederick Doveton Nichols, *The Early Architecture of Georgia* (Chapel Hill, N. C., 1957), p. 26.

[39] There was legislation relating to wooden chimneys at Yorktown and Gloucester in 1734, Fredericksburg in 1742, Richmond in 1744, Port Royal, Newcastle, and Suffolk in 1745, Smithfield in 1752, Staunton, Strasburg, and New London in 1761, Fredericksburg in 1763, Manchester in 1769, Tappahannock in 1769, and Richmond in 1773. Hening, ed., *Statutes,* IV, p. 465, V, pp. 209, 274, 387, VI, p. 274, VII, pp. 475, 651, VIII, pp. 422, 424, 656. For a photograph of a Virginia cabin with a catted chimney, see A. Lawrence Kocher and Howard Dearstyne, *Colonial Williamsburg: Its Buildings and Gardens,* rev. ed. (Williamsburg, Va., 1961), p. 18.

cision may be easily discerned in some of the public buildings of
Williamsburg.[40] It may be observed in the designs of the city's private
dwellings as well.

Systems of proportion employing mathematical formulas may be divided into two groups, the modular and the geometrical. In modular
systems, which are essentially arithmetical, the dimensions of a building
and of its component parts may be stated in terms of a given unit,
the module. The prime example of a modular system is the classical
one as described by Vitruvius and elaborated by the theorists of the
Renaissance in which the semidiameter of a column at its base was
the module which, with its subdivisions, called minutes, was multiplied
or divided to give the correct dimensions for everything else. In geometrical systems, on the other hand, dimensions are derived from a line
of a given length by constructing one or more geometrical figures on
it.

The proportional formulas found in Virginia buildings of the eighteenth century were geometrical. Geometric methods of proportioning
were much used by medieval builders, and their application here followed ancient traditions. Practically, they had the advantage that the
lines of the design on paper could be repeated full-sized on site with
strings as an aid to accuracy in the work. Aesthetically, the geometrical
figures that thus regulated design were still believed to have an inherent
superiority even if the proofs of that superiority advanced by earlier
theorists had been forgotten.

To the early theorists, the most perfect figures were the circle and
the square. In colonial Virginia, the circular plan was confined to simple
utilitarian structures such as dovecotes and icehouses; the square, however, was fundamental to much domestic architecture. In Williamsburg,
houses that are square on plan (or nearly square) are the Peyton Randolph House (earliest section, twenty-eight feet by twenty-nine), the
Palmer House (thirty-six feet by forty), and the Orrell House (twenty-
eight feet by twenty-eight).[41] The Orrell House also measures twenty-

[40] Whiffen, *Public Buildings*, pp. 24, 80–82, 86, 100, 108, 157–160.
[41] Slight departures from geometrical exactitude in the vertical dimensions may well
have occurred in construction; measurements from ground level were of course at
the mercy of changes of grade through the years. Attempts to show that medieval
church plans were based on elaborate geometric figures of the polygram class have
been criticized as being dependent on insufficiently accurate measurements. Rather,
it would seem that owing to inevitable variations in construction, the use of such figures
can never be proved from the buildings alone. In the case of simpler figures such as
the square, the root-two rectangle, and the equilateral triangle, the burden of proof
is not so heavy and greater tolerances can reasonably be accepted.

eight feet from the top of the basement wall to the roof ridge; as a result, its timber structure fits into a regular diagrammatic cube.

More commonly used than the square for overall plan dimensions was the ratio 1 : 1½, which gave a square and a half. The smallest house on Duke of Gloucester Street permissible under the terms of the act that founded Williamsburg was to be of this proportion, or "twenty foot in width, and thirty foot in length." No house with these precise dimensions has survived, and it may be that few were built, but larger buildings of a square and a half on plan are the Archibald Blair House (approximately thirty feet by forty-five), the Coke-Garrett House (the eighteenth-century section is twenty-six feet by forty), the Robert Carter House (thirty feet by forty-five), and the George Wythe House (thirty-six feet, six inches by fifty-four feet, six inches). The 1 : 1½ ratio was also much employed in front elevations. The front elevation between the ground line and the cornice of the Palmer House forms a rectangle of twenty-six feet, six inches by forty. The front elevation of the Dr. Barraud House between the ground line and the roof ridge is thirty-one feet by forty-six. The elevation between the ground floor level and the roof ridge of the Archibald Blair and George Wythe houses forms a 1 : 1½ rectangle. The respective vertical measurements are thirty feet, nine inches and thirty-six feet, six inches; the horizontal, forty-six feet and fifty-four feet, six inches.

End elevations were more frequently controlled by the square. The height of the Archibald Blair House from ground floor to roof ridge and the depth of the plan are both thirty feet. The same dimensions in the George Wythe House are thirty-six feet. Another building that measures thirty feet by thirty feet in these dimensions is the gambrel-roofed Tayloe House. In the Ludwell-Paradise House, the base line of the figure drops from ground floor to ground level, giving a square of thirty-three feet, six inches. In the middle section of the Semple House, the height from the ground floor to the cornice was made equal to the depth of the plan and resulted in a square of twenty-one feet.

The double square was another common figure. The Bracken House is an example of a building twice as long as it is broad, being forty feet by twenty. The John Blair House as first planned was thirty-six feet by eighteen. Examples of elevations that were apparently designed as double squares are numerous. In the Moody House, the height from the first floor to the roof ridge is twenty-two feet, six inches and the total length of the front is forty-five feet. The same measurements in the Ludwell-Paradise House are thirty feet and sixty feet respectively.

In the Robert Carter, Charlton, and St. George Tucker houses, the front elevation between the basement wall and the eaves cornice forms a double square, the respective measurements being twenty-two feet, six inches by forty-five, twenty-two feet by forty-four, and twenty feet by forty. In the Archibald Blair and George Wythe houses, the base of the figure is at ground level and the top coincides with the eaves cornice. The respective measurements are twenty-three feet by forty-six and twenty-seven feet, three inches by fifty-four feet, six inches.

The gambrel-roofed Orrell House measures twenty-eight feet from the top of the basement wall to the roof ridge and thus its walls and roof are the same height. This correspondence seems to be uncommon in houses of two full stories, although it occurs in the Brafferton at the College of William and Mary.[42] It is found frequently in the story and one-half house. Williamsburg examples of one and one-half story houses in which the eaves cornice is precisely half as far from the ground as the roof ridge are the Brush-Everard (twelve feet, six inches), John Blair (thirteen feet), Coke-Garrett (thirteen feet in the eighteenth-century portion), Bracken (thirteen feet, six inches), and Nelson-Galt (fourteen feet).

The root-two rectangle, that is, the rectangle of which the length is equal to the diagonal of a square constructed on the breadth, seems to have been used less often than its frequent occurrence in the public buildings of Williamsburg might lead one to expect. In the Archibald Blair House, the height to the roof ridge can be stated as the length of the diagonal of a square constructed on half of the length of the building. It can also be stated as the length of the radius of a circle having its center at the midpoint of the ground line of the elevation and passing through the extremities of the eaves. Since the height of the George Wythe House ridge can also be stated in the latter terms but not in the former, it seems likely that the circle and not the root-two rectangle was the real determinant.

The equilateral triangle was much used, especially in the design of elevations. In both the Archibald Blair and George Wythe houses (*Figures 15 and 16*) the height of the chimneys is equal to the altitude of a triangle with sides of the length of the house. Outside Williamsburg, Westover, in Charles City County, seems to show the use of the same ratio, since its total length is sixty-four feet and the height to the top of the chimneys is fifty-five feet.[43] In the President's House at William

---

[42] Whiffen, *Public Buildings*, p. 108.

[43] For an elevation of Westover, see Thomas Tileston Waterman and John A. Barrows, *Domestic Colonial Architecture of Tidewater Virginia* (New York, 1932), pp. 80–81.

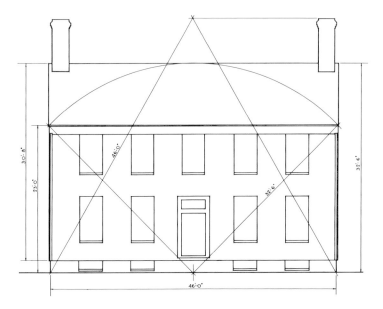

*Figure 15* Archibald Blair House. Diagrammatic elevation showing system of proportion.

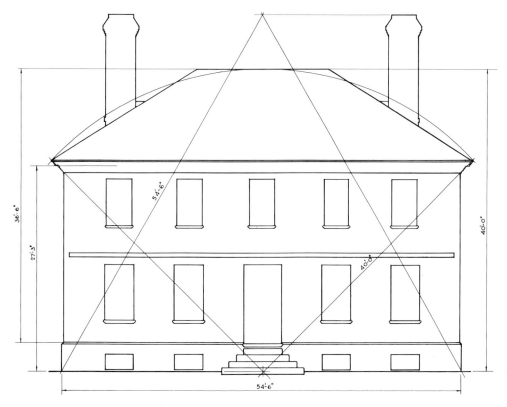

*Figure 16* George Wythe House. Diagrammatic elevation showing system of proportion.

and Mary, however, it is not the chimneys but the roof ridge whose height could have been determined by an equilateral triangle with sides of the longer plan dimension.[44] Other Virginia houses of which the same may be said are Ampthill, formerly in Chesterfield County, and Menokin, in Richmond County.[45]

The diagrammatic elevations of the Archibald Blair and George Wythe houses demonstrate that geometric systems of proportion were employed in eighteenth-century Virginia. The fact that many, indeed most, of these ratios are not perceptible as such to the human eye in the completed building does not detract from their efficacy as controlling factors in the impression that the building makes on the beholder. The eye alone cannot tell when a facade is exactly twice as long as it is high, still less that the height to the eaves is half the height to the roof ridge. But such ratios have distinctive effects on the eye, which will perceive departures from them. The general use of certain ratios to determine the proportions of buildings is one of the factors that give Virginia colonial architecture a homogeneity that transcends the differences of one building from the next—in short, they are significant among the factors that enable it to be recognized as a style.

---

[44] See Whiffen, *Public Buildings*, p. 126, for an elevation.
[45] For elevations, see Waterman and Barrows, *Domestic Colonial Architecture*, pp. 46–47, 154–155.

# 5

## *Houses of Williamsburg: Construction and Details*

HAVING surveyed the materials and "necessaries," native and imported, that went into the houses of Williamsburg, having discussed what is known of the training and the lives of some of the men who built them and seen what tools and books they used in the exercise of their crafts, and having considered the main forms that the houses took and the general factors that influenced their design, it is time to look at those houses rather more closely, to see how they were put together and how they were made pleasing to the eye. Obviously, there is a limit to the minuteness of detail into which such an investigation can lead if this study as a whole is not to be overbalanced. Furthermore, few generalizations can be offered about any architecture, even one so set in its ways as the domestic architecture of eighteenth-century Virginia, to which no exceptions are to be found. When all due qualifications have been made, however, a mind's eye picture of the features that are typical of the time and place, the eighteenth century and the Virginia colony—or, more narrowly, Williamsburg—will emerge.

### THE HOUSE FRAME

Most houses were built of wood, and an account of the frame of a timber-built house (*Figure 17*) logically starts with the groundsills, which rest on the foundation walls and support all of the rest of the structure. There were four groundsills in a house of rectangular plan built all at one time unless one or more was interrupted by a chimney. In Williamsburg they were of square or nearly square section measuring about six to eight by eight to ten inches. When they were not square, they were bedded on their broad sides. Where they met at the corners of the building, they were joined by one of two methods, the mortise-

*Figure 17*  Ewing House. Frame stripped for restoration.

and-tenon or the half-lap. If the mortise-and-tenon joint were employed, the mortise was cut in the longer sills at the front and rear of the building and the shorter sills, at the ends, were tenoned to fit into them. Supported partly by the brickwork of the foundation walls and partly by the front and rear sills, the ground-floor joists were sometimes notched into the sills and sometimes mortised. There was some variation in the scantling, or sectional dimensions, of joists in Williamsburg. In the typical story and one-half A-roof house, they were normally three to four inches wide by about eight inches deep, although in larger houses they may have been three to four inches by ten or even twelve inches.

At the four corners, over the junction of the groundsills, stood the most important upright members of the house frame, the corner posts. In the great majority of cases, they were oblong and the narrower sides were about two inches shorter than the broad faces. An exceptional form occurred in the George Reid House, where to insure that unusually heavy posts did not appear inside the house, each corner post was cut back on its inner face so that in cross section it became an equilateral L. The broader sides of the corner posts, which sometimes were equal in breadth to the groundsills but more often were a little narrower, faced to the front and rear of the building. The length of the corner posts determined the height of the building from sill to roof, and the existence of two posts standing one over the other—as in the central section of the St. George Tucker House—always means that the house has been heightened since it was first built.

Since either of the usual methods of joining the groundsills reduced the amount of wood in their ends to a degree that made any deep insertion of the corner posts into them difficult and risky, the feet of the posts were equipped, at most, with small tenons and often merely rested on the sills. The chief means of holding them in place were the corner braces, a pair to each post, which were diagonal members tenoned into the sill at a point usually between five and six feet from the corner post at one end and into the post some six to eight feet above the sill at the other. The mortise-and-tenon joints, like all other major mortise-and-tenon joints in the frame, were secured with wooden pins called treenails. The corner braces, which were not dressed neatly but were left quite rough, were usually equal in width to the deeper dimension of the studs, while the breadth of their vertical surfaces might have been anything up to, or even greater than, the breadth of the corner posts. Since cutting two mortises into adjoining faces of the posts at the same level weakened the latter unduly, one brace of each pair was tenoned into the post at a higher level than the other and was also somewhat longer. Using this system of bracing, windows and doors could never be placed close to the corners of the building, a point missed by many purveyors of colonial revival houses today. The outer surfaces of corner posts, studs, and braces were all kept flush.

In addition to corner posts, intermediate posts of the same or smaller scantling might have been placed at intervals. Sometimes they had a brace similar to the corner braces on each side, sometimes they were braced on one side only, and sometimes they were not braced at all.

*Figure 18*    Dr. Barraud House. Interior showing normal spacing of studs.

Where intermediate posts existed, there was a natural tendency to abut the internal partitions against them, but it was not the invariable practice to do so and many smaller houses had no intermediate posts. In the George Reid House, where the form of the corner posts was unusual, the intermediate posts were shaped into a T section, the partitions being received by the foot of the T.

The secondary vertical members in the wall frame were the studs, which were much lighter than the posts and had a scantling of two and one-half to four by three and one-half to six inches. The commonest size was about three inches by four; studs as much as six inches deep were rare.[1] Normally they were spaced from twenty to twenty-two inches center to center (*Figures 18 and 19*). The method of framing the studs varied a good deal. Sometimes they were tenoned below and above— that is, into the sill and into the plate—and sometimes they were tenoned below but not above; sometimes they were notched into the plate with a diagonal cut, and sometimes they were simply nailed. There was a relationship between the spacing of the studs and the framing of the

---

[1] Smokehouses, storehouses, and the like were sometimes built with heavy studs, about 4 by 6 inches at 12-inch centers, to prevent forcible entry. Market Square Tavern illustrates an example of such construction in a dwelling house. See Fig. 19.

*Figure 19*  Market Square Tavern. Southeast room showing studs at one-foot center.

diagonal braces because the latter customarily were tenoned into the sill where the third stud from the post that was braced would otherwise have met it. This stud was cut off diagonally at the foot and was fastened to the upper surface of the brace. The two studs between it and the post broke at the brace and were nailed to its upper and lower surfaces.

For the sake of simplicity, the studs have been described as being fastened at the top to the plate. This was true of a single story or story and one-half house, and therefore of most of the frame houses in Williamsburg. But in a frame house with two full stories, the next horizontal member above the groundsill was the one that supported the second floor. Whether or not the term was used in Virginia, we may follow the example of J. Frederick Kelly and call it the girt.[2] The ends of the girts were framed into the corner posts, and from their upper surfaces rose the studs of the second story, which were placed over those of the first. The girts at the front and rear of the house also received the ends of the joists. In a small house, the joists spanned the whole depth of the plan. In a larger one, each joist extended approximately halfway and its inner end was framed into a heavy longitudinal

---

[2] J. Frederick Kelly, *The Early Domestic Architecture of Connecticut* (New Haven, Conn., 1924), pp. 31, 32, 34.

member called a summer beam. Summer beams were used in frame buildings in Virginia less often than they were in New England, however.

In a frame building, the plate was effectively a part of the wall in that it held the upper ends of the studs in place. In a brick building, its function was to provide a homogeneous base for the wooden roof structure. It was therefore of oblong section and was laid flat, its breadth usually being two to four inches less than the thickness of the wall below. In a frame building, if it was not square in section, it was framed with its broader sides, which in Williamsburg measured from six to nine inches across, laid vertically; its breadth in this case was equal to the larger sectional dimension of the studs, which varied in Williamsburg from three and one-half to six inches. The end plates were framed so that their upper surfaces were level with the upper surfaces of the joists, which were notched over the front and rear plates to a depth of from three-quarters of an inch to one and one-half inches and projected outside them from eight inches to one foot, three inches. Unless the roof was hipped, the gable-end studs, which did not necessarily range with the studs below, rose from the end plates.

In the great majority of cases, there was no infilling between the members of the frame. However, a few instances of brick nogging have been found in Williamsburg (*Figure 20*), and there is a reference to the practice in a 1789 memorandum relating to the St. George Tucker

*Figure 20*   Peyton Randolph House. Brick nogging.

House: "M^r William Harwood undertakes to fill in the sides of S. G. Tuckers house with brick bats plaistered in clay, and to cover the same."[3] It may be worth noting that an experiment in brick nogging by Colonial Williamsburg was greeted with enthusiasm by the termites.

## THE ROOF FRAME

The types of roofs commonly used in Williamsburg were the gable roof, which was constructed in the shape of an A or triangle, the gambrel roof, which had a double slope back and front, and the hip roof, which had four slopes. The Robert Carter House is unique in that it has a mansard roof with four double slopes.

In tidewater Virginia, the structural frames of roofs of all types included a member, the use of which was uncommon in England and New England. The member, now termed a false plate, was usually in the form of a board, about one and one-half inches thick by six to eight inches wide, laid flat on the ends of the joists that projected beyond the wall (*Figures 21 and 22*). More rarely, and, it would seem, most often in early buildings, the secondary plate was a scantling of square section let into the upper surface of the joists diagonally (*Figure 23*).[4] The lower ends of the rafters were attached to this false plate instead of into the wall plate as occurred in more conventional systems of roof framing. In the flat type, they were cut off diagonally at the foot and rested on its upper surface, while in the diagonal type, they were notched over its uppermost angle and continued beyond the ends of the joists.

The term false plate is not found in the glossaries. In the eighteenth century, a false plate was called a raising plate. It has been adopted here from William Penn's *Information and Direction to Such Persons as are inclined to America, more Especially Those related to the Province of Pennsylvania*, printed in 1684. In his tract, Penn gave instructions for building a frame house thirty feet long by eighteen broad. After describing the plates "for the *Gists* [joists] to rest upon," he added, "there must be ten *Gists* of twenty foot long, to bear the Loft, and two false *Plates* of thirty foot long to lie upon the ends of the *Gists* for the *Rafters* to be fixed upon."[5] Since Penn's false plates lay on the ends of the joists, they

---

[3] Harwood Memorandum.

[4] No example of this type has survived in Williamsburg, but it was doubtless used here.

[5] Quoted in Harold R. Shurtleff, *The Log Cabin Myth* (Cambridge, Mass., 1939), p. 125. The significance of this passage in relation to Williamsburg practice was pointed out to me by Singleton P. Moorehead.

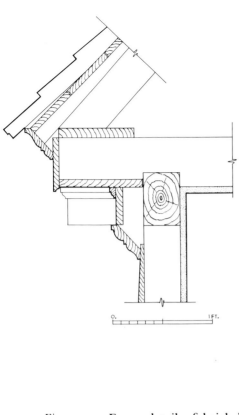

*Figure 21* Eaves detail of frame house (Brush-Everard House).

*Figure 22* Eaves detail of brick house (Palmer House).

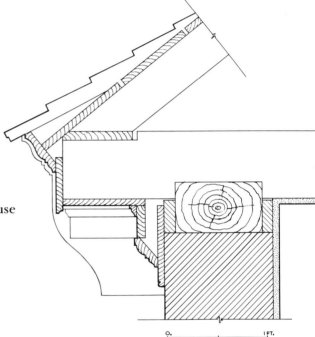

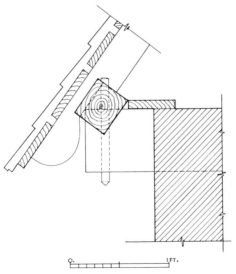

*Figure 23* Eaves detail of brick house showing false plate set diagonally (Lynnhaven House, Princess Anne County, Virginia).

resembled the feature in its commoner Williamsburg form more closely than did either the Connecticut examples of the second plate illustrated by Kelly or Owen Biddle's raising piece, both of which were framed into tie beams or into end girts.[6]

The false plate greatly facilitated bringing forward the eaves to make room for a classical cornice. This could be accomplished by fastening the feet of the rafters directly to the projecting ends of the joists. The spacing of the rafters and the spacing of the joists therefore had to be the same. When the false plate was used, the spacing could be different, and in Williamsburg the rafters, at about two feet from center to center, were in fact usually a little more widely spaced than the joists.

While the use of the false plate characterized Williamsburg roof framing positively, a negative characteristic was the absence of any ridgepiece. The normal A roof of the smaller house was framed with common rafters of three- to four-inch by five-inch scantling, with collar beams, sometimes called wind beams,[7] to tie each pair of rafters together at approximately two-thirds of the height of the roof structure. The rafters were left quite rough except at the joints. At the ridge, the rafters were joined with an open-end mortise-and-tenon and were pegged; the collar beams were joined to the rafters with half-lap dovetails and were nailed.

The gambrel roof may be described simplistically as the lower part of an A roof in which the rafters have been cut off level with the upper surfaces of the collar beams, lengthened to give the rafters a much steeper pitch, with a complete A roof of conventional construction on top of it. The longitudinal members to which the lower ends of the upper rafters were fastened were called the curb plates. They rested on the lower rafters and not on the studs of the gambrel story,[8] although

---

[6] On p. 127 of *Early Domestic Architecture*, Kelly described the arrangement illustrated as "somewhat common." See also p. 124, fig. 126, p. 125, fig. 127, and Owen Biddle, *The Young Carpenter's Assistant; or, A System of Architecture, adapted to the Style of Building in the United States* (Philadelphia, 1805), plate 26, facing p. 34. The term is an ancient one derived from the Anglo-Saxon *raesn*, a beam. Salzman, *Building in England*, p. 203.

[7] Collar beams is a more familiar term today, but wind beams may have been more commonly used in the eighteenth century. The contract for building the Lower Chapel, Middlesex County, Va., in 1717 described the roof, which is of the type now often called the clipped gabled roof, as "hipped above the wind beams." C. G. Chamberlayne, ed., *The Vestry Book of Christ Church Parish, Middlesex County, Virginia 1663–1767* (Richmond, 1927), p. 140.

[8] Virginia practice differed significantly from that in Connecticut, where the curb plates were generally supported by posts resting on transverse beams or girts. Kelly, *Early Domestic Architecture*, p. 60.

the latter, which were fastened to the lower rafters at the top and to the joists at the foot, naturally had some bracing effect, as did the studs in a gable roof.

Only a few buildings had roofs with framed principals, or trusses— among those of brick, the George Wythe House, the Palmer House, and Prentis Store, but not the Ludwell-Paradise House, and among those of timber, Wetherburn's Tavern. The trusses were usually of the king-post type, that is, they had a single vertical post from the tie beam to the ridge with diagonal braces. The Prentis Store, however, had a queen-post roof with two vertical members in each truss. Only in trussed roofs were the longitudinal members called purlins employed. Framed into the principals, they helped to support the common rafters, to which they were joined in a variety of ways. Most commonly the rafters were notched over them, but sometimes the rafters were simply laid against them without any cutting. At the other extreme, the rafters sometimes broke at the purlins and had their ends tenoned into them. Trussed roofs also had a variety of diagonal braces between the trusses that usually followed no regular pattern and were somewhat haphazard, if not chaotic, in effect. Where the braces met the rafters, it was the rafters that were interrupted.

## WEATHERBOARDS AND SHINGLES

The sheathing of surviving eighteenth-century Virginia frame houses is nearly always of sawed weatherboards, most commonly of yellow pine but sometimes of poplar. An alternative for walls as well as for roofs were narrow split boards of oak about four feet long.[9] Such clap-boards, used extensively in the seventeenth century, became less common on substantial houses in the eighteenth. Another possible alternative, horizontal flush boarding, was generally confined to dormers and porches on houses, although it was used extensively on outbuildings. Interiors in Williamsburg finished with original horizontal flush boarding include the Nicolson Shop and Market Square Tavern.

Weatherboards were normally about seven and one-half inches wide. They were made by dividing ordinary boards through their thickness so that each board supplied two weatherboards. The cut was diagonal to give each weatherboard a wedgelike cross section. The right-angled, or outer, arris of the thicker edge of the weatherboard was usually

---

[9] For Williamsburg examples, see chap. 1, n. 19.

beaded for all but the simplest type of buildings, that is, it was given a small segmental molding with a molding plane (*Figure 24*). This bead might be called the hallmark of colonial work in Virginia since it was used for boards of all kinds and in all positions and also on door and window frames. Besides producing a good shadow, it had the practical advantage of preventing splintering.

The weatherboards were nailed to the frame with an overlap of about one and one-half inches so that each had an exposure of about six inches "to the weather." The bottom weatherboard over-lapped the brick of the basement wall about one-half inch. Each corner of the building was finished with a corner board, a narrow, vertical board, also beaded, that was nailed to the front of the corner post. The outer surfaces of the corner board were flush with the beaded edges of the weatherboards that were stopped against it. Where beaded weatherboards ran up against a windowsill, the bead might have been contin-ued along the lower outer edge of the sill. At the top of the wall, there sometimes was a board with a vertical face, flush with the corner boards, to receive the cornice; this board was beaded like the weatherboards, the uppermost of which it overlapped.

The way in which the members of the eaves cornice were fixed to the rafters and the projecting joists is illustrated in *Figure 21.* There was nothing specifically indigenous to Vir-ginia in the details of the cornice, which followed the usual classical patterns with variations, from one building to the next, suggested by the taste and knowledge of the individual carpenter, and the expense of the building. But there is one point to be noted. In colonial Virginia, the treatment of the end of the cornice in A-roof buildings was unusual. In such buildings, the cornice was never returned only a short dis-tance along the gable wall, as was the common practice in New England. If the cornice returned along the gable wall at all, it continued right across it from side to side so as to turn the gable into a pediment. More often than not, it stopped against a shaped endboard, the outer face of which was flush with the rakeboard of the roof. Endboards did not necessarily follow the profile of the cornice, and showed considerable variety of design.

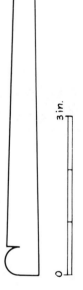

*Figure 24* Section of typical beaded weath-erboard.

A refinement in the design of the rakeboards developed in Virginia. Instead of having parallel edges, they nearly always tapered toward the ridge, and the rakeboards of gabled dormers did the same. It is proper to call this development a refinement, since there can be no doubt that it is one of those details which, although it is hardly noticeable until it is pointed out, contributed materially to the characteristic beauty of the colonial Virginia house.

The shingles were nailed to random-width boards or to shingle laths or roofers (the name they bore until quite recently), which were nailed to the rafters. Roofers varied in width from four to six inches. As a rule, they were abutted edge to edge, with a space of one to two inches left between them to allow the house to breathe.[10] Shingles were of random widths, from three to five inches, and were usually about eighteen inches long. They were laid with about a six-inch exposure.[11] Although square-butt shingles were common enough, those with round butts seem to have been in the majority. The round-butt shingle had a practical advantage in that it did not curl like the square-butt shingle was apt to do, and it seems likely that it was preferred for reasons of appearance also. It should be noted that only a few shingles on any roof would have truly segmental butts because, owing to the fact that their widths varied, a roof covered with such shingles would have presented a series of intolerably erratic lines to the eighteenth-century eye.

The shingles were fantailed at the hips of a roof, as shown in *Figure 25*. Valleys and ridges confronted the colonial builder with difficulties that his modern counterpart overcomes with special tiles or metal flashing, both of which were denied to him. In a valley, which occurred where the main roof met that of a dormer or another roof set at a right angle, the shingles were carried over from one to the other. Whether at the ridge of the main roof or of a dormer, the shingles were laid so that those on one side projected about two inches above and over those on the other. This "comb" at the roof ridge was laid to extend away from the direction of prevailing winds. The choice of which side of the ridge to carry up in this manner was not settled by chance or whim but with a sound regard for orientation since it had to be the side that received the most prolonged rain and heavy winds.

---

[10] In the early days of the restoration, the point was missed and some roofs were redone with closely fitting boards, which rendered the rooms immediately below them practically uninhabitable during summer nights until the mistake was recognized and rectified. Singleton P. Moorehead supplied this information.

[11] For additional information about shingle sizes, see chap. 1, n. 20.

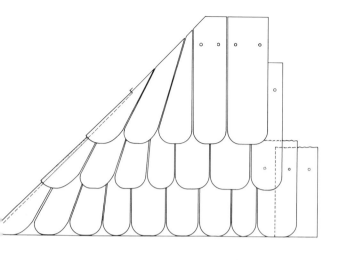
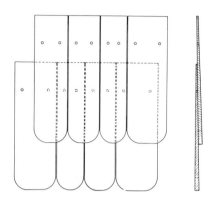

*Figure 25*   Details of shingled roof showing fan-tailing at hip (left) and system of lapping (right).

In Virginia, where it was common knowledge that the northeasterly storms were the ones to be feared, the eighteenth-century builder chose the north or east.

Earlier ages did not regard shingles as a makeshift, a substitute for more durable kinds of roofing. In medieval England, oak shingles were much used on buildings on the royal estates, and it was the rising cost of timber as much as anything else that led to their being superseded by stone slates and earthen tiles.[12] To an eighteenth-century Virginian the relatively low cost and lightness of a shingled roof may have counter-balanced the disadvantages of its short life and inflammable nature.

It was a fixed principle of the eighteenth-century builder that all wood-work exposed to the weather should be given a protective coating. Shingles, as a quantity of evidence shows, were often tarred,[13] but there is no evidence that they were sprinkled with sand while still wet, a practice that an observant Russian traveler described as general in early nine-teenth-century America.[14] Sometimes shingles were painted with oil paint, and sometimes, as the agreement between St. George Tucker and Jeremiah Satterwhite transcribed in Appendix II shows, fish oil

---

[12] Salzman, *Building in England,* pp. 228–229.

[13] Whiffen, *Public Buildings,* p. 212, n. 23.

[14] Avrahm Yarmolinsky, trans., *Picturesque United States of America, 1811, 1812, 1813, being a Memoir on Paul Svinin, Russian Diplomatic Officer, Artist, and Author* (New York, 1930), p. 40. Svinin actually described the roofs "covered with pine or oak shingles" as being "painted with black oil paint," but surely he was mistaken and should have written tarred.

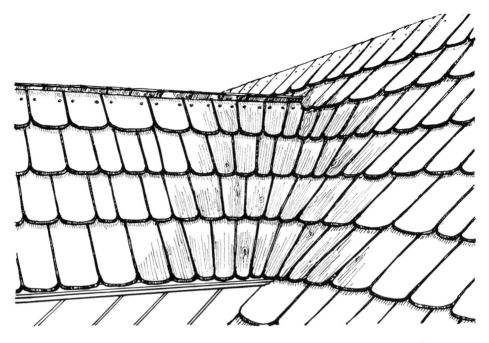

*Figure 26*   Detail of shingled roof showing woven or swept valley.

was mixed in with the paint.[15] Hugh Jones wrote that weatherboards were painted with white lead as early as the first quarter of the eighteenth century,[16] and numerous references to white lead in the documents make it clear that it was often used later as an exterior paint, as well as to lighten other pigments. Reds, browns, grays, blues, greens, and ochres also appeared. The Tucker-Satterwhite agreement tells more about the painting of a Williamsburg house in the late eighteenth century than any record yet discovered.

## BRICKWORK

Although houses built wholly of brick were in a minority in Virginia, there was always enough demand for the bricklayer's services to make his craft a vital and developing one throughout the colonial period.

---

[15] In this case, the roofs were to be painted with Spanish brown, but other colors were used. In 1774 the Scottish tutor John Harrower, newly arrived in the colony, noted that the roofs of the houses in the main street at Fredericksburg were "all covered with wood made in the form of slates about four Inches broad, which when painted blew you wou'd not know it from a house sclated with Isedell sclate." Riley, ed., *Journal of Harrower,* p. 38. See Appendix II.

[16] Jones, *Present State of Virginia,* p. 71: "Here [at Williamsburg] as in other parts, they build with brick, but most commonly with timber lined with cieling, and cased with feather-edged plank, painted with white lead and oil."

Even in frame houses, the foundations and chimneys were normally of brick, and the shortage of stone led to the frequent use of brick for steps and paving.

In the seventeenth century, brick walls were most commonly laid in English bond, which featured alternate courses of headers and stretchers. In the eighteenth, Flemish bond—headers and stretchers alternating in each course—was the rule. For a major example of English bond in Williamsburg, one must go to the oldest walls of the College of William and Mary, which antedate the founding of the town. However, English bond continued to be employed quite often for the foundation walls and chimneys of frame houses, and it was used in brick houses below the water table. Whatever the bond, the mortar joints of all exterior brickwork, which varied in width from one-fourth to one-half inch, were struck, or tooled, so that after the joints had been cleaned with a trowel, an incised line was drawn along the center of the face of the mortar with a special iron tool, sometimes called a jointer,[17] and the aid of a straightedge.

The walls of a brick house could be articulated and given richness and variety through the use of rubbed, molded, cut, and gauged bricks and glazed headers, bricks that developed a dark glazed surface from proximity to the fire in the kiln. Some of the sand used in the brickmaker's molds to prevent the clay from sticking to the wood adhered to the bricks' surfaces when they left the molds. Rubbed bricks took their name from the fact that the sand was removed from the exposed rough surfaces of selected trim bricks by rubbing them with a rubstone or sometimes with other bricks so that they became quite smooth. Bricks whose position in the kiln resulted in their being rather soft and of a light red color were chosen for rubbing. Molded bricks were what today would be called cast, since they were made in specially shaped molds for use in water tables, stringcourses, and doorways. Cut bricks were shaped with a chisel or brick ax. Gauged bricks were shaped with special care, either by cutting or molding, then they were rubbed and laid with very close joints, the mortar being not more than one-eighth inch thick and sometimes as little as one-sixteenth inch.

The techniques of the colonial bricklayer may be observed in Williamsburg at the George Wythe House, which was erected circa 1750. The bond was Flemish above the water table and English below it. All joints, vertical and horizontal, were struck. The small bricks known as closers

---

[17] The mason's jointer should not be confused with the carpenter's tool of the same name. See p. 47.

were used consistently next to the end header in each course that terminated with a header, both at the corners of the building and at the window and door openings. Otherwise, the brickwork was far from uniform since the colonial bricklayer did not aim at mechanical accuracy, which was unattainable with bricks that varied so much in size, but rather at a satisfactory effect. The bond had intrinsic irregularities, the commonest of which was the substitution of a pair of headers for a stretcher, a standard device for reducing by a fraction of an inch the length of the course in which it occurred. Such a solution usually was preferred to the alternative of cutting a stretcher to fit. A scattering of glazed headers was used above the water table, but they did not form any regular pattern. Rubbed brick was used for all quoins and jambs above the water table, but not below it, and the water table itself, a simple chamfer, was of rubbed brick. The flat arches over the windows and doors were of rubbed and gauged brick. True arches, they were self-supporting but only one brick thick,[18] and the wall behind them was carried over the openings on wooden lintels. The stringcourse or belt course at the upper floor level was also of rubbed and gauged work. The three courses, which stopped short of the corners of the building, were equal in height to two courses of the wall bricks. The chimneys were laid in Flemish bond with closers and had substantial caps, each of which consisted of four courses corbeled out to the widest projection, which was two courses high with vertical faces. Above that, four courses of cut or molded brick were drawn into the chimney top, which also had two courses with vertical faces. Finally, the brick steps had oak nosings to minimize wear.

Where a regular pattern of glazed headers existed and it was necessary to lay two or more headers side by side to bring a course to the requisite length, the colonial bricklayer was careful to use unglazed bricks for the extra header, or headers, and so maintained the pattern. At the Ludwell-Paradise House, there were headers in pairs to the left of the front door and in triplets to the left of the window above it. Although closers were invariably used at the corners of a building, convenience sometimes led to their omission at jambs, as occurred in the President's House at the College. In the George Wythe House, as in most of the brick buildings in Williamsburg, the rubbed brick of the quoins and jambs was kept to a minimum and only the last brick in each course,

---

[18] They may be less than one brick thick, since Singleton P. Moorehead told me that he saw arches made of rubbed and gauged bricks cut down the center with the space behind them filled with mortar.

header or stretcher as the case may be, was rubbed. The Prentis Store, however, showed intermediate rubbing, to adopt the late Herbert A. Claiborne's convenient terminology,[19] with rubbed closers also. There is no example in Williamsburg of maximum rubbing, in which the headers next to the end stretchers and the stretchers next to the closers, as well as the end bricks and the closers, were rubbed. Carter's Grove, however, exhibited maximum rubbing in its original brickwork. Plain, unrubbed brick was normally used for the quoins below the water table.

Sometimes—in the Ludwell-Paradise and Palmer houses, for instance, as well as at the College—segmental arches of rubbed and gauged work were employed for the basement windows instead of the flat arches that were used at the George Wythe House. But no brick house in Williamsburg had segmental window arches above the water table. All extant eighteenth-century brick houses in the town have a plain chamfer for the water table,[20] and a stringcourse usually three stretchers in width constitutes the common type of belt course. The Lightfoot House is unique in having a belt course with moldings, a cove below and an ovolo or quarter-round above. Chimney caps varied somewhat in the design of their upper portions, but they usually started with three or four corbeled courses. They tended to become simpler toward the end of the century. The outside chimneys of frame houses, which with their sloping weatherings can become fascinating pieces of abstract sculpture, inspired the bricklayer to use a good deal of ad hoc ingenuity. The best old specimens in Williamsburg are the west chimney at the George Reid House and the east chimney of the Bracken House (*Figure 27*). Fireplace jambs were sometimes lined with gauged bricks as they were in the central room of the Peyton Randolph House.

Brick gutters at the foot of exterior walls are a feature of many houses in Williamsburg. The gutters were intended to catch and carry away the rain that fell from the eaves, and therefore they are not found at gable ends. It is probably erroneous to regard brick gutters as a second-best substitute for lead eaves gutters, since that metal was both costly and scarce. Eighteenth-century builders were well aware of the disadvan-

---

[19] Herbert A. Claiborne, *Comments on Virginia Brickwork before 1800* (Boston, 1957). Of 45 buildings in Virginia having quoins and jambs of rubbed brick that were examined and described by Claiborne, 28 showed minimum, 9 intermediate, and 8 maximum rubbing.

[20] This was by far the most common type of water table in Virginia as a whole. Claiborne, *ibid.*, noted 38 chamfered or beveled water tables, as against 5 simple setbacks, 1 cove, 6 ovolos, and 12 with more elaborate moldings.

tages of eaves gutters under certain circumstances. In the *Builder's Dictionary* (1734) appeared, under the heading "Roof":

> The common pitch [i.e., the pitch resulting from the use of rafters whose length equals three-quarters of the breadth of the building], is not only unpleasing to the Eye, but is attended with this Inconvenience, if there be a Gutter round the Building, the Steepness of the Roof occasions Rain to come with so sudden a Velocity and Force into the Pipes, which are to convey the Water from the Gutters . . . and sometimes to that Degree, that the Water runs under the Covering of the Roof, and very much endamages the Timber, &c. of the Building.[21]

What was true of eaves gutters with a roof of common pitch in England was, owing to the much heavier rain, true of them with any kind of roof in Virginia. The trouble that might have resulted from water running in under the eaves was of course aggravated when the building

---

[21] *The Builder's Dictionary: or, Architect's Companion,* II (London, 1734), s.v. "roof."

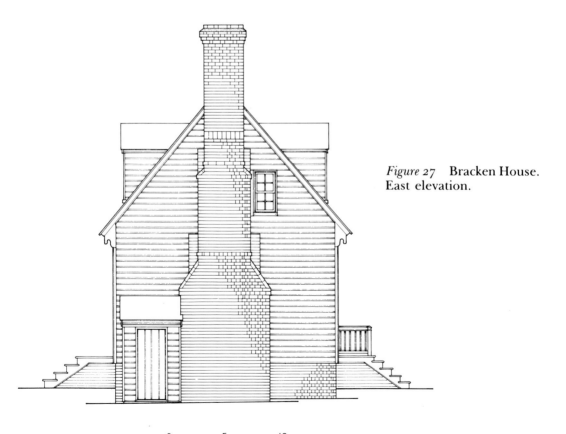

*Figure 27*   Bracken House.
East elevation.

0.          5.          10.

was of wood construction. The brick gutter may therefore be regarded as an eminently rational solution to a special regional problem.[22]

## WINDOWS AND DOORS

Nothing contributes more to the external effect of the Williamsburg house than its sash windows: they give it scale and sparkle.

In seventeenth-century Virginia, casement windows with leaded lights were the rule for houses that boasted more than wooden shutters to keep out the elements. Sash windows were specified for the Capitol in the act of 1699,[23] however, and it is likely that they were universal in the private houses of Williamsburg from the first. They were not a new invention; the *Dictionary of Architecture* of the Architectural Publication Society quoted what sounds like a description of sash windows from a book published in 1519,[24] although the first use of them in any quantity in England seems to date only from 1685–1686, when sash windows appeared in the new wing built for James II at Whitehall Palace by Sir Christopher Wren.[25] That they were beginning to become fashionable is suggested by an advertisement in the *London Gazette* in 1686: "Any Person may be furnished with Glasses for Sashwindows . . . at Mr. Dukes Shop."[26] It was not until Queen Anne's reign, however, that sash windows were generally substituted for casements in the older houses of London,[27] so in this respect, Williamsburg was well abreast of London practice.

Sash windows are usually thought to have been invented in England; certainly it was from England that they were introduced into France (where they never became popular) at the end of the seventeenth century.[28] According to the *Dictionary of Architecture*, the weight-and-pulley device by which the sashes were held at the required height and which by the time of Wren's Whitehall addition had succeeded the notch-and-catch contrivance employed in the earliest examples, "is

---

[22] Considerable remains of brick gutters were found at the Palace and the Palmer House, among many other locations in town. How extensively they were used in eighteenth-century Williamsburg is a speculative question. Their bricks, laid in sand, offered themselves rather readily for diversion to other uses.

[23] Whiffen, *Public Buildings,* pp. 42, 227.

[24] *Dictionary of Architecture,* VII, s.v. "sash," which quotes from William Horman, *Vulgaria.*

[25] *Wren Society,* VII, pp. 98, 108.

[26] *Oxford English Dictionary,* IX, s.v. "sash-window."

[27] Sir John Summerson, *Georgian London,* (London, 1945), pp. 52–53.

[28] Martin Lister, *Journey to Paris* (1699), quoted in *Dictionary of Architecture,* VII, s.v. "sash."

considered to be a Dutch invention."[29] Evidently at least some of the Capitol sashes did not have weights and pulleys at first, because in June 1723 the Council ordered "that Mr. John Holloway and Mr. John Clayton who have the care of repairing the Capitol, do cause all the Windows in the Chambers on the 1st & 2nd floor of the Capitol to be made to run wth Leads."[30] The indications are that by the end of the colonial period, all but the smallest sash windows in Williamsburg were equipped with weights and pulleys, although the vast majority were still single-hung so that only their lower sashes could be moved up and down.[31] The muntins, or sash bars, varied astonishingly little in design (*Figure 28*). It was evidently a rule that the two segmental moldings on the inner side of the glass should have a common center whatever the thickness of the muntin or the relative sizes of its flat faces.

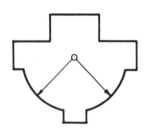

*Figure 28* Section of typical muntin or sash bar.

A feature that distinguished eighteenth-century brick houses in Williamsburg, and indeed in Virginia generally, from their contemporaries in London was the setting of the window frame close to the outer face of the wall. It was forbidden in London by an act of Parliament of 1709 that ordained, as an anti-fire measure, that the frames were to be set back four inches behind the wall plane.[32] The act did not apply to the English provinces, but like other London building acts, it affected them indirectly. Throughout the colonial period, Virginians continued to prefer the decorative effect of the older practice to the appearance of solidity given by deeper reveals.

What may be termed a local peculiarity in the design of fenestration, at least until it is demonstrated that it occurred in other localities, was the scaling down of upper floor windows. Williamsburg examples include the George Wythe and St. George Tucker houses. An earlier example (ca. 1730) outside Williamsburg is provided by Westover.[33]

---

[29] *Ibid.*

[30] McIlwaine, ed., *Legislative Journals*, II, p. 703.

[31] The oldest part of the Peyton Randolph House was found by Colonial Williamsburg architects to be equipped with double-hung sash windows which, by the fixing of the upper valves, had been converted during the eighteenth century to a single-hung arrangement.

[32] Summerson, *Georgian London*, p. 52.

[33] Waterman and Barrows, *Domestic Colonial Architecture*, pp. 80–81. The variation in window size is more easily seen in the quarter-inch scale detail on p. 83.

It was usual enough in classical facades for the vertical dimension of the upper windows to measure less than that of those below; for them to be narrower was by all the rules most improper. Yet in the George Wythe House, whose design had some pretension to academic propriety, the upper window openings are narrower than the lower, being three feet, six inches wide as against four feet, as well as being less tall, six feet, six inches against seven feet, nine inches. This is not immediately noticeable because all of the parts of the upper windows were scaled in proportion: their panes measure eight inches by ten while those in the lower are ten inches by twelve, and their sash bars are one and three-eighth inches wide while those in the lower are one and five-eighths inches. A marked ambiguity of scale resulted.[34]

Dormers are a prime example of a feature that by the eighteenth century had acquired distinctively Virginia forms (*Figures 29 and 30*). Dormers were not an integral part of the roof structure, but were framed separately. Each was fixed to the upper surfaces of two rafters, over the boarding to which the shingles were nailed, the intervening rafters being cut away as necessary for the window openings. They could therefore be added to or removed from a house at will, and they often were. Virginia dormers had noticeably taller proportions than their counterparts in England. It might be supposed that this was the result of the invariable use of single-hung sashes. Although it is true that in England casements were often retained for dormers when the windows of the main floors were equipped with sashes, English dormers exist that were sashed from the first and yet do not approach the Virginia proportions. In the story and one-half Virginia house, the dormers supplied a strongly vertical accent. The proportions of Virginia dormers were distinctive, yet two other important characteristics isolated them as a singular class or category. In eighteenth-century buildings in Virginia, the slope of the roof of a dormer was nearly always the same as that of the main roof from which it projected. When the latter was a gambrel, the dormer roof slope was the same as the upper slope of the gambrel roof. Virginia dormers also approached standardization in the treatment of the boarding on their cheeks, or sides, which nearly always was of flush, beaded boards with lapped joints that ran parallel to the slope of the main

---

[34] Singleton P. Moorehead asked a number of people, architects and laymen, to indicate the height of a man on an elevation of the Wythe House that had been reduced to no standard scale. Estimates of heights of 8 to 9 feet were given, even by architects acquainted with the building. The design of the doors and the exceptionally wide trim of the door frame doubtless contribute to the illusion that the house is smaller than it is.

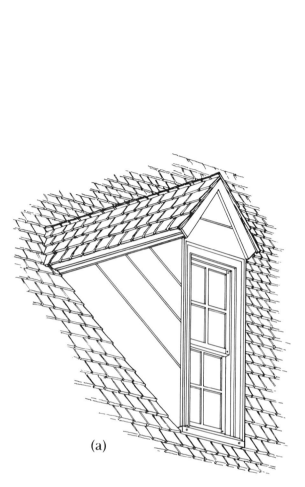

(a)

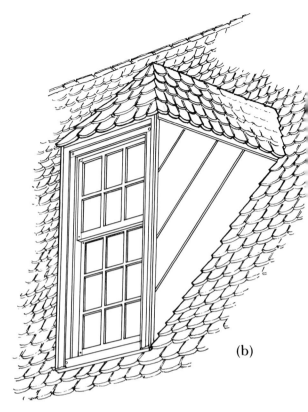

(b)

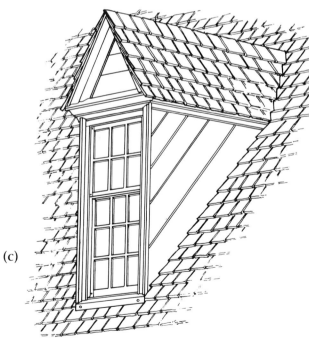

(c)

*Figure 29* Three varieties of dormers used with gable roofs: (a) simple gable; (b) hip roof; (c) pedimental gable.

(a)

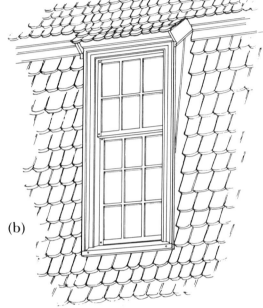

(b)

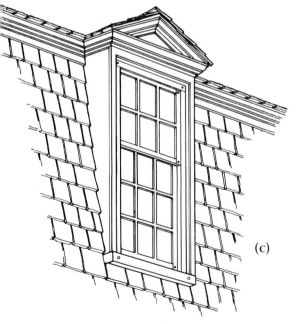

(c)

*Figure 30*  Three varieties of dormers used with gambrel roofs: (a) hipped; (b) shed; (c) pedimental gable.

roof of the house.[35] Their front elevations, with the window flanked on either side by nothing more than a narrow, molded architrave, exemplified that economy of means that was one of the characteristics of colonial building in Virginia.

The only window openings that did not share the sash bar grid pattern were those of cellars used for storage. Unglazed, their grilles of close-set bars, usually horizontal and usually of wood, but occasionally of iron, provided for the free passage of air for ventilation. Exterior shutters were never used on brick houses, although they were general on frame ones. Both the paneled and the louvered types were popular. There is no conclusive evidence for the use of shutters with movable slats, although since they were known in Europe before 1771 when one was illustrated in Diderot's encyclopedia, they may have appeared on some houses later in the century. Similarly, there was little record of exterior cloth or canvas awnings on any private dwelling before the Revolution. They were used at the College in 1766,[36] so it is difficult to believe that a device known in England and obviously appropriate to the Virginia summer would have been ignored by the sweltering householders.

Doors were generally of the six- or eight-panel type. Where double, or folding, doors existed, the two leaves each had three or four panels and, when closed, looked like a single large door of the usual pattern. Elaborate frontispieces with pediments and pilasters such as a few Virginia plantation houses boast were not found, doubtless due to the secondary status given the townhouse, and the molded trim of the frame constituted the greatest degree of elaboration accorded the doorway. Often an oblong transom light with one or at the most two rows of panes was installed above the door. Neither the sidelight nor the semicircular fanlight appears to have been used in any domestic building in eighteenth-century Williamsburg, although there are fanlights in the Courthouse of 1770 and in the Norton-Cole House, which dates from the first decade of the nineteenth century.

## INTERIOR WOODWORK

Boards of yellow pine from five to eight inches wide were normally used for flooring. Edge-grain boards sawed radially from the log were

---

[35] Two Williamsburg exceptions to the rule were the Brush-Everard House, where the boarding was horizontal, and the Benjamin Waller House, where the dormer cheeks were faced with ordinary weatherboards.

[36] Accounts for 1766–1767, College of William and Mary, quoted in Howard Dearstyne, "Shutters, Blinds and Umbrelloes," *Architectural Review*, CXXIII (June 1958), pp. 420–422.

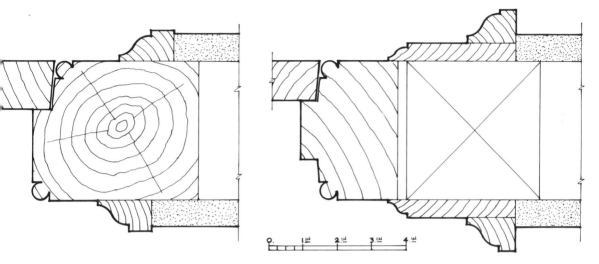

*Figure 31* Details of two types of door frames: (a) stud forming jamb; (b) separate jamb beside stud.

used in the majority of cases, the advantage being that they were much less liable to splinter than those with a flat grain. They were finished with a plane on the upper surface only, and were sized to a thickness of about one and one-eighth inches only where they were to lie on the joists. Not infrequently, they were joined with a tongue-and-groove, although the commonest and most efficient method of joining floor-boards was with splines—long strips of wood slotted into the edges of the boards—supplemented at intervals with wooden dowels. Butt joints might have been employed in inferior rooms and attics. Floor-boards were usually face-nailed or occasionally blind-nailed to the joists, the upper surfaces of which often show holes that were bored to receive the end of a tool used to force the boards tight.

Door frames were of two types: one where two studs form the jambs, and the other, which was more common, where the jambs were separate pieces set inside the studs (*Figure 31*). In the first type, the inner moldings were cut in the stud itself. The face moldings against which the wall plaster was stopped were applied in both types; in the second type, they were wider than in the first since they had to extend over part of the stud to mask its junction with the jamb. A distinguishing characteristic of colonial door frames was the treatment of the rabbet that received the door. It was always slightly more than a right angle on plan, and the door was cut on the bias to fit. The considerations that led to this treatment were perhaps as much aesthetic as practical.

Interior doors were rarely more than one and one-eighth inches thick even when they were paneled on both sides. The commonest type had six panels arranged from top to bottom: two small, two large, two large. The panels in eight-panel doors were usually arranged two small, two large, two small, two large. More rarely—at Williamsburg in the central addition of the Peyton Randolph House, for example—they were arranged two small, two large, two large, two small. Four-panel doors were also much used, while doors with two panels occurred rather less often and then were used mostly for cupboards. Where appearance was not of prime importance, batten doors continued in fashion throughout the colonial period. The Brush-Everard House has an oversized front door that combined the two treatments; paneled on the outside, it has diagonal battens on the interior face. Leather washers were used under the heads of the nails that fastened the hinges to the door as a cushion to take up the expansion and contraction of the wood of the door. The nails were customarily clinched on the side of the door away from the hinge, and were hammered flush with the surface of the wood to permit a smooth paint job.

There are few completely paneled rooms in Williamsburg today, and it is unlikely that many ever existed. The interior wall trim of a modest house consisted, characteristically, of baseboard, chair rail, and cornice. If one element were omitted, it was the cornice, and a plain beaded chairboard frequently sufficed for the more ornate chair rail, but the baseboard was hardly ever omitted. The next additive step toward full paneling was the provision of a wooden dado with the chair rail becoming a dado cap. *Figures 32–35* illustrate typical examples of these features from both paneled and plastered rooms. One general observation may be made about the character of eighteenth-century trim. The use of a bevel in the rabbeting of door frames was ubiquitous. Cornice profiles showed the same tendency to avoid right angles on filets. Similarly, the segment of the full circle in both convex and concave moldings was often ignored, and all half-rounds were slightly flattened. This was certainly not due to any technical deficiency on the part of the eighteenth-century craftsman but to his dislike of mechanical effects—and to his eye for subtle detail.

On the upper floors, the trim generally was simpler. The only unique feature was the use of narrow beaded boards to protect the plaster angles on either side of the dormer openings. Much of the constructive ingenuity and taste of the eighteenth-century carpenter and joiner went into the stairs by which the upper floors were reached. The closed

string stair appeared more often because it was easier to construct.
Some fine stairs of the open string type have survived at Williamsburg,
however, such as the significant examples in the Brush-Everard, George
Wythe, and Tayloe houses. Stairs with an easy rise were the eighteenth-
century ideal, achieved surprisingly often at Williamsburg even in modest dwellings like the George Reid House.

The handrail to the stairs, which was curved or scrolled only with
the open string, was often the only interior woodwork, apart from the
floors and the treads of the stairs, that was unpainted. Two generalizations may be made on the subject of interior paint colors. First, white
was used very little, and cream hardly at all. The popular association
of white and cream with colonial interiors is due to the fact that the
initiators of the Colonial Revival at the end of the nineteenth century
were reacting against the dim and cavelike interiors of the preceding
Brown Decades. Second, the bold colors were marked by a certain full-

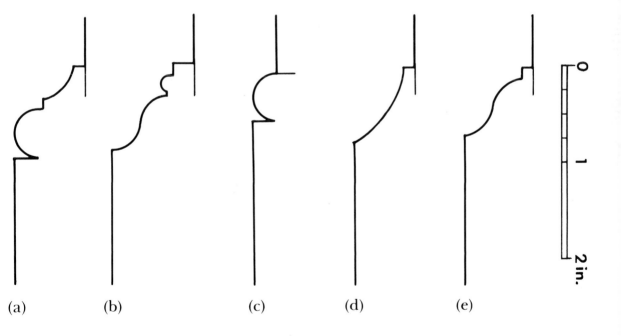

(a)  (b)  (c)  (d)  (e)

*Figure 32* Five baseboards: (a) Powell-Waller House; (b) Tayloe House; (c)
Benjamin Waller House; (d) Peyton Randolph House; (e) Dr. Barraud House.

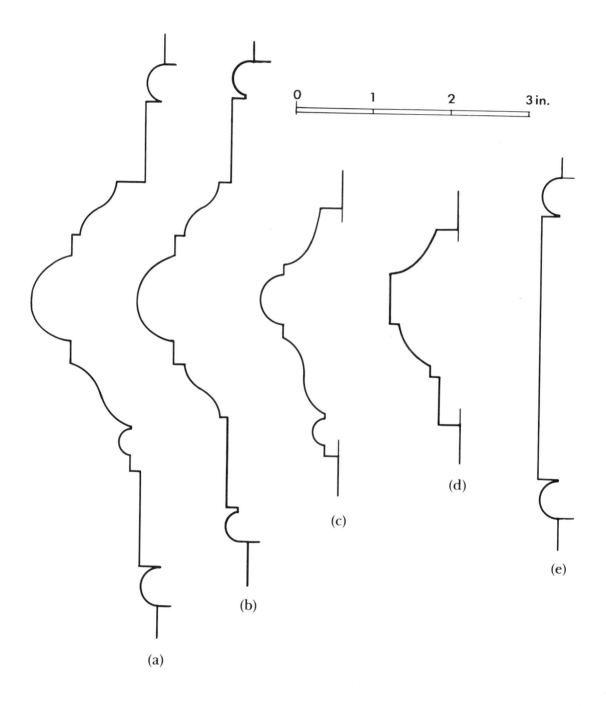

*Figure 33*   Five chair rails: (a) Benjamin Waller House; (b) George Reid House; (c-e) Peyton Randolph House.

bodied quality and by an absence of glare, which was anathema to eigh-teenth-century taste. Both documentary evidence[37] and modern experi-ments indicate that the ingredient lampblack produced the robust strength and resonant qualities of eighteenth-century paint shades.

### PLASTER AND PAPER

When a house is built today, the interior trim is applied after the plasterers have done their work and the plastered surfaces are finished against strips of wood called plaster stops or grounds. In the eighteenth century, all of the interior woodwork was in place before the plasterer came on the scene. Clearly this was the only convenient way of proceed-ing under a system of separate contracts with the different trades, be-cause if the carpenter or joiner had to stop in the middle of his work to allow the plasterer to do his, it would only have led to trouble. What is important is that the procedure left its mark on the character of the eighteenth-century interior. The plaster being stopped against the trim itself reduced the relief or salience of the latter and tended to soften the transition between one material and the other.

In frame houses, the plastering was done over hand-split laths nailed to the studs, while in brick houses, the plaster was laid directly on the brick walls. This helps to account for the condensation that so trou-bled colonial Virginians, and it also accounts, in no small measure, for the complete disappearance of early wallpaper in brick houses. Some-times, as in the George Wythe House, the backs of fireplaces were plastered since plaster could be renewed so much more easily than brick.

The time-honored way of treating all plaster surfaces was to whitewash them, and walls and ceilings in Williamsburg houses were whitewashed over and over again, even after the introduction of wallpaper.[38] Wallpa-

---

[37] See, for instance, Dr. James Carter's order to John Norton & Sons quoted on p. 23. The small quantity of lampblack ordered shows that it was to be used as a toning agent, and the same may be said of the "3 lb. Lamp-Black" sent for by John Page of Rosewell the same year in an order that included "100 lb. of white Lead," "20 lb. yellow Ochre," "20 lb. of Venetian red," and "5 lb. of Red Lead." Mason, ed., *John Norton & Sons,* p. 199. The price of lampblack in the decade 1760–1770 was 7s. 6d. per barrel and 5s. 6d. per small barrel. Allason Letter Book.

[38] John Blair's account with Humphrey Harwood included the following charges for whitewashing:

1789
June 23
   To whitewashing 7 Rooms & 4 passages
      @ 3/9 . . . . . . . . . . . . . . . . . . . . . . . . . . . . . . . . £2 . 1 . 3

per apparently was first imported into Virginia by George Washington in 1757 for use at Mount Vernon.[39] It seems to have reached Williamsburg in the mid-1760s. In 1766 William Siddall, bookbinder and paperhanger from London, announced in the *Virginia Gazette* "that he proposes carrying on his Business opposite the Rawleigh Tavern in *Williamsburg* . . . and that he hangs Paper genteel and secure on reasonable Terms."[40] The following year, an advertisement of a house for sale stated that it was "elegantly papered."[41] There was wallpaper in the Palace in the early 1770s, and in 1777 John Baker, surgeon dentist, advertised for sale his "VALUABLE House . . . on the market square in this city, having four handsome rooms below, neatly papered."[42] Fragments of old wallpapers have been found in several Williamsburg locations, two in the Brush-Everard House, one in the Nicolson Shop, and another at the Robert Carter House. That a wide variety of papers was available at local shops was substantiated by Benjamin Bucktrout's advertisement in 1771:

A NEAT and ELEGANT ASSORTMENT of PAPER HANGINGS, of various Kinds, and of the newest Fashions, for Staircases, Rooms, and Ceilings; namely, embossed, Stucco, Chintz, striped, Mosaick, Damask, and common.[43]

---

| | |
|---|---|
| To do. 2 clossets 2/6 . . . . . . . . . . . . . . . . . . . . . . . . . . . . . . . . . | 4 . 6 |

1790
September 22

| | |
|---|---|
| To whitewashing 7 Rooms @ 3./- . . . . . . . . . . . . . . . . . . . . | 1 . 1 . 0 |
| To do . . . 4 passages @ 2/- . . . . . . . . . . . . . . . . . . . . . . . . . . . | 8 . 0 |
| To ditto 2 clossets & porch 3/- . . . . . . . . . . . . . . . . . . . . . . . | 3 . 0 |

1791
April 3

| | |
|---|---|
| To whitewashing Room 3/- . . . . . . . . . . . . . . . . . . . . . . . . . . | 3 . 3-3/4 |
| To whitewashing 3 Rooms & 2 passages @ 3/6- . . . . . . . . . . . . . . . . . . . . . . . . . . . . . . . . . . . . | 17 . 6 |
| To do the Porch 1/3- . . . . . . . . . . . . . . . . . . . . . . . . . . . . . . | 1 . 3 |

Harwood Ledger, C, pp. 13, 44.

[39] John C. Fitzpatrick, ed., *The Writings of George Washington, 1745–1799*, II (Washington, D. C., 1931), p. 23. A valuable research report on the subject of wallpaper in Virginia has been compiled by Miss Mary A. Stephenson, typescript, Department of Research, CWF.

[40] *Virginia Gazette* (Rind), Dec. 4, 1766.

[41] *Ibid.* (Purdie and Dixon), Oct. 8, 1767.

[42] Whiffen, *Public Buildings*, p. 220, n. 8; *Virginia Gazette* (Purdie and Dixon), Aug. 21, 1778. The house was the predecessor of the one known today as the Norton-Cole House.

[43] *Virginia Gazette* (Purdie and Dixon), May 9, 1771.

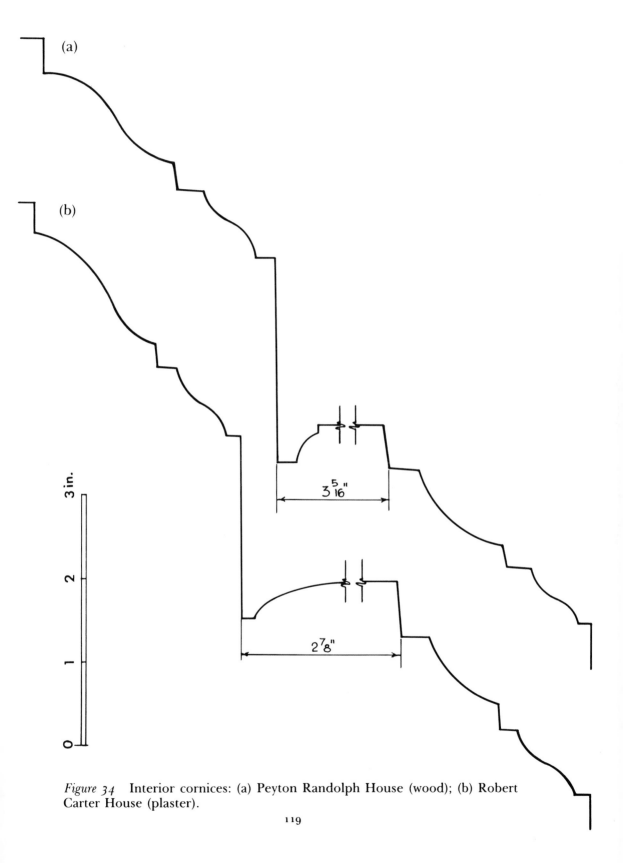

(a)

(b)

3 in.

2

1

0

$3\frac{5}{16}$"

$2\frac{7}{8}$"

*Figure 34*  Interior cornices: (a) Peyton Randolph House (wood); (b) Robert Carter House (plaster).

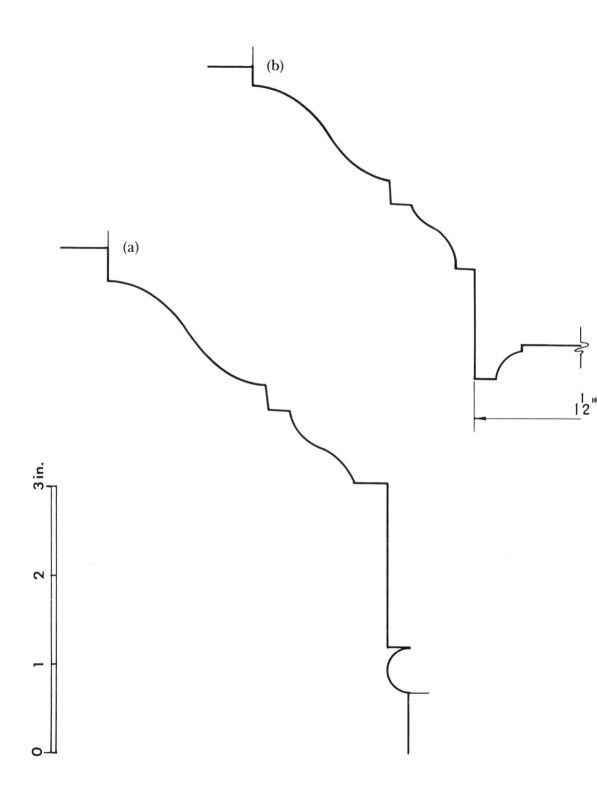

(a)

(b)

$1\frac{1}{2}$"

3 in.

2

1

0

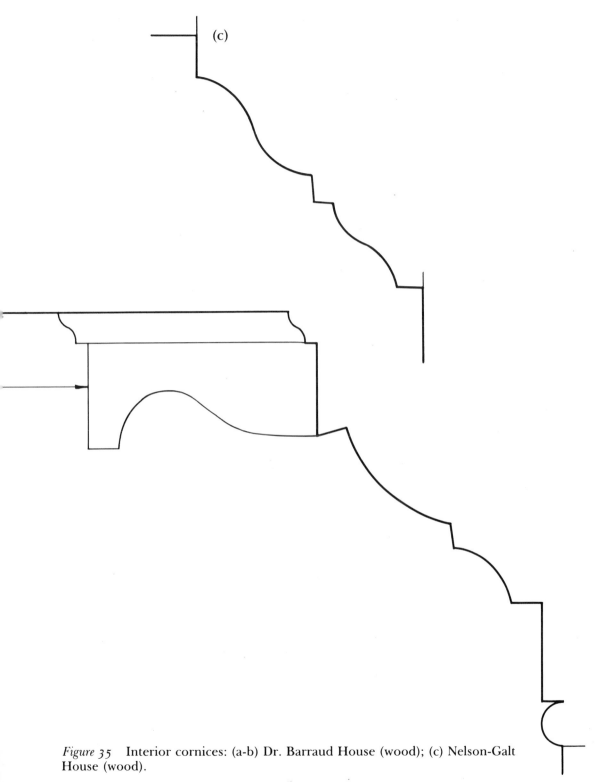

(c)

*Figure 35*  Interior cornices: (a-b) Dr. Barraud House (wood); (c) Nelson-Galt House (wood).

How best can the domestic architecture of eighteenth-century Williamsburg be characterized? First, its ancestry was English, and it remained English to such an extent that no one could suppose for a moment that it was French or German or Dutch or anything but English. Moreover, such stylistic innovations that occurred during the course of the century followed English modes.

None of the brick houses of Williamsburg would look out of place in an English country town, even though they show the effects of local or regional conditions in their planning and in certain matters of detail. With the frame houses, the case is rather different. There still was a certain amount of building in timber in eighteenth-century England, but even in the eastern and southeastern counties where most occurred, it was pretty well confined to utilitarian structures such as mills and barns and to houses of no great architectural pretensions—to cottages and to the lesser manor houses. Where style was a consideration, brick was preferred. Not so in Virginia. Here, as Jefferson tells us,[44] there was a definite sentiment in favor of frame houses that led, quite late in the century, to the execution in timber of such highly sophisticated designs as the Semple House, the result in that case being a building which is quite unimaginable in England. At the same time, according to Hugh Jones, the Virginians of the colonial period regarded themselves as Londoners,[45] and so if it was convenient or necessary, as it often was, that their dwellings in Williamsburg should be cottages, then they had to be cottages worthy of Londoners. Consequently, as all of the evidence goes to show, there was a remarkable consistency in both the kind and the quality of the details of houses in Williamsburg, whatever their size. The smallest were finished with a care and a regard for classical propriety in such features as the cornice that speak of a very general insistence on the things that were held to constitute style, or fashion, and that it would be difficult to parallel in similar buildings in England.

On the other hand, elaboration was eschewed. No doubt this was partly because the life of a frame house was reckoned at no more than fifty years. But the generalization is true of brick houses too, and the main reason must have been that the wealthy planter who had a house in Williamsburg in addition to his plantation home thought of it as the nobleman or landed gentleman in England thought of his London

---

[44] Jefferson, *Notes on Virginia*, pp. 153–154.
[45] Jones, *Present State of Virginia*, p. 43.

house—as a secondary dwelling for use during relatively short periods each year. As for the tradesman, it was as unthinkable for him as it was for his London cousin that he should appear to try to set himself up above the gentry by architectural ostentation.[46]

It is not surprising to find a high degree of standardization in the designs of the eighteenth-century houses of Williamsburg, or of Virginia. The eighteenth century was an age that built according to the rules handed down in the shops of the various crafts and the rules set down in the books on architecture. This is not to say that the two categories did not overlap, for shop rules were the staple of the authors of many handbooks, and book rules doubtless became the rote-learned formulas of the shops. The rules were believed to provide a discipline, not a straitjacket, and always the final appeal in any disputed question of design was to the eye. And so there was plenty of variety within the accepted limits, as the reader's eye may see for itself in the architectural survey of the eighteenth-century houses of Williamsburg that forms the second part of this book.

---

[46] It is a well-known fact, which has been called unexplained, that eighteenth-century houses in the provincial cities and towns of England tended to have much richer and more elaborately detailed fronts than their London contemporaries had. Surely the explanation is that in such places the standard was set by what were the *first* houses of rich merchants and not, as in London, by the *second* houses of the nobility and gentry.

# Part II

*Figure 36* Nelson-Galt House. South front.

# NELSON-GALT HOUSE

THE two lots nearest the Capitol on the south side of Duke of
Gloucester Street were granted to William Robertson, clerk of
the Council, in 1707.[1] The deed contained the usual building
clause, and later deeds recording Robertson's sale of parts of the lots,[2]
including most of the Duke of Gloucester Street and Capitol Square

---

[1] York Co. Recs., Deeds, Bonds, II, p. 268.

[2] *Ibid.*, p. 295, III, p. 267. The Nelson-Galt House stood behind the Francis Street
building line, which was thought to indicate that a house was located there before
Williamsburg was laid out, but the absence of any mention of one in the 1707 deed
sufficiently disproved the theory. The acts of Assembly of 1699 and 1705 did not estab-

*Figure 37*    Nelson-Galt House. East room.

frontages, made it fairly certain that this was the house that he built
in the twenty-four months following his acquisition of the site. The
house took its present name from its ownership, first by members of

lish the building lines on the "back streets," which was left to "the directors . . . or
. . . the incorporation of the Mayor, Aldermen, and Commonalty of the City of Williamsburg." Robertson's house was one of the first on Francis Street, and it is reasonable
to suppose that the building line had not yet been established when it was built.

*Figure 38*   Nelson-Galt House before restoration.

the distinguished Nelson family of Yorktown, and later by the Galt family, which was long associated with the Public Hospital in Williamsburg.

To hold two lots adjoining Duke of Gloucester Street, a frame house with a brick cellar and two brick chimneys had to be forty feet long and twenty feet broad. As it stood, this house was twenty feet broad and forty-eight feet long, which complied with the law with eight feet to spare, although there was some evidence in the framing that the house was lengthened at each end at one time—perhaps during construction as an afterthought—and that as originally planned, it had outside chimneys as did most of the story and one-half houses in Williamsburg.[3]

---

[3] Heavy posts, braced on each side, were located in the north and south walls about 6 inches inside the line of the chimney breasts and closet partitions. Mortises, as if for braces, had been cut in their inner faces, which suggested that they were intended to be corner posts. If they were originally the corner posts of the house, the chimneys must have been rebuilt when it was lengthened. Although not impossible, it is at least as likely that the plan was altered before construction was completed.

The four chimney closets, each of which had its own small window while the northwestern one contained a secondary fireplace of uncertain purpose, gave the house an unusual plan. Unorthodox too was the placement of the stair in a separate compartment off the north end of the central passage. The partition framing and the narrowness of the passage, which was only five feet wide, suggested that the space for

*Figure 39*    Nelson-Galt House during restoration.

*Figure 40*    Nelson-Galt House. South elevation.

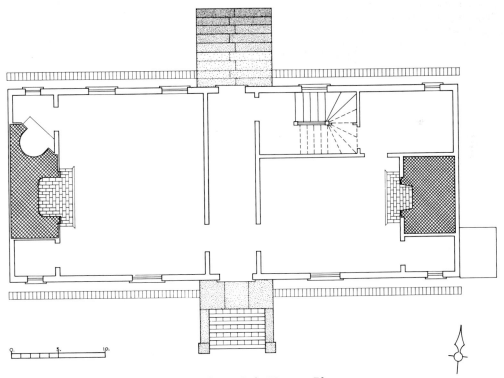

*Figure 41*    Nelson-Galt House. Plan.

both stairs and passage was taken out of the east room. As first built, the east room was a hall of the old, medieval form entered directly from the outside. The paneled mantel was a noteworthy feature of the room. The west room had a paneled dado and a stone chimneypiece restored from fragments that were found embedded facedown in the hearth.

The grouping of the windows and the variations in their sizes gave the street front a certain formality that was affected little by the inequality in the spacing of the hip-roofed dormers. Its uncommon features may have been the result of alterations, or signs that when it was built, the type was not yet standardized. In any case, the Nelson-Galt House was one of the most interesting and attractive of the smaller houses of Williamsburg, as well as one of the oldest.

## CONDITION

The Nelson-Galt House was restored during 1951–1953. The basement wall and the east chimney had to be rebuilt, and the frame was reinforced where necessary. Late door hoods were replaced with new ones of eighteenth-century character. The one over the south door rests on the original brackets, while the design of the one to the north was based on evidence found in the framing. Generally, the house had been little altered since the eighteenth century, and it needed only repairs rather than extensive restoration. Among the rarer survivals were two pairs of eighteenth-century shutters on the west pair of large windows on the north side and eighteenth-century wood grilles in all four of the basement openings.

*Figure 42* John Blair House. South front.

# JOHN BLAIR HOUSE

THIS house took its name from John Blair, Jr., a late eighteenth-century owner and the first whose name was known. In part, however, it was one of the oldest houses in Williamsburg.

As it was first built early in the eighteenth century, the house was a typical central passage, story and one-half dwelling, thirty-six feet by eighteen feet on plan, with end chimneys. It probably had a lean-to or shed, nine feet deep, behind. Evidence for claiming that the shed was contemporary with the oldest part of the structure came from the framing of the roof, which had a two foot, four-inch jut or overhang at the rear that seemed to indicate the plan was altered after construction had begun. The inequality of the foundation walls—the one on the street front was one foot, ten inches thick while the others were a more usual one foot, one inch—also suggested that early plan changes were made.

Later, probably in the third quarter of the century, the house was

lengthened twenty-eight feet to the west. The west chimney was enlarged, a second staircase was built, and a second street door was inserted. The stone steps at both entries were added during the same
period. Tradition in the town always maintained that they came from
the Palace Street theater.

Transom lights above the doorways were a necessary device where
there were no windows to light the interior passages. Also noteworthy
were the early type of dormers with hipped roofs. Bricklayer and plasterer Humphrey Harwood's accounts for work done in the years 1789–
1791 mentioned a marble mantelpiece still located in the west room,
and indicated that one of the rooms was called the library.[4]

---

[4] Harwood Ledger, C, p. 13: "THE HON'BLE, JOHN BLAIR ESQ[R] . . . 1790 March
16 To building up the Jambs of the library Chimney."

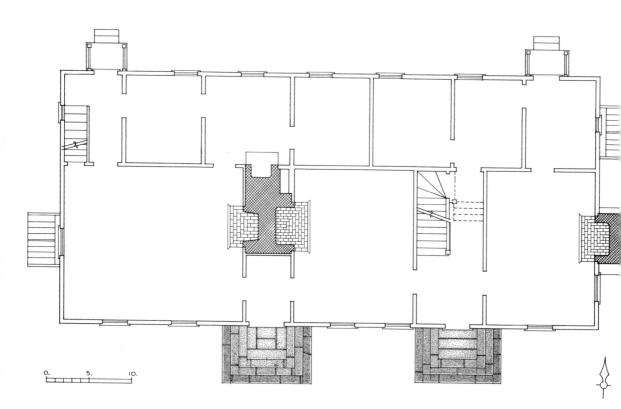

*Figure 43*  John Blair House. Plan.

## CONDITION

In outward appearance, the John Blair House had changed less than most houses between its construction in the eighteenth century and its acquisition by Colonial Williamsburg in 1928. The south dormers were rebuilt to their original form following the example of an unaltered dormer on the north side. The eighteenth-century west street door is original to the building and served as the model for the east one. Shutters, corner boards, and cornices date from the restoration. Some of the frame of the house was renewed, the west chimney was rebuilt, and most of the present interior trim was installed in 1929. The east staircase, however, is largely original, and most of the floors are old. The partitions were altered and partly rebuilt in 1923 when the building belonged to the College of William and Mary and was used as a sorority house. The old partitions were of poplar with an infilling of four-inch brick nogging, portions of which are preserved in situ along with remnant oak clapboards against the earlier west wall of the house.

*Figure 44*  Ludwell-Paradise House. South front.

# LUDWELL-PARADISE HOUSE

P HILIP Ludwell II of Green Spring, a large estate some six miles west of Williamsburg that for thirty-five years (1642–1677) had been the seat of Governor Sir William Berkeley, was granted the lot on which this house stood by the trustees of the city of Williamsburg in 1700.[5] Since the lot did not escheat to the city (while two lots immediately west of it, which were granted to him at the same time, did), Ludwell must have built a house on it within two years. Although it seems improbable that this was the house that Ludwell built, it is conceivable that it was constructed during the period 1710–1716 when he was

[5] York Co. Recs., Deeds, Bonds, II, p. 30.

deputy auditor general of the colony. In view of the architectural character of the house, however, it is more likely that it was built by Philip Ludwell III after he came of age and entered into his inheritance in 1737. Ludwell rented the house for many years, although it was later occupied by his second daughter, Lucy Ludwell Paradise.

The house consisted of a two-story front portion, one room deep on each floor, and a single-story lean-to, or shed, that extended along the length of the rear. Unlike all of the other outside walls, the north wall of the shed was of frame construction covered with weatherboards. It might be argued that it had been the intention to build the whole house to two stories, a course that was abandoned for lack of funds. But two things militated against this conclusion: the basement walls of the north, or shed, section were only one foot thick and therefore were evidently never intended to be carried up two stories; and the centers of the chimneys fell nearly two feet south of the longitudinal

*Figure 45*  Ludwell-Paradise House. South elevation.

axis of the ground plan instead of coinciding with it as they surely would have done if it had been designed as a two-story house in the usual manner.

The wide expanses of wall between the windows gave the front of the Ludwell-Paradise House a certain reticence, which but for the rich pattern of the Flemish bond brickwork, with its regular pattern of glazed headers, would have amounted to austerity. This brickwork and most of the cornice were all that was original on the exterior of the house, which had suffered in many hands before it was acquired for restoration

*Figure 46*   Ludwell-Paradise House. Northeast view.

in 1926 as the Reverend W. A. R. Goodwin's very first purchase on behalf of John D. Rockefeller, Jr. The Abby Aldrich Rockefeller folk art collection was exhibited in the Ludwell-Paradise House from 1935 to 1957.

## CONDITION

The house was restored in 1931. It had been much altered from time to time. The greatest number of changes occurred in the early 1920s when, among other things, the front door was framed in a pedimented frontispiece of wood, which subsequently was removed. The arches and the sills of the first floor windows on the street front were raised and lowered respectively to their original positions as indicated by the brickwork. Upper floor windows had preserved their original sills, frames, and trim, which, being too decayed to retain, were replaced with copies. The modern chimneys were taken down to the top of the old portion just below the roof and were rebuilt to a design indicated by a nineteenth-century photograph. All of the framing of the shed, both roof and wall, was renewed with old materials and its north wall was refaced with old weatherboards from an old house in Norfolk, Virginia. The framing of the roof and floors is in the main original, as is the stairway, although balusters are new following the original design indicated by the profile of the half-balusters found on the original newel posts. Some old woodwork from other Virginia buildings was used in the interior, such as the paneling in the southwest room on the ground floor that came from the Bolling House in Petersburg. The interior was converted into a residence in 1959.

*Figure 47*    Prentis Store. Southeast view.

## PRENTIS STORE

UILT in 1738–1740,[6] this was the oldest surviving store in Williamsburg. With its brick walls, pedimental gable, and trussed roof,[7] surprising in so small a building, it represented the commercial architecture of the time and place at its most substantial and highly finished. The store's dimensions on plan, twenty-four feet wide by thirty-six feet deep, were very close to those of the shop illustrated

[6] The evidence for so dating the building was in the annual accounts of Prentis and Company, Webb-Prentis Papers, Alderman Library, University of Virginia, Charlottesville. When the building was reexamined in 1959, 1740 was found scratched in the plaster of the gable end of the loft. The Prentis accounts also showed that the building was valued at the considerable figure of £200.

[7] Its four framed trusses originally had queen posts and an unusually regular system

in Joseph Moxon's *Mechanick Exercises,* which was twenty feet wide by forty feet deep.

The walls were laid in Flemish bond throughout with a plentiful, although far from uniform, use of glazed headers. The water table, composed of alternate headers and stretchers, was a plain chamfer.

*Figure 48* Prentis Store before restoration.

Rubbed brick enframed all openings and defined the quoins. The roof, with its pronounced kick at the eaves, closely resembles the roofs of contemporaneous dependencies at Shirley plantation in Charles City County, which were constructed around 1740.[8] The door opening in the gable to the street was undoubtedly used for hoisting goods directly

---

of wind braces. Each wind brace was tenoned into a principal rafter at one end and into a purlin at the other, and each set of four wind braces formed a St. Andrew's cross between each pair of trusses on either side of the roof.

[8] Waterman, *Mansions of Virginia,* pp. 173–174.

*Figure 49*    Prentis Store. Detail of roof framing.

to the upper floor, although no evidence of a cat head, or hoist, was
found in the surviving brickwork.[9]

The interior followed the standard shop arrangement with the salesroom, which was about twenty-one feet square and probably sheathed
with vertical boards, in front facing the street, and the counting room

[9] A contract for a store to be built at Petersburg, Va., in 1785 specified "one large
dormant window in the front & fixed with a beam . . . to draw goods up." Folder
67, Tucker-Coleman Papers. There was no evidence that Prentis Store had had such
a beam.

and stairs behind.[10] The counting room had a fireplace and was lighted by two small windows in the east wall, while the shop, where all of the wall space was needed to store and display goods, got its light from the front windows only.[11] The upper floor was used not only for storage but also to house one or more clerks or apprentices. When William Prentis died in 1765, it was furnished with "a Bed, Bedstead, Cord, Hide, Sheets, 2 Pillows and Cases," and a "Ship's stove."[12]

## CONDITION

The Prentis Store was restored during 1928–1931. It was being used as an automobile service station when acquired by Colonial Williamsburg. Although it had been gutted and the existing shop front was nineteenth-century, the main structure, including the roof and its trim, had been little altered. It was necessary to rebuild partly the north and south walls and, owing to its poor condition, to renew much of the roof trim. The interior was adapted for commercial use in 1972 and the exterior was substantially restored, yet Prentis Store still awaits a complete restoration of its fabric.

---

[10] The term counting room was frequently found in advertisements of storekeepers in eighteenth-century Virginia. See those of John Pagan, William Rand, and James Buchanan and John Finner, *Virginia Gazette*, Apr. 25, 1751, *ibid.* (Purdie and Dixon), Nov. 6, 1766, June 20, 1771.

[11] Windowless store walls were common, perhaps due to the fact that shops and stores in Williamsburg were often densely situated. The Prentis Store, built within 5 feet, 6 inches of an adjacent frame storehouse on the west, would consequently have received little light from that side even if the interior wall space had not been fitted more profitably with shelving.

[12] York Co. Recs., Wills and Inventories, XXI, p. 260.

*Figure 50*  Moody House. Southwest view.

# MOODY HOUSE

THE eighteenth-century history of the house that stood here until 1939 when it was razed and virtually reconstructed was little documented. The Frenchman's Map showed two buildings, joined end to end, on the lot, while Williamsburg land tax records indicated that the property was purchased by Josias Moody, a blacksmith, in 1794.

The fabric of the building had an interesting story to tell. The framing of the walls and roof made it clear beyond all reasonable doubt that as it was first built, probably in the second quarter of the eighteenth century, the house measured thirty-two feet by eighteen and had a central chimney that served both rooms. Between the front door and the chimney was a small entry measuring six feet, four inches by four feet, six inches with a door to each of the rooms and presumably, since there was no room for any kind of stair, a ladder to the loft. It was therefore a type of house common enough in New England but which is represented by only a small number of Virginia examples.[13] The first addition to this little house was a lean-to, or shed, at the back. Later the building was lengthened thirteen feet to the west, the central chimney was taken down to permit a through passage and stairway of the normal type, and end chimneys were erected. The result was a hall-passage-parlor plan of the usual form with a shed extension, and outwardly there was nothing to show that the course of development by which it arrived at that form was unusual, if not unique.

## CONDITION

The structural condition of the Moody House was so poor that it was decided to reconstruct it completely rather than to attempt restoration. The work was carried out during 1939–1940. Outside, only the two chimneys up to a point just above their second weatherings are original. Within, three of the doors, most of the floorboards, some interior woodwork, and all visible parts of the simple but handsome stairway are original. In 1950 the interior was altered for residential occupancy.

---

[13] For plans of some New England examples of the type, see Kelly, *Early Domestic Architecture*, pp. 8–12.

*Figure 51*   Moody House before restoration.

*Figure 52*  Wetherburn's Tavern. Northeast view.

# WETHERBURN'S TAVERN

HENRY Wetherburn, tavern keeper, had erected the east section of this building by 1743.[14] About ten years later, the better to house his thriving business, he added a west extension.[15] The junction between the two sections was marked on the facade by a beaded corner board close beside the west doorway and a break in the brick foundation directly below the corner board.

---

[14] Henry Wetherburn purchased this property in 1728 and began to build on it while he operated the Raleigh Tavern diagonally across the street. York Co. Recs., Deeds, IV, pp. 540–541.

[15] The addition was probably completed by March 1752, when Wetherburn advertised a ball to be held in his tavern and had 100 tickets printed. *Virginia Gazette*, Mar. 5, 1752; Virginia Gazette Day Books, Mar. 6, 1752. The original east section alone would not have been large enough to accommodate so many people.

The earlier part of the building had a typical plan—a stair passage in the center and two rooms, one behind the other, on each side. The only unusual feature was the location of the chimneys, which provided fireplaces on short diagonal walls at the interior corner of each first floor room. This first building had a jerkin head or clipped gable roof, and the same roof form was followed when the west addition was built. Where the newer roof framing abutted the older, the framing for the first jerkin head was left in place. This roof form at Wetherburn's Tavern was the only original example that survived in Williamsburg. Architectural investigations revealed that the framing of both sections was so similar in details and arrangement as to indicate that the same builder was responsible. When a shed room added to the rear of the first building was investigated, several courses of the original round-butt juniper (white cedar) shingles were found in place on the rear roof where they had been covered and protected by the addition. They served as the prototypes for the cement asbestos shingles used on the restored building.

The restoration of Wetherburn's Tavern was assisted by the 1760 inventory of Henry Wetherburn's estate,[16] which, by listing furnishings according to room names, corroborated the original floor plan as deduced from architectural examinations. In the tradition of London coffee houses, the "Bull head Room" may have been a private dining room or club. The presence of a "Porch Chamber" upstairs suggested the holdover of an early room name rather than a plan feature, since structural evidence precluded any jutting two-story porch chamber of the type found at the Peyton Randolph and Orlando Jones houses. The specific notation of "Mr. Pages Room" implied a special occupancy of some sort, perhaps that of a permanent lodger or the tavern keeper's resident factotum. The building's wide-span braced frame, an expensive structural system used infrequently in Williamsburg, consisted of a framework of heavy beams and girders supporting a trussed roof. It achieved a single-pile plan in what appears to be a double-pile building, a construction technique that allowed for the large "Great Room," measuring twenty-five feet by twenty-five.

The building continued in use as a tavern long after Wetherburn's death under the management of successive occupants, including Mrs. Ann Craig, who kept a public house that was one of the last in Williamsburg at the close of the eighteenth century.

---

[16] York Co. Recs., Wills and Inventories, XXI, pp. 36–43.

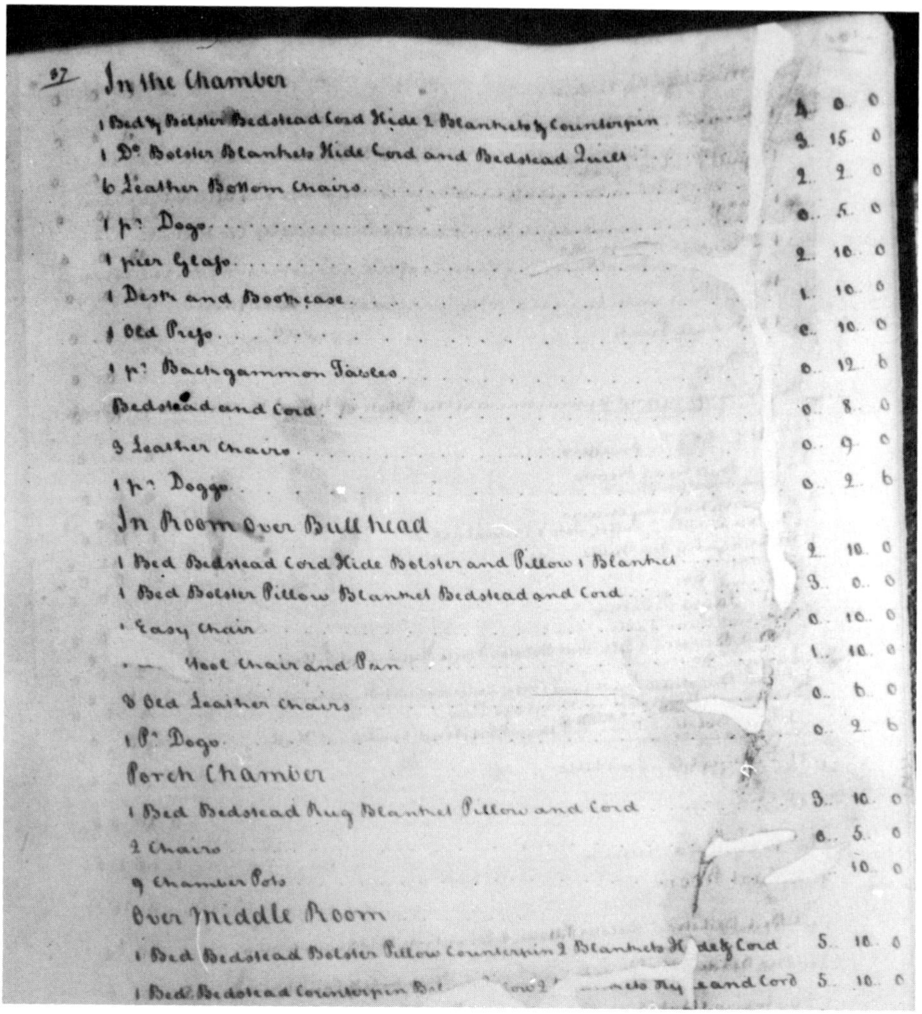
In the Chamber
1 Bed & Bolster Bedstead Cord Hide 2 Blankets & Counterpin 4. 0. 0
1 Do. Bolster Blankets Hide Cord and Bedstead Quilt 3. 15. 0
6 Leather Bottom Chairs 2. 2. 0
1 pr. Dogs 0. 5. 0
1 pier Glass 2. 10. 0
1 Desk and Bookcase 1. 10. 0
1 Old Press 0. 10. 0
1 pr. Backgammon Tables 0. 12. 6
Bedstead and Cord 0. 8. 0
3 Leather Chairs 0. 9. 0
1 pr. Doggs 0. 2. 6
In Room over Bull head
1 Bed Bedstead Cord Hide Bolster and Pillow 1 Blanket 2. 10. 0
1 Bed Bolster Pillow Blanket Bedstead and Cord 3. 0. 0
1 Easy Chair 0. 10. 0
1 — Stool Chair and Pan 1. 10. 0
8 Old Leather Chairs 0. 6. 0
1 Pr. Dogs 0. 2. 6
Porch Chamber
1 Bed Bedstead Rug Blanket Pillow and Cord 3. 10. 0
2 Chairs 0. 5. 0
9 Chamber Pots 10. 0
Over Middle Room
1 Bed Bedstead Bolster Pillow Counterpin 2 Blankets [illegible] Cord 5. 10. 0
1 Bed Bedstead Counterpin [illegible] and Cord 5. 10. 0

*Figure 53* Page from inventory (1761) of Henry Wetherburn's estate recording room names.

## CONDITION

The building was restored during 1966–1967. The framing was found to be almost entirely original and it was substantially reinforced. The brick foundation walls are largely original and were patched and repaired as necessary. A few original beaded weatherboards remain on the south elevation, but the porch across the rear is entirely reconstructed, as are both front porches. Most of the first floor sashes are original; the details of the rest were copied from the remaining originals. The front cornice and the rear door to the west addition are largely original. An unusual exterior paint treatment, consisting of whitewash applied over a prime coat of Spanish brown paint, was discovered at Wetherburn's Tavern and accordingly was restored.

Inside the tavern, the flooring is almost all original, as are a few doors, some trim, and the top portion of the marble surround of the west room's fireplace. During archaeological excavations, fragments of the side panels were found scattered in the yard and they provided the molding profile for their replacement. Lead sash weights, apple wood pulleys, and strands of red and white sash rope discovered undisturbed within window frames in the west room likewise provided examples that assisted in duplicating the original double-hung window mechanisms. One wall of eighteenth-century plaster dating from an alteration that removed two second story windows remains intact in the east bedchamber. Otherwise, missing features were restored on the basis of structural indications such as the nail pattern discernible in the chimney

*Figure 54* Wetherburn's Tavern. The great room restored.

brickwork of the northwest room on the first floor, which revealed the overmantel panel design. Fortunately, almost every feature restored could be based on evidence found in situ during intensive architectural investigations.

The dairy in the service yard behind the tavern retains its original framing, but the rest of the outbuildings, including the kitchen with its huge fireplace, were reconstructed on their original sites.

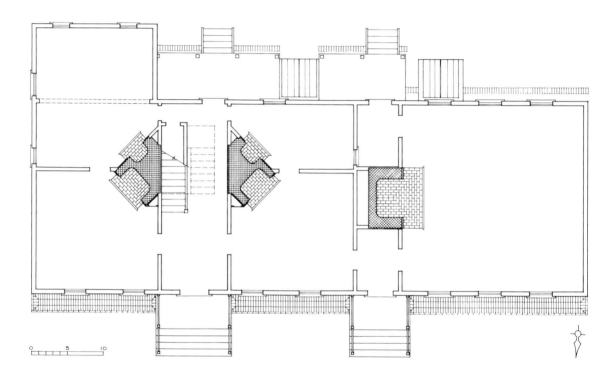

*Figure 55*   Wetherburn's Tavern. Plan.

*Figure 56*   Benjamin Waller House. Northeast view.

# BENJAMIN WALLER HOUSE

THE destruction of the James City County records during the Civil War left little certain knowledge about the early history of the land on which this house stood. In the early eighteenth century, it was part of a large tract owned by Mann Page of Rosewell in Gloucester County. A plan made in 1749 by William Waller, burgess for Spotsylvania County, showed that by then it belonged to his brother Benjamin, a lawyer.[17] Five years before, at the age of twenty-six, Benjamin Waller had been appointed an advocate of the Court of Admiralty by Governor William Gooch, and he was to play an increasingly impor-

---

[17] York Co. Recs., Deeds, V, p. 334.

*Figure 57*    Benjamin Waller House before restoration.

tant part in the affairs of the city and colony. It may reasonably be
assumed that Benjamin Waller was living on the lot in 1746, the year
of his marriage, when he was certainly a resident of Williamsburg. Waller
continued to own the property until his death in 1786, when his youngest
son inherited it.

The Frenchman's Map established that the house had assumed its
present L-plan form by about 1782. The stages through which it passed
before it did so were found to be clearly distinguishable, although not
datable, when the framing was examined prior to restoration. The original dwelling consisted of one room only, the present east room in the
front portion, which was twenty-four feet long by eighteen feet wide.
Although outside the town limits when it was built and so not subject
to Williamsburg's building laws, the house comfortably exceeded the
twenty- by sixteen-foot minimum required to hold a lot on any back
street.[18]

Instead of shingles, the roof was covered initially with overlapping
boards, some of which were found still in position. There were no
dormers. The first addition was a nine-foot-wide entry or stair passage

---

[18] Waller acquired this land from Mann Page II in 1743 as part of a large tract located
east of Williamsburg's boundaries. Articles of Agreement between Page and Waller,
Dec. 13, 1743, Waller Collection, 1737–1759, CWF. During the early 1750s, he developed the area as a residential "suburb" by negotiating deeds of sale, resembling the
town's early building laws, that required purchasers to finish within three years "one

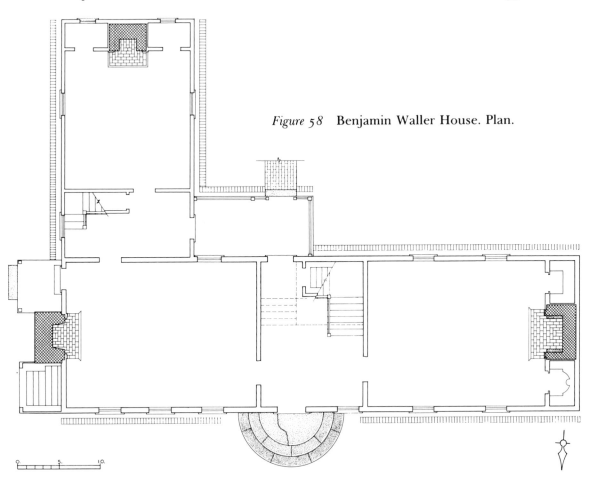

*Figure 58*   Benjamin Waller House. Plan.

at the west end whose width was later increased to twelve feet, three inches when the present stairway and the west room were added. The second addition brought the total length of the house, exclusive of the east chimney and attachments flanking it, to sixty-three feet. The roof of the west part was framed for dormers from the first, so it is reasonable to suppose that the east dormers were cut into the roof of the old part at the time of this second addition. The last major addition, made before 1782, was the gambrel-roofed wing to the rear. The south porch of the main range was added before the end of the century.[19]

good Dwelling House containing Twenty feet in Width and fifty feet in length" or forfeit their lot(s) to him for resale. Deed to John Stretch for Christiana Campbell's Tavern site, 1754, York Co. Recs., Deeds, V, pp. 627–628. Waller's suburb was annexed by the city in 1756.

[19] It is interesting to compare the history of the development of the Benjamin Waller

A most unusual detail of the exterior was the facing of the cheeks of the dormers of the main range with horizontal beaded weatherboards, instead of the diagonal flush boarding nearly always used for longevity.[20] Contrary to all expectations, an examination of the framing of the dormers showed that the weatherboards were original.

East of the house stood the old smokehouse. Of undetermined date, it was a ten-foot-square building with a pyramidal roof. The framing of the walls consisted of four-inch by six-inch sills, plates, and corner posts with no intermediate studs, and the weatherboards were nailed to random-width vertical planking. The tulip-headed pales of the fence between the street and yard at the east end of the house were copied from an eighteenth-century specimen found nailed to one of the rafters in the house.

## CONDITION

The house was restored during 1951–1952. The frame was reinforced throughout, all groundsills were renewed, and the basement walls were partially rebuilt. The east chimney was rebuilt completely after a design determined by the base of the chimney then existing and markings on the framework; the west chimney was rebuilt above the level of the collar beam of the roof. All weatherboarding was renewed except on the west elevation of the main range where nearly all of it is old. The new cornice on the street front is modeled on the original surviving cornice on the south front. Some of the shutters are old, but window sashes were renewed throughout. The front door is original; its steps were reconstructed with the aid of surviving fragments and foundations. The south porch is reconstructed on the original foundations. Much of the interior woodwork, including many of the doors, the closets flanking the fireplace in the west room,[21] and both stairs, is original. There is also considerable original hardware in the house. During the restoration of the smokehouse, the brick foundation was rebuilt, the sills were replaced, and the roof framing was renewed.

---

House with that of the Moody House a quarter-mile to the west on the same street. Both were enlarged by stages, and in neither case could one guess what those stages were from the outward appearance of the building in its final form.

[20] Wetherburn's Tavern also had horizontal weatherboards on the dormer cheeks.

[21] The closets were converted to cabinets, or beaufets, at an undetermined date in the eighteenth century by the removal of both doors, the insertion of simple archway motifs, and the probable addition of shelves, which were curved or butterfly in the north closet but plain and U-shaped in the south.

*Figure 59* Market Square Tavern. Southeast view.

# MARKET SQUARE TAVERN

ORIGINALLY part of Market Square, the site of this building was first leased in two parts to a private occupier by the trustees of the city of Williamsburg in 1749 and 1750.[22] The lessor, John Dixon, built a store on it, and a subsequent tenant, Thomas Craig, a tailor, took in lodgers until 1767, when he began to operate a licensed public house.[23] Having determined "to discontinue tavern keeping" in 1770, he advertised the dwelling in the *Virginia Gazette*, describing it as "very well calculated for publick business, being in the centre of the city, and every convenience to it for a tavern."

---

[22] Memorandums of leases dated July 3, 1749, and Feb. 9, 1750, MS, CWF. The term was twenty-one years, the ground rent £5 per year, and there was "a Covenant for renewing the lease upon paying a fine of 3 years Rent provided the Same is Sued out at least 3 years before this lease Expired and with a like Covenant for Renewing from Time to Time for ever." This leasehold arrangement, resorted to because Market Square was inalienable, represented an interesting departure from the usual kind of grant.

[23] *Virginia Gazette* (Purdie and Dixon), Feb. 12, 1767.

There are fine cellars, an exceeding good stable for thirty horses, with a large fodder loft, a very good kitchen, with a room adjoining, a large and strong smokehouse, at one end of it a place for people to sleep in, an excellent well of water, and a good garden. There is likewise a very good shop, on the main street, which might be converted into three or four lodging rooms; and there is a cellar under it. The house might be made much larger, at a very trifling expence, by taking in a store, at one end of it, which rents for 20£. year.[24]

The house was sold the next year to Gabriel Maupin, who shortly after purchasing it announced in the *Gazette* that he was "making considerable Additions and Improvements, for the purpose of KEEPING TAVERN" and that he was moving his shop to the site and would continue to carry on "the SADDLERY and HARNESS MAKING Business . . . in all its Branches."[25] Maupin continued to own the property until his death, which occurred about 1800.

Restored and in large part reconstructed, Market Square Tavern consisted of a two room deep, story and one-half house parallel to the street with two small buildings forming a lower and narrower wing at the west end. Its chief feature was the northeast room, known as the parlor, which retained the original horizontal board sheathing of natural pine that was similar to the eighteenth-century interior finish found at the Nicolson Shop.[26] The framing of this room, with studs at one-foot centers, was unusual[27] (*Figure 19*). The restored tavern represents the period of its final colonial enlargement, around 1771, when it had grown from a one room structure to the considerable size it later attained.

## CONDITION

Market Square Tavern was restored during 1931–1932. Late in the nineteenth century, the main range was lowered two feet by removing the top courses of the basement wall, after which the fireplaces were closed and a second story was added. At the same time, a southeast wing was built. The small buildings that have been reconstructed to form the southwest wing had already disappeared when these changes

---

[24] *Ibid.*, Aug. 30, 1770.

[25] *Ibid.*, Sept. 26, 1771. One of Maupin's customers was Patrick Henry, who in 1776 was billed by Maupin for £19 11s. for saddles, harness, etc. MS, CWF.

[26] See MS, pp. 62–63.

[27] See Fig. 19 and p. 92, n. 1.

occurred. Two original rear windows survived to supply a model for restored ones. Only the south elevation was faced with old weatherboards, all of which were removed to the street front to constitute the only old work visible there. In the northeast room or parlor, wainscot boarding, wood trim, one door, and floorboards are original, but door hardware is unauthentic. There are several other original interior doors. The mantel is old but not original to the house.

*Figure 60* Market Square Tavern. East room with horizontal board sheathing restored.

*Figure 61*  William Lightfoot House. Northwest view.

# WILLIAM LIGHTFOOT HOUSE

THE lots on which this house stood were owned by members of the Lightfoot family for a period of more than one hundred years that ended in 1839.[28] The first owner was Philip Lightfoot, councillor, planter, merchant, and attorney—and one of the richest men in Virginia in the second quarter of the eighteenth century. It is likely that he built the house between 1733, when he was appointed to the

[28] In 1747 Philip Lightfoot devised to his son John his "Lots and Houses in the City of Williamsburg" and bequeathed to him "the Furniture in the House at Williamsburg." York Co. Recs., Wills, Inventories, XX, pp. 103–106. John Lightfoot died without

Governor's Council, and 1740, when William Byrd recorded a visit to "Colonel Lightfoot's."[29] William Lightfoot of Tedington inherited the lot from his grandfather's estate and owned the property until his death in 1809. He twice represented James City County in the Virginia House of Delegates.

The plan of the William Lightfoot House, with two rooms back and front on each floor and the stairs to one side, was like that of an isolated London terrace house. Its urban ancestry was revealed not only by the general arrangement of rooms but also by its proportions on plan— its depth exceeded its length—and by the total enclosure of the chimney as if by a party wall. As usual, the front rooms were larger than the back ones.

The street front was well proportioned. Its satisfactory effect was due largely to the synchronized three-bay arrangement offset by the diagonal balance of chimney and entrance doorway at opposite ends of the facade. The reconstructed porch arrangement and details were conjectural, although the width of the original platform was established by the discovery of a fragment of one of its foundation walls and by other structural indications.

The roof may have been the earliest gambrel in Williamsburg, and owing to the gentle rake of the upper slopes, it was the lowest in relation to its span. The tendency as the century progressed was for the upper part of the gambrel to become steeper, as a comparison with the slightly later Tayloe House and the considerably later Ewing House shows. The lower slopes, on the other hand, were very nearly vertical, with the result that the faces of the dormers projected beyond the walls of the principal story instead of lying in the same plane as exhibited at the Tayloe House.

The simple interior had neither wainscot nor paneling. The stairway, which was of the closed string type with turned balusters and square newel posts, was peculiar in three respects. First, the newel post at its foot was paneled while the rest were plain; second, the newel post at

---

male issue in 1751, and in accordance with the terms of his father's will, the property went to his brother William. When William died in 1767, it was inherited by his son, later well known as "William Lightfoot of Tedington." His heirs sold the property to George W. Southall of Williamsburg in 1839. Lyon G. Tyler, "Lightfoot Family," *WMQ*, 1st Ser., III (July 1894), p. 109. The earliest indication of the location of the Lightfoot lots was in the act of Assembly of 1769 defining the boundary between York and James City counties within the city. Hening, ed., *Statutes*, VIII, pp. 405–406.

[29] Maude H. Woodfin, ed., Marion Tinling, trans., *Another Secret Diary of William Byrd of Westover 1739–1741* (Richmond, 1942), pp. 75–76.

the half-landing continued down to the floor below;[30] and third, the upper flight ended, not at the beam across the entry at the edge of the stairwell in the normal manner, but two feet short of it, the gap being spanned by a projection of the landing.

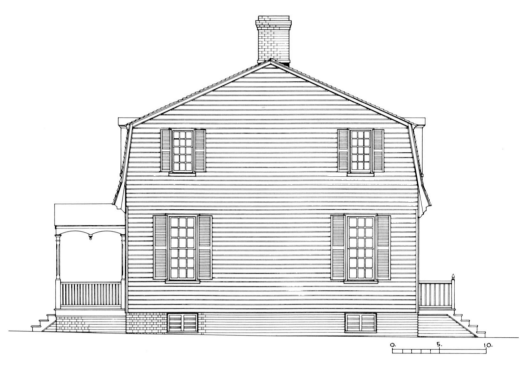

*Figure 62*   William Lightfoot House. East elevation.

Two of the outbuildings, the smokehouse and the dairy, were in large part original. Both were frame structures a little more than ten feet square with pyramidal roofs. The eaves of the dairy, which projected more than three feet, had a flat soffit instead of a cove like the one under the eaves of the Archibald Blair dairy.

## CONDITION

The house was restored in 1931. Three nineteenth-century additions, a porch on the front, a two-story wing to the east, and a lean-to at

---

[30] For a newel post going up to the ceiling, see the description of the James Geddy House, p. 187.

the rear, were removed. Most of the framing is old and was reinforced. The chimney was taken down for the practical purpose of putting in terra cotta flue linings and then was rebuilt as before. Most of the weatherboarding is old, although it did not necessarily date from the eighteenth century. The main cornice on the street front is the original, slightly repaired; that at the rear is old except for the bed mold and fascia. The original curb or gambrel cornices were still in position but had to be replaced because of their rotted condition. First floor window sashes, frames, and trim on the street front are old; dormer sashes on this front are based on the design of old sashes found in the dormers at the rear. Two of the shutters are original and served as models for the others. The front door and transom light had to be restored. Inside, the stairway and some of the doors and trim are original. The smoke-house and dairy had been moved from their foundations; they were replaced and were repaired as necessary.

*Figure 63*   Charlton House. North front.

# CHARLTON HOUSE

THE history of the lot on which this house stands was obscure at many points. At one time it belonged to William Byrd II of Westover, and it is possible that the "store at Williamsburg," which he mentioned in his diary as his and Richard Bland's, stood here.[31] There was a warehouse on the lot in 1750, when it was referred to in a deed as having "formerly belonged to the late Colonell William Bird."[32] Henry Wetherburn, whose tavern was next door, owned this

---

[31] Wright and Tinling, eds., *Diary of Byrd,* p. 161.
[32] York Co. Recs., Deeds, V, p. 393. The deed is a conveyance of three lots, whose numbers are not given but can be identified as nos. 22, 23, and 24, from James Crosby to Alexander Archibald Buchanan and Company.

property around mid-century. At his death in 1760, it was inherited by his widow, Anne Marot Ingles Shields Wetherburn, as her one-third dower-right legacy. Its disposition thereafter is unclear, although Mrs. Wetherburn's name continued to appear in local records until 1769.[33]

Structural evidence in the plan and the brickwork of the basement indicated that the foundations of a smaller building were reused when the house took its present form, which must have happened by 1782, when a building of the right size appeared on the Frenchman's Map. Probably it did so before 1772, the year in which Edward Charlton,

[33] *Ibid.,* Judgments and Orders (1759–1763), pp. 216–217.

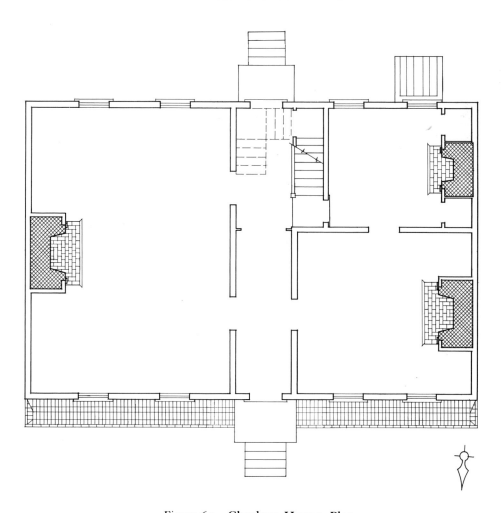

*Figure 64*   Charlton House. Plan.

wigmaker, paid a considerable sum for the property.[34] In the course
of the nineteenth century, the house was bisected along its east-west
axis, the southern half being taken down to ground level. Various additions were then tacked on behind. The front half of the house is the
original and was restored, while the rear half was reconstructed on
the original foundations. It has a well-mannered but unremarkable street
elevation and a plan in which the chief departure from orthodoxy was
the placement of the staircase in an alcove west of the rear passage
instead of within the passage itself.

## CONDITION

The Charlton House was restored, and the southern half was reconstructed, during 1929–1930. Original features that were retained, with
necessary repairs, included the basement walls, the front cornice, all
weatherboarding on the street front and some on the west, exterior
trim and sills of second floor windows on the facade, the front door
and several other doors, first floor and some second-floor framing, floorboards in three rooms and ground floor passage, and paneled dado
in the northwest room on the ground floor. The roof, chimneys, stairs,
sashes, and window frames were renewed.

---

[34] Glasgow agent Adam Stewart received £240 from Edward Charlton; he probably
was acting as a representative of Buchanan and Co. Ledger of George Washington,
B, p. 4, Manuscripts Division, Library of Congress.

*Figure 65*   Powell-Waller House. Northwest view.

# POWELL-WALLER HOUSE

L IKE the Benjamin Waller House, which faced the opposite end of the street on which this L-plan dwelling fronted, the Powell-Waller House developed through stages of alteration. Here the upright of the L, which extended to the rear of the part lying parallel to the street, was constructed first of brick. It was probably standing when Benjamin Powell, a builder, bought the property in 1763.[35] The Frenchman's Map indicated that the front frame portion had been added by 1782, the year in which Powell sold the house.[36] In 1791 it became

[35] York Co. Recs., Deeds, VIII, p. 4.
[36] *Ibid.*, VI, p. 118.

*Figure 66* Powell-Waller House before restoration.

*Figure 67* Powell-Waller House. Northwest room.

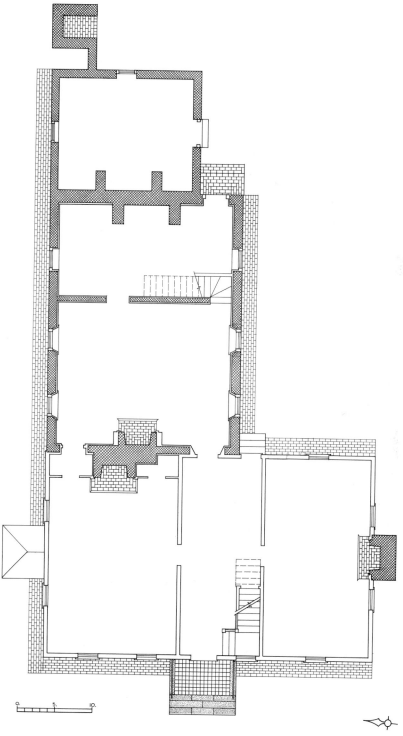

*Figure 68*  Powell-Waller House. Plan.

*Figure 69*   Powell-Waller Dairy before
restoration.

*Figure 70*   Powell-Waller Dairy after
restoration.

the property of Benjamin Carter Waller,[37] son of Benjamin Waller, from
whom Powell had purchased the site in the first place.

The brick house originally had three rooms, one of which was the
kitchen, and a small stair hall on the ground floor, with a laundry or
scullery or perhaps the carpenter's shop in the single-story projection
to the east. It faced south toward the part of Page Street that ran east
and west.[38] Probably late in the eighteenth century, the two west rooms,
which had corner fireplaces served by the central chimney to the west,[39]
were opened into one in which a mid-eighteenth-century paneled dado
clearly brought from elsewhere was installed. The wood front portion
of the house had the most common plan, with two rooms and a central
passage on both floors. The paneled dado in the north room was similar
to the one in the west room of the brick portion and obviously came
from another house. It also had a wood cornice and a mantel with a

[37] *Ibid.*, VII, p. 44.
[38] Page Street was an eighteenth-century street that connected Waller Street and
York Road. Today, Waller Street is considered to run to the end of Nicholson Street,
but in the deed of 1763, the boundary of the property to the west was described as
"the street leading to Queen Mary's Port," i.e., Capitol Landing.
[39] The triangular foundations of the chimney still existed in the basement.

shelf enriched with dentils and molded paneling. The passage and the south rooms had plain dados with molded chair rails. Only the balusters of the stairs were original.

Outbuildings at the Powell-Waller site are nineteenth-century examples. The kitchen dates from the period 1820 to 1840, although the smokehouse and dairy may have been built earlier. A temple-style brick office at the southwest corner of the lot, similar to one nearby at the Coke-Garrett House, is probably the "Doctor's Shop" mentioned in an 1814 deed.[40]

## CONDITION

The house and outbuildings were restored during 1955–1956. In the nineteenth century, the house had acquired a full second story and a two-story veranda along the street front, all of which were removed. Everything above the eaves, including the cornices, roof framing, and trim, had to be rebuilt. The weatherboards were replaced everywhere except on the south gable of the frame portion, where all the usable old weatherboards were collected. The north windows in the frame portion are original; elsewhere, window sashes were replaced. The east outside door in the frame portion is original. The single-story wing and an exterior oven at the east end of the brick portion were reconstructed on original foundations. A porch in the angle between the brick and frame portions was added as a feature of convenience. The staircase in the rear passage had been rebuilt in the nineteenth century and so it retained only its original balusters when it was restored to its eighteenth-century location. Much early paneling and trim were extant, and some of the inside doors and flooring had also survived. In 1972 the south room was restored to its original size by removing nineteenth-century partitions.

---

[40] York Co. Recs., Deeds, VIII, p. 268. The physician was Robert Page Waller, son of Benjamin Carter Waller.

*Figure 71*    Robert Carter House. East front.

# ROBERT CARTER HOUSE

THE Robert Carter House had an unusual plan and design features that distinguished it from other eighteenth-century houses in Williamsburg. The date of its construction was uncertain. The earliest definite information about the lots on which it was constructed appeared in an indenture of 1746 that recorded their sale by Charles Carter to Robert Cary of London, merchant.[41] The lots may have been included in the Williamsburg property left in 1732 by Robert "King" Carter to his son George, Charles Carter's eldest brother, and Charles may have purchased them from the trustees appointed to administer George's estate in 1744, but the evidence is tangled. Cary sold the property to a physician, Kenneth McKenzie, in 1747; in 1751 it was purchased by the colony to house Governor Robert Dinwiddie while the Palace was being repaired.[42] Robert Carter Nicholas bought it in

---

[41] York Co. Recs., Deeds, V, pp. 167–169.
[42] *Ibid.*, pp. 299–301, 468–471.

1753 and sold it in 1761 to Robert Carter of Nomini Hall,[43] in whose possession it remained until it was purchased by Robert Saunders sometime between 1796 and 1801.[44] The house probably had taken its present form by 1751, when it was chosen as a temporary residence for the governor. A graph of the prices at which the property changed hands showed the steepest rise between Dr. McKenzie's purchase and its sale to the colony, so it may be that Dr. McKenzie was responsible for giving it that form.[45] A date in the late 1740s would coincide well with the stylistic evidence.

The most unusual exterior feature of the Robert Carter House was its roof, which by alteration became a true mansard, a type more common

---

[43] *Ibid.*, pp. 585–588, VI, pp. 356–361.

[44] Carter wrote to Saunders about the latter's "Proposal to purchase my Property in Palace Street" in April 1796. Robert Carter Letter Book, 1794–1796, Manuscript Division, Library of Congress. The Williamsburg land tax records show that Saunders owned the property by 1801.

[45] The property changed hands at the following prices: Charles Carter to Robert Cary, £103 8s.; Cary to Dr. Kenneth McKenzie, £224 13s. 2d.; McKenzie to Philip

*Figure 72* Robert Carter House before restoration.

in late seventeenth-century England than in eighteenth-century Virginia. Ampthill, formerly in Chesterfield County, but rebuilt in 1929 in Richmond, had one of the few other Virginia examples. At an earlier stage in its development, however, the Robert Carter House roof had two parallel ridges, with a valley between, at the level of the present lower roof slope. The roof was M-shaped. The upper slope, which covered the valley and produced the mansard shape, was added later in the eighteenth century. An examination of the altered framing revealed traces of shingle laths on members now inside the attic. It was known that the house had a porch in the eighteenth century, although it was replaced in the nineteenth by a heavy, two-story portico in Greek Doric style. The design of the reconstructed front porch was therefore hypothetical.

The unusually wide spacing of openings on the street elevation produced an under-windowed effect on a front measuring forty-five feet, six inches long. The plan was unique in Williamsburg, if not in Virginia. Instead of a broad passage through the middle of the house with the stairs ascending by one of its side walls, there was an L-shaped entrance hall with the stairs to the right in the horizontal stroke of the L. Among colonial buildings, the Brice House at Annapolis, Maryland, had a similar arrangement; among British ones, Milton House in Edinburgh, Scotland, provided a precedent. Milton House was designed by architect William Adam, father of the famous brothers, and the design was one he had had engraved and published. The resemblance between the Brice House and Milton House plans may be too close to be coincidental, especially when other evidence indicated that the engravings of William Adam's works, although they were not collected into the volume entitled *Vitruvius Scoticus* until 1810, were known in the colonies at an early date.[46] In two respects, however, the Robert Carter House resembled Milton House even more closely: it had only three openings in each story of the entrance front, which was only one foot shorter than the facade of the Edinburgh building.[47] The likelihood that Milton House served as the model would be even greater if in fact the Williamsburg structure was given its present form during the ownership of the Scotsman, Dr. McKenzie.

Grymes, receiver general of Virginia, £537 10s.; Grymes to Robert Carter Nicholas, £450; Nicholas to Robert Carter, £650.

[46] Waterman, *Mansions of Virginia,* pp. 246–250, 336–337.

[47] The length of the front of Milton House is given in the engraving as 44 feet, 6 inches; the Brice House front extends 41 feet.

**CONDITION**

The house was restored during 1931–1932, while the front porch and the lateral additions connected by north and south colonnades were reconstructed between 1950 and 1953. Much of the weatherboarding is old and original to the house, as are many of the shutters. Most window frames are original, but all sashes were renewed to a design established by the old sashes that remained. Other exterior features that were renewed included the cornice and the front door. The rear porch was added for convenience. Inside, the Robert Carter House retained its original stairway, some plain early mantels, some eighteenth-century wood chair rails and cornices, and the only surviving eighteenth-century plaster cornice in Williamsburg, located in the southeast room on the second floor. The flooring is original, as are eight of the doors. An original brick outbuilding remained northwest of the house.

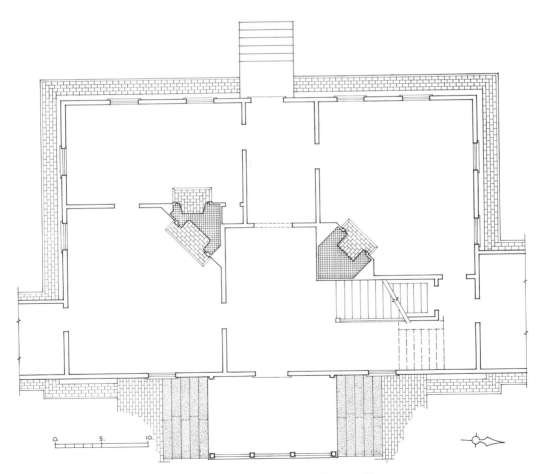

*Figure 73*   Robert Carter House. Plan.

*Figure 74*   George Wythe House. East front.

# GEORGE WYTHE HOUSE

THIS house, generally and not unjustly considered the most hand-some colonial house in Williamsburg, was built circa 1752–1754 by Richard Taliaferro.[48] A planter who on occasion undertook building works and may have designed those structures he erected, Taliaferro was at the time repairing the Governor's Palace and adding the ballroom wing.[49] The proximity of his new house to the Palace would clearly have been convenient in terms of supervision and the

---

[48] The date was previously given as "about 1755." However, Taliaferro was granted the western lot of the two that constituted the property in 1748, and the usual building clause was included in the deed. York Co. Recs., Deeds, V, pp. 256–258. No record survived of his purchase of the eastern lot, but it is reasonable to assume that he obtained it from a private owner at the same time and that the house was built within two years in order to save the two lots.

[49] Whiffen, *Public Buildings*, pp. 140–143.

supply of building materials, so it was conceivable that practicality influenced Taliaferro's undertaking of the private work at the same time he executed the public project.

George Wythe married Taliaferro's daughter, Elizabeth, about 1755, and probably moved into the house then. He continued to live in it until 1791. By 1755 Taliaferro, who on his death in 1775 gave the couple a life right to the property, was living at Powhatan in James City County in a house that afforded an interesting comparison with his Williamsburg dwelling.[50]

With four rooms and a wide central passage on each floor, the George Wythe House had a regularity of plan common in colonial Virginia, where domestic functions were removed to separate kitchens and other service outbuildings. The arrangement was balanced on the east-west axis only, since the front rooms were slightly deeper than those behind. All four exterior elevations, however, were symmetrical.[51] The geometrical system of proportion controlling the design has been described on page 86, and so has the variation in the sizes of the windows and their component parts. An unintentional variation of another kind that was due to a bricklayer's inaccurate workmanship—the failure to center the upper north window on the east front over the one below—is noticeable on close scrutiny (*Figure 11*). The brickwork was of the generally high quality characteristic of mid-century craftsmanship, with rubbed brick judiciously used as an articulating element. It demonstrated, as did the brickwork at Powhatan plantation, that Taliaferro's abilities as a designer and overseer favored geometric order and decorative restraint.

## CONDITION

The George Wythe House was restored during 1939–1940. The walls are original, except where patched, in some places with bricks from the original chimneys that had to be rebuilt for safety reasons. The identical steps on both fronts were rebuilt after their original design was established by the holes for, and in three places the profiles of, the oak nosings in the walls. The cornice dates from the nineteenth

---

[50] The date when Taliaferro purchased Powhatan was uncertain; it is likely that he bought it from Benjamin Weldon, who advertised land for sale there in 1752. *Virginia Gazette*, Sept. 15, 1752. For a photograph of the house, see Waterman, *Mansions of Virginia*, p. 202. Its hipped roof, which burned during the Civil War, has since been restored.

[51] See MS, p. 128.

century, but its pattern was eighteenth-century and surely followed the design of the original. The double doors and transom sashes on both fronts are original. The bulkhead near the southeast corner of the house was reconstructed. Most of the window frames and sashes are original, with considerable repairs. Framing generally is original. The stairs (except treads), most of the flooring, most interior doors together with their hardware, and most of the window shutters on the ground floor, including all those in the southeast room, are original. All wood and stone chimneypieces were restored.

*Figure 75*   George Wythe House. Stair passage.

*Figure 76*   Tayloe House and Office. Southwest view.

# TAYLOE HOUSE

THE Tayloe House was the most spacious of the isolated terrace houses with gambrel roofs in Williamsburg. The house must have been built during the period 1752–1759 when the lot on which it stood was owned by surgeon and apothecary James Carter. Carter sold the property in 1759 for the considerable sum of six hundred pounds, which was three times what he paid for it,[52] and stylistic evidence definitely supported a construction date in the 1750s. John Tayloe, who had just completed Mount Airy, his fine stone mansion in Richmond County, Virginia, bought the property from Carter.

Although the Tayloe House resembled the William Lightfoot House in some respects, its exterior differed most significantly in the rake of the lower slopes of the roof, which was less steep, giving a greater projection to the dormer roofs. An unusual refinement was the elongated

---

[52] York Co. Recs., Deeds, VI, p. 234, V, p. 475.

*Figure 77*  Tayloe House before restoration.

kick at the lower eaves. The front porch was reconstructed on original foundations; the back porch, which has been boarded in as a modern convenience, was original.

The interior of the Tayloe House was trimmed with woodwork considered to be among the finest joinery extant in Williamsburg. The floor-to-ceiling paneling of the first floor front room, together with its crowning cornice and the four foot, six inch paneled dado and ceiling cornice in the room behind, were exceptional among eighteenth-century treatments. Other noteworthy features were the paneled shutters inside the dormers, an oddity found elsewhere in Williamsburg only at the Nelson-Galt House, and the marble console table supported by handsome wrought-iron brackets near the front door. Yet even more remarkable was the design of the stair hall and upper passage. The normal arrangement was for the stairway to ascend against one wall to an intermediate landing and then return against the opposite wall to the second floor. In the Tayloe House, however, while the first flight ascended conventionally against the stair hall's inner lateral wall, the upper flight returned free of the outer wall. On the upper floor, the open stairwell was bound by wall on one side only, the other three sides being protected where necessary by the balustrade. This admirable scheme produced a spatial continuity between the two floors rarely found in colonial domestic architecture.

178

*Figure 78*　Tayloe House. Stair passage before restoration.

Three outbuildings were original in some degree. To the northwest was a storehouse, of which only the brick basement dated from the eighteenth century, and to the northeast, beyond the reconstructed kitchen and laundry, stood a square wood smokehouse that retained much original fabric. Remarkably, the door was hung on old strap hinges and still had its old rim lock. The most interesting, as well as the most conspicuous, of the surviving outbuildings was the ogee-roofed office that stood eastward in line with the front of the house. Although unique in Williamsburg, its roof was of a type common enough in Britain before 1770, as illustrated by many eighteenth-century design books. Most of the surviving examples in America were later, dating from the end of the eighteenth century or from the first two or three decades of

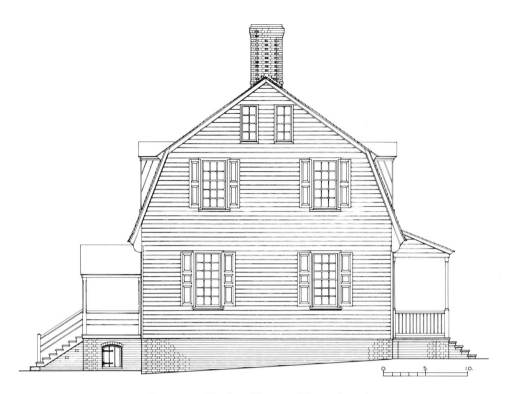

*Figure 79*   Tayloe House. West elevation.

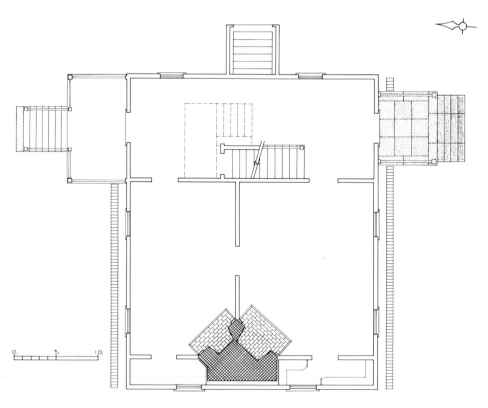

*Figure 80*   Tayloe House. Plan.

*Figure 81*   Tayloe House. Paneling in southwest room before restoration.

the nineteenth.[53] Structural evidence suggested that the Tayloe Office dated from the 1750s and thus was contemporary with the house, further complementing its stylishness.

## CONDITION

When the Tayloe House was obtained for restoration in 1950, it had a two-story extension to the east and a single-story wing on the west, both built in the 1870s, although the house itself and the office had

---

[53] A notable exception to this rule was Mulberry, on the Cooper River in South Carolina, which had four corner pavilions covered by ogee roofs and dated from the second decade of the eighteenth century. Another Virginia example was the roof of the octagonal summerhouse at Federal Hill, Fredericksburg, which the Historic American Buildings Survey assigned to the late eighteenth century.

*Figure 82*   Tayloe Office. Framing stripped for restoration.

been little altered. The frame of the house had spread at the bottom, a condition that was corrected by inserting tie rods between the ground floor joists. To strengthen the roof structure for the installation of heavy asbestos shingles, the original rafters, which were nearly square (four and one-half by four and three-fourths inches), were supplemented by new rafters, and some of the vertical members of the frame were also reinforced. The north and south cornices had survived and needed only repairs and slight replacements, while much of the original upper gambrel cornice and parts of the rakeboards had also survived. The weatherboarding on the south front is all original, although not necessarily to this front; the rest of the weatherboarding was replaced. The north and south doors are both original, and so are the sashes in all of the upper windows and in five of the eight windows on the first floor. The interior woodwork, including paneling, ceiling cornices, stairs, and most doors, is largely original. The mantel in the north room on the ground floor is original, while those in the front room and upstairs were reconstructed. The house was refurbished in 1974.

*Figure 83*    Archibald Blair House. South front.

# ARCHIBALD BLAIR HOUSE

D R. Archibald Blair acquired the lot on Nicholson Street just west of England Street in 1716.[54] Inasmuch as the lot did not revert to the grantors, he presumably built a house on it within the next two years.[55] The present house, however, a later structure, probably was erected in the third quarter of the eighteenth century.

Its proportions determined by a geometrical system, the Archibald Blair House was a simple yet satisfying building. The main house was

[54] York Co. Recs., Deeds, Bonds, III, pp. 126–127.

[55] In 1728 Sarah, a mulatto slave belonging to Blair, was charged in the York County court with setting fire to the house and burning part of it. She was found guilty and was sentenced to death by hanging. Sarah was valued at £18. *Ibid.*, Orders, Wills, XVI, p. 511.

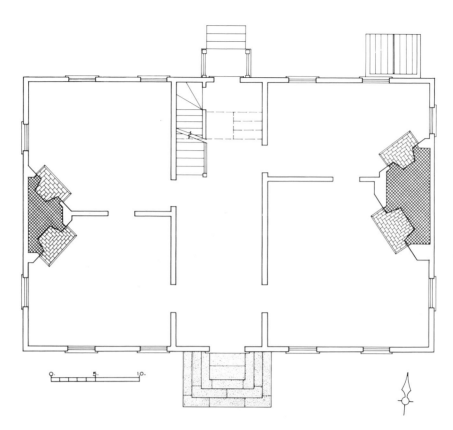

*Figure 84*   Archibald Blair House. Plan.

*Figure 85*   Archibald Blair Dairy
before restoration.

*Figure 86*   Archibald Blair Dairy
after restoration.

two rooms deep, with four rooms on each floor and a central passage containing the stair. As occurred in the contemporaneous part of the Peyton Randolph House on the opposite side of England Street, a fireplace was set diagonally across one corner in each room. This arrangement was common in England during the last quarter of the seventeenth century, but Palladian ideals of symmetry led to its abandonment in the eighteenth. In Virginia, it was found in many of the major houses of the first half of the eighteenth century, and remained a commonplace of the minor ones to the end of the colonial period. The neat porch with its Doric columns and pediment dated from the early nineteenth century. It was retained when the house was restored for its intrinsic merit and because it belonged to the classical continuation of the eighteenth-century tradition. Beneath its platform, archaeological excavations revealed the brick foundations of original three-sided steps, the stones of which were found scattered about the yard.

The outbuildings included two of eighteenth-century date, a pyramidal-roofed smokehouse and a dairy with a deep plaster cove under the eaves. The brick kitchen, whose deep red painted walls provided a note of contrast in this corner of Williamsburg, was built between 1815 and 1823.[56]

## CONDITION

The house and outbuildings were restored during 1930–1931. The house had been extensively altered after the eighteenth century: the chimneys had been rebuilt; the original stair had been replaced by a new one built in the northeast corner of the house; and the windows had been equipped with Gothic sashes. The frame and the framing of the roof, however, had survived unaltered. Of the exterior trim, the lower members of the cornice on the south front and the rakeboards and corner boards of the main house are old, as are the weatherboards on the south front and the west end. No eighteenth-century trim survived indoors. The framing, weatherboarding, and door of the smokehouse are original. Its cornice was copied from the original, which remained but had to be replaced. The structure of the dairy is original; it was repaired, and the plaster cove was renewed.

---

[56] To judge from Mutual Assurance Society policies, nos. 1523 and 5045, Virginia State Archives.

*Figure 87*   James Geddy House. Southwest view.

# JAMES GEDDY HOUSE

T HE lot on the corner of Duke of Gloucester and Palace streets
was granted to Samuel Cobbs in 1716.[57] The deed contained
the usual building clause, and Cobbs clearly fulfilled his obliga-
tions; not only did the lot not escheat to the city, but when Cobbs
conveyed it to the next owner in 1719, he received forty pounds instead
of the thirty shillings he had paid for it.[58]

James Geddy, gunsmith, had acquired the property by 1738, living
and carrying on his trade there until he died six years later. Ownership
passed to his widow, who built the present two-story house and its
attached one and one-half story extension to the east about 1750. The
second east addition, whose gable end faced Duke of Gloucester Street,
was completed before 1760 when Mrs. Geddy sold the property to her

[57] York Co. Recs., Deeds, III, pp. 149–150.
[58] *Ibid.*, pp. 297–298.

son James Geddy, Jr., silversmith.[59] He continued to own and occupy
the property until 1778 and rented out the east wing as a separate
shop.[60]

The L plan of the old part of the house was uncommon in Williamsburg and possibly was the result of an attempt to utilize the advantages
of the corner site. Its low-pitched roof, without dormers, related it to
the Archibald Blair and Peyton Randolph houses, with which it might
have been contemporary. An interior feature of special interest was
the stairway, which at landing level had a turned newel post that extended all the way to the ceiling, a peculiarity that may have been a
throwback to the scheme from which the English open well stairs
evolved.[61] The mantel in the southwest room on the ground floor was

[59] *Ibid.*, VI, pp. 276–278.

[60] *Ibid.*, pp. 288–290.

[61] Marcus Whiffen, *An Introduction to Elizabethan and Jacobean Architecture* (London, 1952),
pp. 33, 60. In Williamsburg, the William Lightfoot House (see pp. 159–160) had a
newel post that descended from the half-landing to the first floor. Walnut Valley, Surry
County, which probably dated from the mid-eighteenth century, had a stair with two
newel posts rising from the upper landing to the ceiling. Singleton P. Moorehead supplied this information.

*Figure 88* James Geddy House.
Mantel in southwest room.

*Figure 89*  James Geddy House. Beaufet in north room.

an example where form triumphed over the material in a way that Isaac Ware would have approved. Its moldings had a character usually executed in marble rather than wood, indicating that it may have been copied directly from an English patternbook design by a joiner heedless of nuances in his trade. No other like it existed in Williamsburg.

The large north room, unadorned by typical cornice and chairboard trim, might have been wallpapered originally. Its most interesting feature is a crude yet intriguing cupboard next to the fireplace. Converted from a closet with scrap materials, including an old window frame with its sash pulleys left chopped in half and visible, it was related to other alteration cabinets at the Benjamin Waller House and Bassett Hall.

## CONDITION

The James Geddy House, the only eighteenth-century structure on the site, was partially restored in 1930 and again restored in 1967.

The porch and front door were replaced, and the chimneys were rebuilt above the ridge of the roof; otherwise, the street elevations of the two-story part of the house are practically all original, or at least old. Exact evidence for the porch was found in silhouette against the exterior weatherboarding, and was confirmed by the rare presence of a transomed original doorway at second-floor level. Its classic design was adapted from the pre-1801 Semple House porch details. On the rear elevations, some window frames and sashes, some shutters, and all weatherboards were renewed. Inside, all doors, floors, mantels, wooden trim, and the stairs are original with minor repairs. The hinges are old throughout, but most of the other door furniture had disappeared and was replaced with modern reproductions. The story and one-half east extensions were reconstructed on the original foundations.

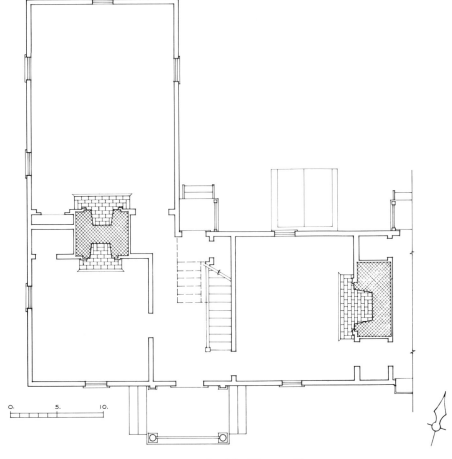

*Figure 90* James Geddy House. Plan.

*Figure 91*   Peyton Randolph House, South front.

# PEYTON RANDOLPH HOUSE

THIS house was built in three sections, as its plan revealed. The earliest was the west part, a square house of two stories with a central chimney serving all the fireplaces on both floors, which was built in 1715 or 1716.[62] A smaller one and one-half story house, represented by the reconstructed east wing, stood on the neighboring lot by 1724. A few years later the two houses, having come into common ownership, were linked by the two-story middle addition. The easternmost section may have been removed by 1783, when the house was described as having "four rooms on a floor."[63]

The west house, which was built by William Robertson, clerk of the Governor's Council from 1701 until 1739, had an early plan and some

---

[62] The lot on which the house stood was granted in November 1714 to William Robertson with the usual stipulation that he should build a house on it within two years. York Co. Recs., Bonds and Deeds, II, p. 28.

[63] *Virginia Gazette, and Weekly Advertiser* (Richmond), Feb. 15, 1783. The stair passages in the west and central portions, although somewhat room-like in plan, would no more have been counted as rooms in the eighteenth century than they would be so counted today.

unusual exterior features, among which was the two-story porch with its porch chamber on the north side. The present feature was reconstructed, but conclusive proof of the existence in the eighteenth century of such a porch was found in the framing and trim of the north wall and in archaeological investigations of the ground nearby.[64] Two-story porches seem to have been quite common in Virginia in the seventeenth century. This was a late, rare example in Williamsburg. Another unusual feature was the belt board at the second floor level that continued along the central section of the house; it had no structural purpose but was imitative of the belt courses common to brick houses.[65] The west and central sections of the house were covered by a continuous roof that was hipped to the west and gabled to the east. As first built, however, the west section had a roof hipped at the four corners with a hollow center containing a secondary W-form roof whose two valleys drained into a large wooden gutter that probably was connected with an indoor

---

[64] The evidence consisted of sawed off upper-floor joists flanked by large studs (5 inches by 8 inches) 8 feet apart, patching of the corresponding section of the cornice with indications of another cornice having returned into it at the ends, and remains of foundations, 8 feet wide, that projected a little more than 5 feet from the center of the north front.

[65] Tuckahoe, Goochland County, which was built about 1712 and enlarged after 1730, was a wooden house that had a molded string at this level.

*Figure 92*   Peyton Randolph House. North view.

*Figure 93*   Peyton Randolph House. Oak paneling in second floor northeast room.

*Figure 94*   Peyton Randolph House. Central room showing marble mantel and walnut trim.

cistern. At an early date, this secondary roof was covered, later to be found still in place in the attic when the house was restored.

Inside, the Peyton Randolph House was distinguished by having the best series of original paneled rooms in Williamsburg. There were four on the ground floor and three on the upper floor. The central stair hall was paneled also. In all but one instance, the paneling was the usual yellow pine, although the northeast room on the second floor in the west section of the house was completely paneled in oak. The doors, sashes, and window trim in the first floor room of the central section were walnut, and it contained a simple yet handsome mantelpiece of gray-veined marble. This mantel and all of the original paneling must have dated from the mid-eighteenth century. Perhaps the older paneling was installed during the period 1724–1737, when Sir John Randolph owned the house. In the course of an active public life, he served as clerk of the House of Burgesses and as attorney general, speaker, and treasurer of the colony. Sir John's son Peyton, speaker of the House of Burgesses from 1766 to 1775 and president of the Continental Congress in 1774, lived in the house from 1745 until his death in 1775.

## CONDITION

The house was partially restored during 1939–1941 when a north wing of recent date was removed. Restoration was completed in 1968. The two-story porch on the west section and the whole wing of the house are reconstructions. The latter was planned for modern convenience and was not intended to reproduce the eighteenth-century interior arrangement. The framing in the old parts of the house was found to be original, generally sound, and was retained with necessary repairs.

*Figure 95*   Peyton Randolph House. South elevation (ca. 1724).

The chimney of the west section, which had been rebuilt in 1920, was restored to its original form. The cornice on the west and south fronts is original, as is the belt board at the second-story level. A few of the weatherboards are old. The sashes of the first floor west windows date from the first half of the eighteenth century and provided the model for necessary replacements elsewhere. Outside doors date from the restoration, and so do the north porch and south door hood of the central section. Flooring in the house is original, along with some of the inside doors and most of the paneling, the principal exceptions being the paneling on the diagonal, or chimney, walls in the west section, where the mantels are also replacements. Two of the chimney breasts, one in the second floor southeast room and the other in the oak room, received their restored paneling in 1968.

This recent restoration involved few major changes other than general refurbishment. Antique wool flock wallpaper was installed in the second floor southeast room of the west section to reflect structural evidence for eighteenth-century decorative hangings. At the same time, however, an eighteenth-century east partition wall in that room, dating from the period of the middle addition, was removed for exhibition purposes.

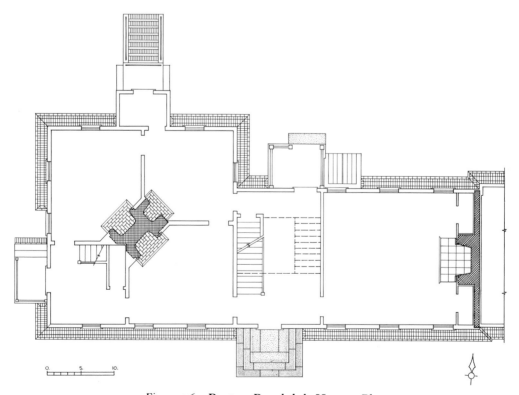

*Figure 96*   Peyton Randolph House. Plan.

*Figure 97*    Palmer House. North front.

# PALMER HOUSE

THERE was a house on this corner site near the Capitol by 1732, when it was bought by Alexander Kerr, jeweler, for one hundred pounds.[66] Four years later, in September 1736, a complaint was brought against Kerr in the House of Burgesses:

> The House was informed, That Mr. *Alexander Ker* has made several Encroachments upon the Capitol Square, particularly in setting a Brick-Kiln upon the Capitol Bounds. *Ordered,* That the Directors of the City of *Williamsburg,* take Care to remove the Nuisance of the said Brick-Kiln that is preparing to be burnt near the Capitol.[67]

---

[66] York Co. Recs., Deeds, IV, pp. 150–151.
[67] H. R. McIlwaine, ed., *Journals of the House of Burgesses of Virginia, 1727–1740* (Richmond, 1910), p. 312.

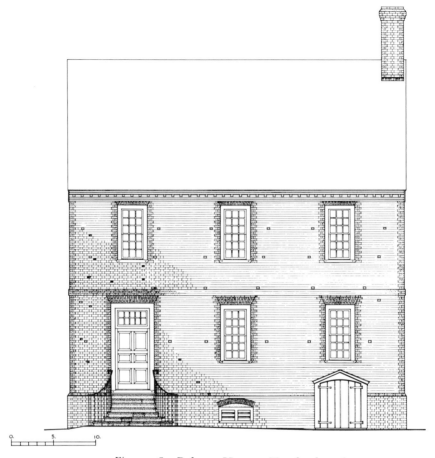

*Figure 98*   Palmer House. North elevation.

Was the kiln to have burned bricks for a new house for Kerr? It was a likely enough conjecture, since after his death in 1738, his executors advertised for sale by auction "a well finished Brick House, in good Repair," with "a convenient Store, Coach-House, Stables, and other Office-Houses, and a large Garden."[68] Sometime before 1749 the house was acquired by John Palmer, a lawyer who became bursar of the College of William and Mary. On April 24, 1754, it was destroyed by a fire— one of the most devastating in eighteenth-century Williamsburg accord-ing to contemporary descriptions—which started at night in the counting room of a nearby store and spread to adjoining buildings.[69]

[68] *Virginia Gazette*, Nov. 17, 1738.
[69] The *Maryland Gazette*, May 9, 1754, reported that two dwelling houses and a jeweler's

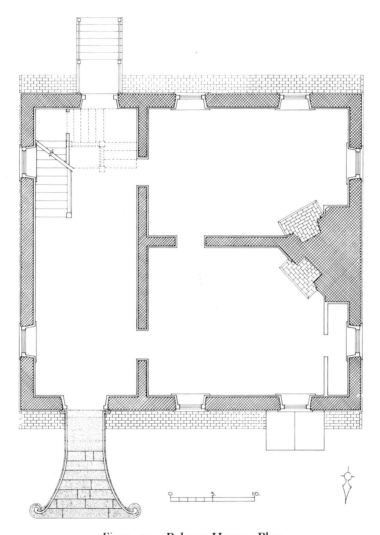

*Figure 99*   Palmer House. Plan.

The present house was built soon afterward by Palmer to replace the one that burned. Its style was decidedly urban, and archaeological evidence suggested that it was somewhat larger than its predecessor.

Of all the isolated terrace houses in Williamsburg, the Palmer House proclaimed most clearly its London ancestry. The high brick walls, rising

shop were destroyed by the fire, as well as the store in which it started, and put the loss at "upwards of Five Thousand Pounds," which was probably an exaggeration. Lyon G. Tyler, ed., "Narrative of George Fisher," *WMQ,* 1st Ser., XVII (January 1909), pp. 150–153, gives a fascinating eyewitness account.

two full stories above the water table and accentuated at the gable ends by the steep pitch of the roof, typified such townhouses, although in London or Bristol they would have been three to three and one-half stories tall. Other characteristic features, such as the off-center placement of the front door, which implied the side passage plan, its double-pile construction with the front rooms being slightly deeper than those at the back, its room arrangement of three upper chambers over two rooms and a stair passage on the first floor, its austere fenestration, and its sober, bulky mass, all linked the design to English prototypes. True, its wood cornice would have been illegal in London, where the law restricting flammable building materials also required that window frames be recessed farther back from the plane of exterior walls.[70] Yet the only fundamental difference between the Palmer House and London counterparts was in the treatment of the foundation walls. Small segmental openings in the brickwork, fitted with wood grilles whose sills rested at grade, provided light and ventilation for the cellar of the Palmer House, whereas the English examples had full-sized basement windows that opened onto a sunken area below street level in the seventeenth-century manner.

One is tempted to wonder if its original builder envisioned the whole of this important section along Duke of Gloucester Street as one day being lined with formal rows, or terraces, of such residences.

A striking feature of the Palmer House was the array of putlog holes punctuating its walls. In eighteenth-century brickwork, such apertures always marked regular spaces where horizontal scaffolding poles were positioned to raise the walls of a building. Normally, putlog holes were infilled at the completion of construction as the scaffolding was dismantled. A 1779 entry in Humphrey Harwood's ledger, however, recorded a lapse of twenty-five years before this routine masonry work was finished at the Palmer House.[71] Because the restoration was intended to re-create the dwelling as it appeared at mid-century, all of the late eighteenth-

---

[70] Williamsburg's 1699 and 1705 building acts did legislate measures to reduce fire hazard in a comprehensive way, but the Virginia General Assembly's codes were less specifically stringent than London ordinances. Fortunately, Williamsburg's early planners had the wisdom and foresight to introduce subtle constraints that minimized the crowded conditions so conducive to disastrous fires in many towns.

[71] The entry in the Harwood Ledger, B, p. 20, Feb. 22, 1779, indicated that the work was done for the then owner, William Page: "To putting in Cellar window frames 48/-& Stoping pudlock Holes 40/- . . £4 · 8 · -" Harwood did some fairly extensive repairs both to the house and to the snuff factory that stood behind or beside it, for a subsequent owner, John Drewidz, in 1782–1785. *Ibid.*, pp. 45, 47, 81.

century brick fillings were removed. Fragments of the sawed-off putlogs that had been left from the time colonial brickmasons built the house were found still embedded when the holes again were exposed.[72]

## CONDITION

Restoration of the Palmer House took place in 1952. An 1857 brick addition to the east, which nearly doubled its size, and various frame additions of the same period to the south were demolished. The windows of the original house, lowered at the sills to match larger windows in the nineteenth-century extension and then capped with cast-iron pediments, were restored to their proper dimensions and trim. Unauthentic late dormers were removed from the roof, and the walls were cleaned of paint. The structural condition of all original brickwork and framing members was sound and needed only minimal repairs for reinforcement.

Exterior features that are wholly or mostly original include the main cornice, except its crown mold, the front steps, lacking only the bottom one whose shape was revealed by archaeological investigations, the rakeboards and endboards on the west elevation, and the south or back door with its hardware. All window frames and sashes, the front door, the wrought-iron railing to the front steps, the north bulkhead (authenticated by structural and archaeological evidence), and the part of the chimney stack above the roof date from the restoration. The south porch is a reconstruction. The only noteworthy original feature inside the house is the stairway, a closed string type with square newel posts and turned balusters of simple but customary design.

---

[72] There were also putlog holes in the east end of Bruton Parish Church.

*Figure 100*   Coke-Garrett House. South front.

# COKE-GARRETT HOUSE

THE story and one-half west section was the only part of the house on the property that dated from the eighteenth century, although the one and one-half story east section was an eighteenth-century structure moved to this site from an unknown location sometime around 1837. The two-story frame center portion was built circa 1836–1837 during the Garrett family's ownership. The brick office that served as Dr. Robert M. Garrett's surgery, where many of the wounded of both armies were treated after the battle of Williamsburg in 1863, apparently dated from about 1810.[73]

John Coke, goldsmith and tavern keeper, bought the two lots on which the house stood from Christopher Ford, Jr., carpenter, for thirty-two pounds in 1755.[74] Coke already owned a house and three lots immediately to the east.[75] Neither the deed that recorded the purchase nor

[73] In the Williamsburg land tax records for 1837, the estate of Richard Garrett was charged with "2 new buildings recently erected, and assessed . . . at $1200." Virginia State Archives. It seems reasonable to suppose that these were the two late frame additions. The east office brickwork, in Flemish bond with regular glazed headers and closers, suggested an earlier nineteenth-century date.

[74] York Co. Recs., Deeds, VI, p. 15.

[75] Lots 361, 281, and 282, purchased from John Mundell, gaoler, in 1740. *Ibid.*, IV, pp. 610–611.

any earlier reference mentioned buildings on the two lots, although when Coke died in 1767, there were "houses" on his five lots.[76] One must have been the house on the eastern three lots.[77] Another probably was the west section of the Coke-Garrett House, which therefore may be dated within the twelve-year period 1755–1767.

Measuring forty feet by eighteen feet on plan, it was a typical story and one-half house with two rooms and a passage on each floor. The railing on one of the few surviving eighteenth-century porches in tidewater Virginia anticipated the best original feature inside, a Chinese trellis stair railing. Several similar stair rails were installed in Virginia houses in the third quarter of the eighteenth century. The design of the trellis panels in the Coke-Garrett example closely resembled the stairway at Weyanoke, twenty-five miles west of Williamsburg in Charles City

---

[76] *Virginia Gazette* (Purdie and Dixon), Jan. 12, 1769.

[77] Excavations carried out in 1958–1959 revealed little of the character of this house, but established that it had been destroyed by fire about 1820.

*Figure 101* Coke-Garrett House. "Chinese" stair railing.

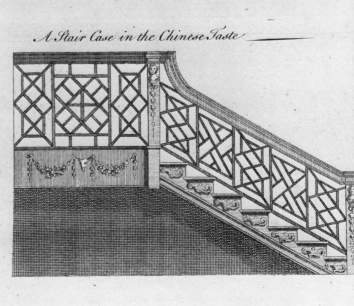

*Figure 102* Stair railing design from William and John Halfpenny, *Rural Architecture in the Chinese Taste* (London, 1752), Plate 50.

County, although there the handrail ran into the caps of the newels instead of into their posts.[78]

## CONDITION

The Coke-Garrett House was partially restored in 1928 and again in 1932. Final restoration occurred in 1961. Additional interior renovations were accomplished in 1971. Only the west section survives from the eighteenth century. On its south elevation, most of the weatherboards were replaced; the basement wall and porch are original but rebuilt; the cornice, windows, and dormers were repaired where necessary; the front door and the shutters are original. A lean-to or shed on the north elevation, removed in 1932, had protected most of the fabric there. Inside, the stairway, all doors and floorboards, and some trim features had survived.

---

[78] According to Robert A. Lancaster, *Historic Virginia Homes and Churches* (Philadelphia, 1915), p. 70, Weyanoke was built in 1740, but it is hard to believe that the stair should be dated before the third quarter of the century. Other examples in Virginia were at Battersea in Petersburg, and Brandon in Prince George County, both attributable to the period 1765–1770. All three are illustrated in Waterman, *Mansions of Virginia*, pp. 221, 371, 377.

*Figure 103*   Bracken House. North front.

# BRACKEN HOUSE

T HE Bracken House was named after the Reverend John Bracken,
who was president of the College of William and Mary in 1812–
1814 and rector of Bruton Parish from 1773 until his death.
Bracken owned the house,[79] but there was no record that he lived in
it, although he did reside in the Lightfoot House, situated farther west
on Francis Street.

The house stood in the part of Williamsburg that in Bracken's time
lay in James City County. Since the county's records were lost or destroyed during the Civil War, the early history of this house was poorly

[79] His name appears on the property in two contemporary maps, the Browne Map
(after 1800) and the College Map (ca. 1800).

documented. It appeared on the Frenchman's Map, so it must have existed by 1782. Stylistic evidence would assign it, at the latest, to the decade 1760–1770. With central passages, four rooms, two upstairs and two down, and end chimneys, the Bracken House was a very typical one and one-half story example of the hall-passage-parlor plan. The T-shaped chimneys with weatherings on their three outer faces were among the most attractive, both in form and in texture, of the outside chimneys in Williamsburg. Like its neighbor, the Orrell House, which never had exterior shutters, the building may originally have lacked shutters also. The interior stair design that combined turned balusters with a closed string was rather awkwardly executed in comparison to similar original examples at the James Geddy and Nicolson houses. One baluster was even upside down, perhaps the result of clumsy alteration.

## CONDITION

The Bracken House always looked much as it does today. When restoration was begun in 1928, most of the structural framing was found to be in good condition and only the roof rafters, of which about three-quarters had to be replaced, needed reinforcement. On the other hand, the external woodwork needed extensive replacements owing to decay, the dormers were rebuilt, and the window sashes were renewed throughout the house. A new front door, door frame, and transom light of colonial pattern were substituted for the nineteenth-century doorway that had replaced the original. The cornice on the street front is nine-tenths original; the chimneys are wholly so. Original woodwork inside includes all floorboards, the doors and door frames of the first floor rooms, and the stairway.

*Figure 104*    Lightfoot House. North front.

# LIGHTFOOT HOUSE

THE Lightfoot House, while related to other two-story brick structures in Williamsburg such as the George Wythe and Ludwell-
Paradise houses, the Brafferton, and the President's House at
the College of William and Mary, nevertheless was distinctive among
local buildings. Presumably built early in the eighteenth century as a
tenement, its restored appearance reflected alterations introduced sometime before 1750. Its setback from the street line was the deepest of

any original residence in town[80] and gave it an aura of remoteness sur-
passed only by Bassett Hall, which was situated outside the colonial
city limits.

The earliest history of the Lightfoot property, which was located in
James City County, was lost, although research confirmed some facts
of its post-Revolutionary ownership. It has been speculated that the
Lightfoot ownership of this site on Francis Street, along with other
Williamsburg properties including the nearby William Lightfoot House,
dated from the early years of the town's establishment. Architectural
evidence strongly suggested that the present house was first built for
rental. Furthermore, certain structural elements hinted that the building
might have been used for commercial as well as residential purposes
during its tenement era. The substantial renovation that converted it
into a townhouse might indicate, however, that it was acquired by the
Lightfoot family around mid-century.

The earliest specific reference to Lightfoot family ownership of the
property occurred in 1783 when Philip Lightfoot III of Bowling Green,
Carolina County, advertised the house for sale, describing it as "a large
two story brick dwelling house with four rooms on a floor . . . lying
on the back street near to the market."[81] In 1786 his nephew and heir,
William Lightfoot of Tedington in Charles City County, sold the house
and parcel of six lots to the Reverend John Bracken, rector of Bruton
Parish Church and subsequently president of the College of William
and Mary.[82]

A British traveler gave an indication of the Lightfoot family's wealth
in 1736 when he described their Yorktown residence as "equal in Mag-
nificence to many of our superb ones at St. James."[83] No such account
has been discovered to document their Williamsburg holdings, but York
County records revealed that in 1747 Philip Lightfoot I, a prosperous
merchant who owned widespread Virginia plantations and served as

---

[80] Williamsburg's 1699 and 1705 building acts stipulated a uniform 6-foot building
setback for Duke of Gloucester, the main street, where the houses all had "to front
alike," but such restrictions on the town's back streets were left to the discretion of
the directors appointed to supervise the laws. The Palace and John Custis and Nicholas-
Tyler houses had deep setbacks similar to that of the Lightfoot House, while among
original structures, the Nelson-Galt and Chiswell houses were situated farther than
6 feet from the street lines yet closer than the other dwellings cited.

[81] *Virginia Gazette or, the American Advertiser* (Richmond), Aug. 16, 1783.

[82] Williamsburg City Land Books, 1782–1861, entries for 1786 and 1787, Virginia
State Library.

[83] "Observations in Several Voyages and Travels in America in the year 1736," *WMQ*,
1st Ser., XV (April 1907), p. 222.

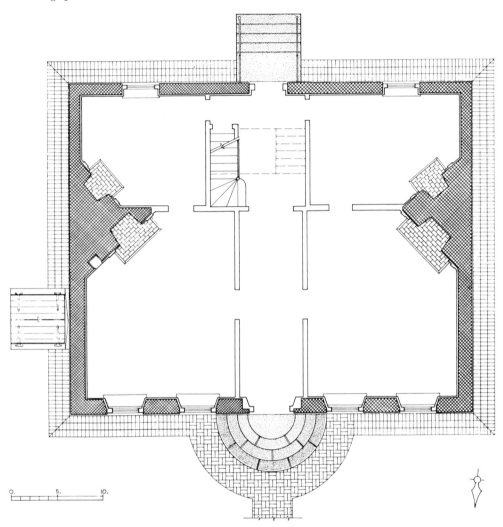

*Figure 105*   Lightfoot House. Plan.

clerk of York County until appointed to the Governor's Council in 1733, willed to his son John all his "Lots and Houses in the City of Williamsburg" including "the furniture in the House in Williamsburg."[84]

Rather surprisingly, in view of the Georgian regularity of its exterior, when restoration was undertaken, the house was found to have some baffling features that were signs of previous radical changes. Evidently the house had three distinct plan types at successive periods. Heavy

---

[84] York Co. Recs., Wills and Inventories, XX, pp. 104–106.

floor framing timbers for the studs of partitions that crossed from front to back precisely at the middle of both floors showed that at one time the doors in the north and south elevations must have been off center, an indication of a floor plan unlike the present central passage type. The remains of corner fireplaces, still strewn with ashes, that were discovered in the attic could not have coexisted with the hipped roof found in place. At one stage, the Lightfoot House may have resembled the Ludwell-Paradise House in form, with a one-story shed across the rear elevations and a second story that was only one room deep, a plan inferred from the presence in the cellar of foundation walls of unequal size. Yet the abandoned cross partitions and garret fireplaces suggested that at another period the building might have been a two and one-half or three-story multipartite tenement. An eighteenth-century floor plan among the papers of John Custis (1678–1749), an early resident of Williamsburg, depicted a similar four-family tenement.[85]

Other unusual features were evident at the Lightfoot House. The ornate gilded balcony above the front door, reconstructed according to structural indications, constituted a rare domestic embellishment in local architecture documented only at public buildings and at Marot's Ordinary. Its windowless side walls were characteristic of shops and stores, rather than houses, in Williamsburg. A contrast in fenestration differentiated the front and rear elevations: the north facade had five bays while the south elevation had only three. When compared to customary window-to-wall ratios at the Ludwell-Paradise and George Wythe houses, which were considered almost ideal, the Lightfoot House had a rather over-windowed front. The rich molded brick stringcourse at front and back that returned at the ends instead of encircling the house was unprecedented among decorative refinements on Williamsburg buildings. Perhaps singular also were the interior ceiling heights that measured almost exactly the same on both floors, eleven feet, ten inches on the first floor, and eleven feet, six inches on the second. Those dimensions emphasized another exceptional condition—the first floor framework was set below the line of the dwelling's exterior water table.

## CONDITION

The house was restored during 1940–1941 and refurbished in 1961. Only the walls, the cornice, and the framing of the roof, floors, and

---

[85] "Plan for a four family dwelling," Papers of John Custis (1678–1749) of Williamsburg, Custis MSS, Virginia Historical Society.

partitions were eighteenth-century in date. The brickwork was cleaned of exterior paint and was repaired and patched where necessary. Late windows in the east and west elevations were infilled. The chimneys were rebuilt above the level of the cornice. Circular stone steps at the front door were restored according to the outline of old foundations, while their design duplicated the original north steps to the Brafferton at the College of William and Mary. The balcony was restored according to the circumstantial evidence of holes in the brickwork, the enlarged size of the central second story windows, and the uncharacteristic returns of the stringcourse that left a space over the front door.

Few original elements survived in 1940 after repeated alterations. Besides interior partitions, the only old features extant are the frames and partial trim of two doors in the first floor passage. The present stairway is a facsimile of one found in place at the beginning of restoration. The antique yellow pine floorboards throughout were installed when the house was restored. Paint colors were derived from fragmentary pieces of woodwork that remained.

The first and second floor plans were adapted for modern residential convenience. The addition of two archways fitted with doors in the front passage provided closets, the southwest room was converted to a kitchen, and the rear passage was enclosed. Originally, the two first floor front rooms were fully paneled to the ceiling, but this replacement was omitted in restoration. Dados were substituted below the chair rails, cornices were applied, and antique wallpaper was introduced in the northwest room. Fireplaces on the second floor were not restored. All lath and plaster, glass, and hardware were replaced. The Lightfoot House required slight exterior restoration, but the interior's unsound and fragmentary condition necessitated almost complete renovation.

*Figure 106*  Brush-Everard House. West front.

# BRUSH-EVERARD HOUSE

JOHN Brush, a gunsmith, bought the two lots on which this house stood from the trustees of the city of Williamsburg in 1717.[86] Thomas Everard, clerk of York County from 1745 until his death in 1784 and mayor of Williamsburg in 1766 and 1771, owned the property in the 1770s.[87] Since Brush was granted the lots with the usual stipulation that he must build a dwelling house on them within two years, since he still owned them at his death in 1726, and since there were no other foundations on the street building line, the front part of the Brush-Everard House, which measured twenty feet by forty-four feet on plan, must have dated from 1717–1719 and so have been one of the earliest structures in Williamsburg.

[86] York Co. Recs., Deeds, III, pp. 246–247.
[87] *Ibid.*, VIII, p. 374.

The plan of the front part also suggested an early date. The chimneys were situated on the back elevations instead of against the end walls as was usual in the great majority of story and one-half houses in Virginia. Some seventeenth-century houses at Jamestown whose foundations have been excavated also had chimneys at the back. The condition here, however, probably was intended for planned enlargements. An unusual exterior detail was that the dormer cheeks were sheathed with horizontal boards instead of with diagonal cheek boards parallel to the slope of the main roof.[88]

Judging from the inventory of his personal estate, Brush was hardly a wealthy man, and the house in his day was probably a modest hall-parlor dwelling, without one of the existing passage partitions. The front door would have led directly into the hall, a large multipurpose room, where in lieu of a separate passageway, the stair would also have been located. Plastered walls were whitewashed from floor to ceiling.[89]

---

[88] The dormers were cut in after the roof had been framed. This was common enough practice when a house was designed to have dormers from the first. But in this instance a rather rough and ready job was made of it, which may indicate that the house was originally built without dormers.

[89] When the house was restored, conclusive evidence that the parts of the walls now behind paneling were once plastered was discovered.

*Figure 107*   Brush-Everard House before restoration.

The date when the house was equipped with the woodwork that makes its interior one of the richest in Williamsburg has been a matter of speculation. The character of the woodwork suggested a date during the second quarter of the century, and perhaps it was installed while the house was owned by Henry Cary, Jr., the builder of the President's House at the College of William and Mary. Cary's ownership ended in 1742, when he sold the house to William Dering, a dancing master.[90]

The stairway and its accompanying paneled dado are especially noteworthy, the stair for an easy rise and sophisticated trim; the dado for the ramps and easings of its capping on the intermediate flight and the two landings. The foliated brackets at the ends of the treads, a feature found similarly at Tuckahoe and at Carter's Grove, were elaborate for a house of this size. The stair brackets at the Brush-Everard House, although less graceful in execution, were almost exact copies of those at Carter's Grove, which the English joiner, Richard Baylis, probably carved. Unusual too were the north and south door frames of the first floor passage and rooms, which were eared or lugged at both top and bottom with crossettes. The front rooms had paneled dados surmounted by an unusually massive chair rail instead of the customary dado cap, a peculiarity indicating that the chair rail was installed first. The molded ceiling cornices and mantels were also late additions. Certain eccentricities in the fitting of the woodwork suggested that whoever installed it may have reworked elements from another house.

The addition of the rear wings, which must have been considerably facilitated by the unorthodox placement of the chimneys, could have been initiated by Thomas Everard. The south wing burned at an unknown date and was entirely reconstructed on old foundations identical to and contemporary with those of the north wing. Excavations revealed that an even earlier south wing with a cellar predated the one reconstructed.

The Frenchman's Map showed an array of outhouses on the Brush-Everard property. Only two outbuildings survived, the smokehouse and the brick kitchen, one of the two eighteenth-century kitchens extant in Williamsburg.

---

[90] The discovery of fragments of a yellow and white wallpaper under the cornice of the south room, which must therefore have been papered before the cornice was installed, may suggest a later date because there is no definite record of wallpaper being used in Williamsburg before George III's reign. More wallpaper, patterned in blue and gray, was found in the northeast room on the ground floor.

*Figure 108* Brush-Everard House. Stairway.

## CONDITION

The house was restored during 1949–1951. The south wing is a recon-struction, as is half of its south chimney. The west part of the house rests on the original brick foundation walls, which were strengthened with concrete underpinnings. The foundations of the north wing were rebuilt. The west part of the house and the north wing had original framing and were reinforced with steel when the house was restored. The roof framework is old. Although little original weatherboarding remained, the exceptionally wide seven-inch exposure of the boards on the west portion was based on the discovery of an old piece in a protected position just below the cornice. The cornice had to be largely renewed. First floor window sashes are old on the west front, and at the northwest of the house. Dormer sashes were copied from old sashes found in the basement that fitted the dormers. Shutters, with one exception, were missing. They were reproduced from one found in use as a door in the kitchen, which fitted the first floor windows exactly. It was refitted at the south window on the west elevation. Most of the interior woodwork, including doors and all floors as well as the decorative features of note, had survived. The first floor of the brick kitchen was restored in 1968.

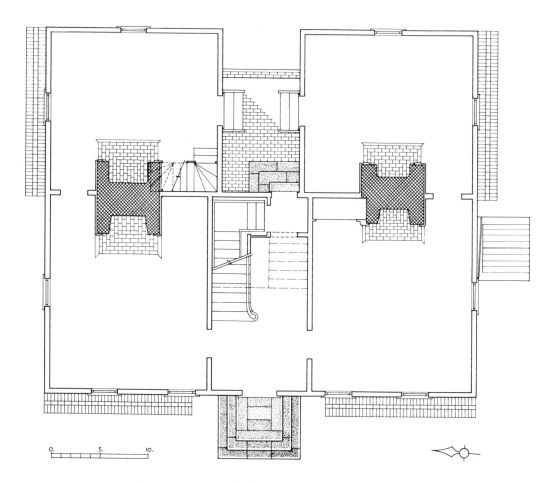

*Figure 109*    Brush-Everard House. Plan.

Dr. Barraud House. South front.

# DR. BARRAUD HOUSE

THE early history of this site is ambiguous, although tangible evidence suggested that the Dr. Barraud House was erected sometime around the third quarter of the eighteenth century. The brickwork of foundation walls and partitions dated from two construction periods, both of which antedated the foundation of an early kitchen discovered behind the house. Probably two dwellings occupied the lot in sequence, and the present structure may once have been a smaller building, the plan of which resembled the William Lightfoot and Tayloe houses. It certainly existed by the time the 1782 Frenchman's Map depicted its initial, almost square, shape, and it must have attained its present form before 1796, when it was first insured as a "wooden dwelling house one story high 46 feet by 33 feet."[91]

---

[91] Mutual Assurance Society, policy no. 108, Virginia State Archives.

The owner in 1796 was Dr. Philip Barraud, who was born in Virginia in 1757 and studied medicine at Edinburgh University after active service in the Revolutionary War. His correspondence with Henry St. George Tucker and others indicated that he was a prominent resident of Williamsburg. He served on the Board of Visitors at the College of William and Mary in 1791 and was a visiting physician at the Public Hospital

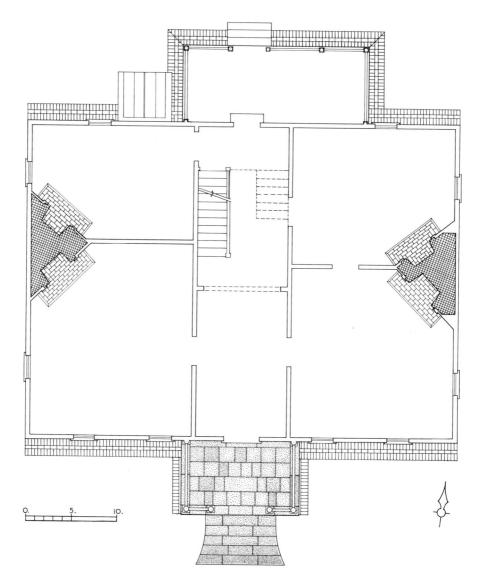

*Figure 111*   Dr. Barraud House. Plan.

from 1795 until he moved to Norfolk in 1799.[92] Dr. Barraud was already settled in Williamsburg by 1783, when Humphrey Harwood's repair accounts began to show entries against his name in November of that year.[93] He sold the property to Mrs. Otway Byrd in 1801.

The house appeared to be a conventional medium-sized frame dwelling, but it was atypical in several respects. The older portion lay at the southeast corner of the property, actually overstepping the surveyed street line, and was located diagonally opposite the area where a series of outbuilding foundations were clustered. It was one of the many dwellings built on a back street that occupied only a portion of the normal half-acre lot. On plan it was much deeper in relation to its length than any other story and one-half, gable-roofed house in town, which may have been because it once had an isolated terrace plan with two rooms on each floor. It also contrasted with others in details such as the asymmetrical placement of its two interior end chimneys. The later west one stood off center toward the rear; as a result, the pairs of first floor rooms flanking the central stair passage had unequal depths. The house was considered to date from the late eighteenth century, yet it had the type of corner fireplaces regarded, in a stylistic sense, as quite early. The difference between the slopes of the main roof and the companion dormer roofs, calculated at 45 degrees and 42 degrees respectively, was highly unusual. The refinement of molded windowsills was common in Williamsburg's domestic architecture, but the treatment of the basement grilles, with molded mullions, molding encircling the frames, and bolted inner iron bars, was unparalleled. The interior woodwork was remarkable for its quality, which was comparable in style and craftsmanship to trim at the Brush-Everard House. Distinctive features included some doors, which retained their original hardware fixtures, two restored mantels, the cornices, and paneled dados in the first floor passage and southwest room. The stairway was reconstructed.

## CONDITION

The Dr. Barraud House was restored in 1942. Nineteenth-century porches were removed from both front and rear elevations. The present

---

[92] Wyndham B. Blanton, *Medicine in Virginia in the Eighteenth Century* (Richmond, 1931), p. 343.

[93] Ledger B, p. 58. Harwood continued to perform various small bricklaying, plastering, and whitewashing jobs for Barraud until 1788; his son William did more in 1790–1792.

south porch was then built to conform to the delineations of old foundations as well as to traces of the original framing visible against the exterior wall facing and roof. Its Chinese lattice railing, combined with attenuated columns to support the pedimented roof, conveyed a Federal motif adapted from various local examples and patternbook designs. Antique stone paving found on the site was incorporated into the porch platform, but the steps were gone. The large rear screen porch, although reconstructed for residential purposes, remained problematical because its foundations apparently dated from the very early 1800s. A ground-level brick gutter, unearthed almost intact along the south front, was restored. Basement grilles were replaced, although they duplicated the unusual design of deteriorated original ones. New window sashes and frames followed the appearance of windows that survived in the gable ends, while the shutters were based on local precedents. All weatherboards were replacements. The cornices are repaired original features; the chimneys too are original except that their stacks were rebuilt above the line of the roof ridge. On the interior, the yellow pine flooring and most original elements of the woodwork and hardware were preserved. Structural indications verified the stairway reconstruction that incorporated original baluster and handrail designs revealed when the removal of paint from a wood post on the second floor showed the profiles. A preponderance of the original fabric survived at the Dr. Barraud House.

*Figure 112*   Travis House. Southwest view.

# TRAVIS HOUSE

THE Travis House stands on the north corner of France Street. It has been returned to its original location after much wandering about town. Before it was transferred to the Williamsburg Holding Corporation in 1928, this house served as the residence of the superintendent of Eastern State Hospital.[94] In 1929 it was moved to a site on the south side of Duke of Gloucester Street opposite the James Geddy House where it was restored. It was moved temporarily to the south side of France Street adjacent to the Griffin House in 1951. A final move in 1968 returned the dwelling to its present site.

The Travis House was a long gambrel-roofed frame structure with one brick end, a rarity in Williamsburg. It was built at different times

---

[94] Mutual Assurance Society, policy no. 14,390, Virginia State Archives.

in successive additions, each differentiated on the street front by perpendicular boards that were originally the corner boards of their respective sections.

The west portion of the house was the earliest, dating from about 1765.[95] Later additions were made during the last quarter of the eighteenth century and the first quarter of the nineteenth.[96] The house

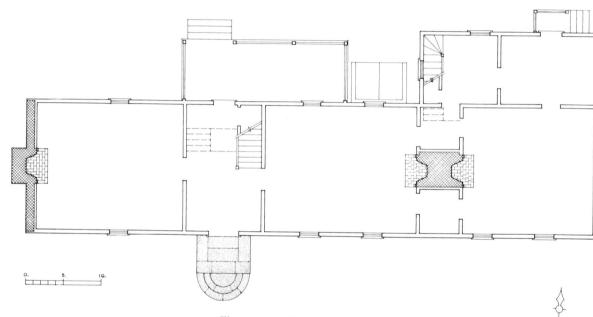

*Figure 113*    Travis House. Plan.

was owned and occupied by Champion Travis and his sons Samuel and Robert from about 1797 to 1830. When it was insured in 1796, the dwelling measured seventy feet by twenty feet,[97] evidence that it must have achieved its final form by then.

### CONDITION

Travis House was damaged by fire soon after its acquisition by Colonial Williamsburg, but the loss was confined to the second story of

---

[95] John Pendleton Kennedy, ed., *Journals of the House of Burgesses of Virginia, 1761–1765* (Richmond, 1907), p. 335, entry for May 11, 1765.

[96] Mutual Assurance Society, policies nos. 186, 957, 2355, and 10,736, Virginia State Archives.

[97] *Ibid.*, policy no. 186.

the west end. After a large Victorian porch and bay window on the front elevation were removed, the house was restored during 1929–1930 and the interior was adapted for use as a restaurant. Much of the original fabric has been renewed, although significant elements of the structural framework, including door, window, and dormer frames, survive, along with the rear door and trim, corner boards, and end-boards. On the interior, plastering and floors were restored. Several original mantels and two stairways remain in addition to remnants of baseboards, dados, cornices, and architraves. Interestingly, all of the interior woodwork is white pine, which would be unprecedented in Williamsburg were there not a question of its having been installed much later than completion of the house in its present form. Some interior repairs and renovations were accomplished in 1968 when the house was replaced on rebuilt foundations at its original site.

*Figure 114*    Orrell House. Northeast view.

# ORRELL HOUSE

NOTHING at all was known about the early history of this house, which took its name from John Orrell, who owned it during the first two decades of the nineteenth century. The Frenchman's Map of 1782 showed what appeared to be a long, narrow building on this site. There were other cases of individual buildings not having been given their true proportions on the Frenchman's Map, and stylistic evidence strongly suggested a construction date in the third quarter of the eighteenth century.

The house formed on plan an exact square whose sides measured twenty-eight feet, and because the roof ridge was twenty-eight feet above the top of the basement wall, it was proportioned as an ideal geometric cube. Its resemblance to the William Lightfoot House was close and surely was due to design rather than to coincidence. Outside, the only important difference was in the form of the gambrel roof, whose later date was indicated by the steeper slope of the upper roof planes. A clever innovation, which improved the interior function of the Orrell

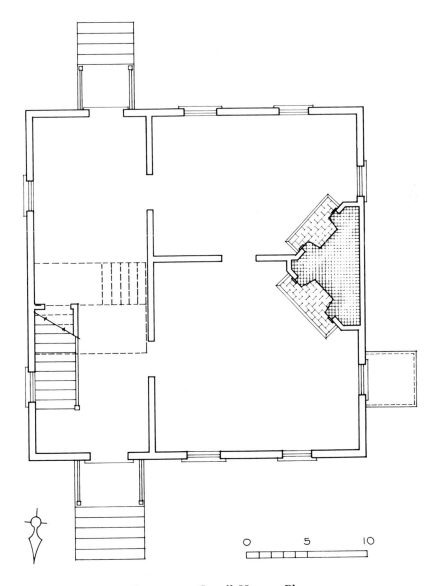

*Figure 115*   Orrell House. Plan.

House, resulted from rearranging the stairs. Instead of occupying the rear end of the entry passage, the stairs started near the front door, ascended against the outside wall to a half-landing, turned right, and finished at a short landing near the center of the upper floor. This space-saving arrangement allowed three rooms instead of two on the first floor, and four instead of three upstairs. The Orrell House was one of the few in town for which no evidence of window shutters could be found.

## CONDITION

The Orrell House was restored in 1929–1931. It was dilapidated, but it had not been greatly altered. A front porch and rear shed, both of mid-nineteenth-century date, were removed. The brickwork of the basement and west chimney was patched, mended, and repointed, and the framing was repaired and partially replaced. The eaves cornice on the north front is original but patched. Practically all of the weatherboards and all of the window sashes were renewed. Original grilles on basement windows were repaired and retained. A modern front door was replaced by an eighteenth-century type with a transom light, and the steps and platform were reconstructed. Within, the original stair was repaired, as were the floors. The interior work was designed for modern convenience rather than exact restoration.

*Figure 116*  Nicolson Shop. Southwest view.

# NICOLSON SHOP

A shop apparently stood on this site during most, if not all, of the
second half of the eighteenth century. Robert Nicolson, a tailor
and merchant, acquired the property in 1773,[98] and in 1796 he
insured a "Wood Store two Story 34 feet by 20 feet" in this location.[99]
The building was described in similar terms in insurance policies of
1806 and 1815.[100] Later it became part of an L-plan house that extended
to the west, although the framing—including the roof timbers—some

[98] York Co. Recs., Deeds, VIII, p. 311.
[99] Mutual Assurance Society, policy no. 112, Virginia State Archives.
[100] *Ibid.*, policies nos. 645 and 1521.

partitions, the fireplace, and much of the stairway remained intact and were extricated when restoration was undertaken in 1949.

The building was planned in a standard English manner, the shop in front taking up most of the ground floor, with the counting room and stairs at the back. Between the two rooms was an original glazed door, unique among eighteenth-century interior features found in Williamsburg and probably related to the structure's function as a shop. The full two-story construction of the Nicolson Shop differentiated it from other extant shops in town, although it resembled the oldest part of the Taliaferro-Cole House, which was almost certainly built for commercial purposes. That the upper rooms of the Nicolson Shop were lived in and not used simply as storage space was established by the 1806 insurance policy that described the building as "a Wooden Store and Dwelling house."[101] Yet the presence of only one rear chimney, a feature typical of shop architecture, indicated that the salesroom and large room above it were unheated originally.

---

[101] *Ibid.*, policy no. 645.

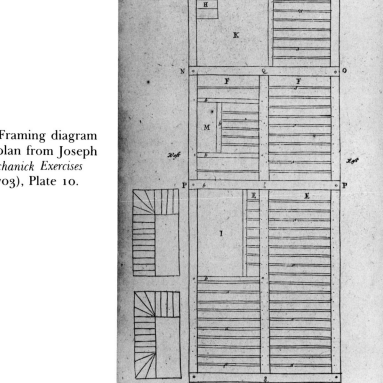

*Figure 117* Framing diagram for a shop plan from Joseph Moxon, *Mechanick Exercises* (London, 1703), Plate 10.

## CONDITION

The Nicolson Shop was restored in 1949–1950. It had been incorporated into an early nineteenth-century house, which was demolished. Enough of the original structure had survived to indicate the form of the building and significant interior features. None of the visible work on the street front or the side elevations was original, but on the north elevation, the chimney up to cornice level and the east window on the upper floor are eighteenth-century features. Evidence of horizontal board sheathing, along with possible shelves, in the front room where the side walls were devoid of windows reinforced documented facts of the structure's shop history. An original mantel remains in the rear first floor room. Old flooring survives throughout although it was patched in some places.

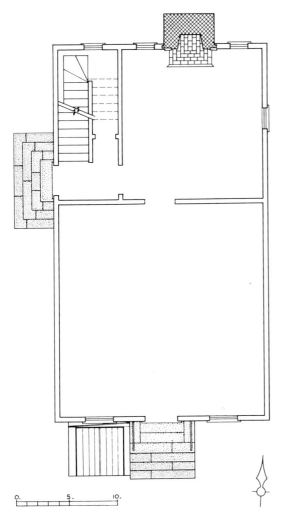

*Figure 118*  Nicolson Shop. Plan.

*Figure 119*  Semple House. North front.

# SEMPLE HOUSE

IN a letter written in 1809, St. George Tucker called the Semple House "the handsomest house in town."[102] It is Williamsburg's sole surviving example—and a very distinguished one—of the classicism that began to change the American architectural scene toward the end of the eighteenth century.

James Semple, the lawyer and judge after whom the house was named, acquired it in 1800 and insured it and all of its outbuildings for $2,000.[103] A sketch of the street front on the insurance declaration documented that the house looked then just as it does today. The house and the other buildings on the property were by no means new. Although the insurance policy stated that it would have cost $4,000 to rebuild the structures in 1800, $2,000 was deducted because of their poor condition. The Frenchman's Map indicated that a house of roughly the same proportions on plan stood there in 1782. Since archaeological investigations

[102] Letters of American Jurists, Gratz Collection, Historical Society of Pennsylvania, Philadelphia.
[103] Mutual Assurance Society, policy no. 486, Virginia State Archives.

of the property failed to reveal signs of earlier foundations on the site, the house depicted on the map must have been the present one.

The year 1782, then, was the terminus ante quem for dating the house, and intrinsic evidence revealed techniques of late eighteenth-century workmanship. Records indicated that the house was erected between 1772 and 1778 by William Pasteur, a physician and apothecary of Williamsburg.[104] The entrance porch was added to the central pavilion about 1791–1801, which accordingly caused the front second story windows to be reduced in height by one light.[105]

The individuality of its early Federal design, and the fact that it seems to have been imitated outside Williamsburg, pose the question of attribution more insistently than in the case of any other house in Williamsburg. Thomas Jefferson has been proposed as its author by Thomas Waterman, among others, and the possibility that it was he cannot be dismissed.[106] The case for attributing the design to Jefferson, however, rested mainly on a drawing in the Coolidge Collection at the Massachusetts Historical Society.[107] Could this drawing (*Figure 122*), a plan in ink and pencil, have been a preliminary study for the Semple House? That it represented a brick building was not really evidence to the contrary, since Jefferson had a poor opinion of frame houses, although the choice of material would not have been his but the owner's. Most significantly, while the dimensions and proportions of the individual parts differed in the two plans, their total areas were exactly equal. The plan of the Semple House was an elongated version of the one drawn by Jefferson, the length of each wing having been increased by as much as the projection of the central pavilion on each front was reduced. Yet the use of lead pencil in the drawing presented a difficulty, because there was no authenticated instance of Jefferson's drafting in that medium before his stay in Europe in 1784–1789,[108] and the Semple House must have been built by 1782.

---

[104] Mary A. Stephenson, "Semple House," pp. 5–10, research report, 1964, CWF.

[105] Mutual Assurance Society, policy no. 486.

[106] Waterman, *Mansions of Virginia*, p. 380. Dr. William Pasteur was related to Thomas Jefferson through marriage, since his wife, Elizabeth Stith Pasteur, and Jefferson were second cousins.

[107] The drawing was first published by Fiske Kimball, *Thomas Jefferson, Architect* (Boston, 1916), plate 119. Kimball suggested that it might be a study for Brandon, Benjamin Harrison's house in Surry County, Virginia; Frederick D. Nichols suggested that Kimball later came to regard it as an early study for Monticello. The possibility that it was a study for the Semple House was first noticed by A. Lawrence Kocher and Howard Dearstyne, "James Semple House," research report, 1950, Architects' Office, CWF.

[108] Kimball, *Thomas Jefferson*, pp. 105–149.

*Figure 120*  Semple House. North elevation.

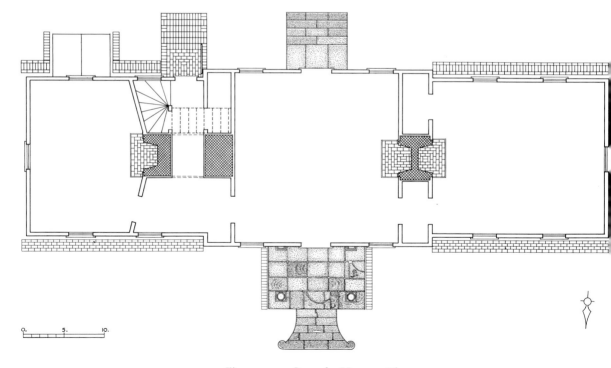

*Figure 121*  Semple House. Plan.

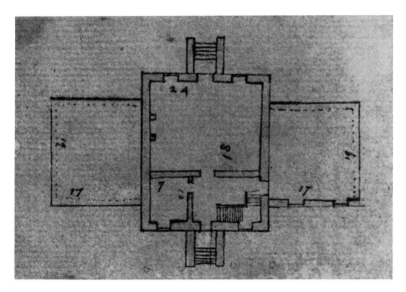

*Figure 122*   Plan of an unidentified tripartite house by Thomas Jefferson.

A design in Robert Morris's *Select Architecture,* a book that Jefferson is known to have owned and consulted, has been proposed as a prototype for the Semple House.[109] The resemblance between the two increases if the porch of the Semple House, which structural evidence proved to have been a later addition (although it was there by the time of the 1801 insurance declaration), is ignored. On the other hand, the resemblance diminishes if the sills of the upper floor windows are lowered to the level that structural evidence showed they occupied before the addition of the porch necessitated their shortening. Another published design that had something in common with the Semple House was in William Halfpenny's *Useful Architecture.*[110] But perhaps it would be a mistake to look for a specific prototype: the high pedimented centerblock with low wings that had roofs at right angles to the main roof was a scheme implicit in many Anglo-Palladian designs. Perhaps its application at the Semple House was an experiment in pure aesthetic design, because the adaptation for a relatively small house constructed of wood sacrificed functional utility for high stylism. It would be erroneous to regard all houses that repeated the *parti* of the Semple House

[109] Waterman, *Mansions of Virginia,* pp. 378–379.

[110] 2nd ed. (London, 1755), plate XVII, No. 1, "The Plan and Elevation of a small Farm, House, &c."

*Figure 123*   Fortsville, Southampton
County, Virginia.

*Figure 124*   The Rowe, Charles City
County, Virginia.

as imitations of it, since they more likely emerged as individual creations
from a common source of influence.[111] Fortsville (*Figure 123*) in Southampton County, Virginia, which was built between 1792 and 1794 by
Lewis Fort, may, however, have been modeled on the Semple House,
and so may The Grove in Halifax, North Carolina, which was built by
a personal friend of Jefferson.[112] Two other houses of the type in North
Carolina, which probably derived from The Grove rather than from
the Semple House itself, were the Williams-Reid-Macon House near
Airlie, and the Junius Tillery House at Tillery, both in Halifax County.[113]
Nearer Williamsburg, The Rowe in Charles City County might have
been indebted to the Semple House for its final form (*Figure 124*), but
in this case, one of the wings was earlier than the center, whereas the
other houses were all built as a whole. The relationships are enigmatic.

Some of the details of the Semple House were of a style and richness
found nowhere else in Williamsburg. The guilloche on the architrave
of the porch could have been taken from the *Builder's Companion* of
William Pain, published in London in 1765, and the same book might
have inspired the diaper-patterned frieze on the mantel in the west

---

[111] From 1830 to 1860 an outwardly similar type of house with Greek details that
often included a portico was popular. Propagated by the pattern books of Asher Benjamin, it of course had no connection with the Semple House.
[112] Thomas Tileston Waterman and Frances Benjamin Johnston, *The Early Architecture
of North Carolina* (Chapel Hill, N. C., 1941), p. 37.
[113] *Ibid.*, pp. 90, 93.

room. It was the most architecturally refined room in the house, with a full modillion cornice and a wooden dado that broke forward under the windows to form pedestal bases.

## CONDITION

The Semple House was restored in 1932, and further restoration work was completed in 1952. A fire about 1900 had destroyed part of the roof of the central pavilion, including the facing of the tympanum of the north pediment, but the fabric was mostly original. It remains so today. Necessary structural reinforcements and the renewal of all interior plaster were carried out as standard restoration procedures. A south wing on the central pavilion that insurance policies showed was built between 1806 and 1823 was removed during the restoration. The east and west windows, which had been closed, were reopened, and the east chimney was rebuilt above the second floor level. Dilapidated stone steps to the front porch were rebuilt, and fluted columns and pilasters were restored in place of the square piers that had replaced the original columns. The guilloche on the architrave of the porch was restored according to evidence provided by traces of the original. The Semple House required very minimal restoration, perhaps the least of any house in Williamsburg.

*Figure 125*   Semple House. Detail of mantel in west room before restoration.

*Figure 126*　Ewing House. North front.

# EWING HOUSE

T HE terminus ante quem for dating this house was established
by its appearance on the Frenchman's Map of 1782. Extensive
construction work by local carpenter and bricklayer Humphrey
Harwood for Peter Moyer, a baker and the first known owner of the
property, indicated the house had achieved its present form in 1787.[114]
Its name derived from Ebenezer Ewing, a Scotsman who owned the
house when he made his will in 1795, having "lately" purchased it
from the estate of Frederick Myers.[115] That he had been living in Wil-

[114] Harwood Ledger, B, p. 111.
[115] Ewing's will is in folder 199, Southall Papers, Swem Library, College of William
and Mary. Local records show that Myers's name was also spelled Mayers.

liamsburg for some time before his purchase was proved by entries in Humphrey Harwood's ledger relating to work done for "Mr. E. Ewing" that went back as far as 1786.

The Ewing House defied classification. It resembled the Orrell House because it had three rooms on each floor instead of two and a gambrel

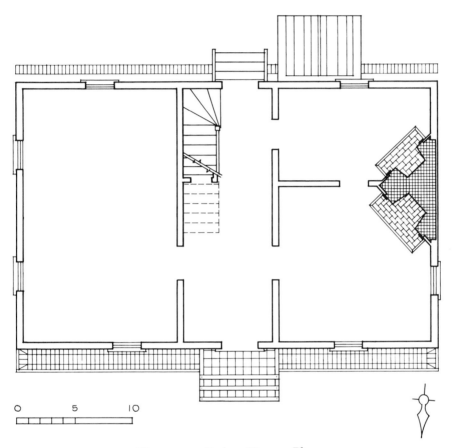

*Figure 127* Ewing House. Plan.

roof, although with shed dormers instead of gabled ones. Unlike the Orrell House and the other gambrel-roofed houses in Williamsburg, it was much longer than it was broad, and the entrance was in the middle of the front, so it did not fall into the category of isolated terrace houses. The presence of only one chimney, along with structural evidence in the east unheated room, indicated that it might have served some commercial purpose.[116] It had a central passage plan, but other features separated it from houses with a standard hall-passage-parlor arrangement. Its corner fireplaces suggested an early construction date, but subsequent modifications have blurred distinct periods in its development.

## CONDITION

The Ewing House was restored in 1940. The original framing was largely retained, although some reinforcement and renewal of structural elements was necessary. On the exterior, about all that remain of eighteenth-century date are parts of the north and south cornices. The weatherboards, window frames, sashes, shutters, and doors were all restored. The weatherboards followed an old sample that was found, and the locations and sizes of the windows were determined by indications in the framing. An east chimney of late date was demolished and the west chimney, which is original, was taken down, clay flue linings were added, and it was rebuilt. Inside, the stairway is original with some replacement. Some doors and most of the floors are original.

---

[116] The east room on the ground floor was originally unplastered. The studs and the backs of the weatherboards were whitewashed and the joists and undersides of the floorboards above were painted. It might have been a storeroom, or perhaps served some commercial purpose.

*Figure 128* George Reid House. North front.

# GEORGE REID HOUSE

THE George Reid House was a late example of the one and one-half story, central passage, single-pile house type in which the axial symmetry had been modified. The stair passage was situated in the exact center on plan, but the disposition of the chimneys at each end, with one inside and the other placed outside, created an obvious imbalance. The room to the west, the hall, had more wall space for windows because it was four feet longer than the room east of the passage. The presence of an inside chimney benefitted the plan by allowing closets flanking the first floor east fireplace.

On the exterior, however, these conditions caused an uneven arrangement in the fenestration of both front and rear elevations. A middle doorway stood between paired windows on one side and a single window opening on the other.[117] To counteract this effect somewhat, one of the three dormer windows in each gable roof slope was set uncharacteris-

*Figure 129*   George Reid House before restoration.

tically above the wall surface between the paired windows rather than directly over an opening as was almost always done in colonial construction.

Another unexplained eccentricity, found nowhere else in Williamsburg, was evident on the end elevations. The second floor framing projected beyond the depth of the first story, leaving an asymmetrical two-foot roof overhang at the back which, in turn, caused an awkward cornice resolution at the eaves.

---

[117] Cf. the John Blair House and the Moody House.

The history of the George Reid site also posed questions. The lot was owned by Edward Barradall, lawyer, burgess, mayor of Williamsburg, and judge of the Court of Vice Admiralty until his death in 1739. Hugh Orr acquired the property from Barradall's estate in 1743 through a mortgage to Benjamin Waller,[118] and lived there until he died in 1764. Orr was a blacksmith, or "hammer man" as his epitaph in Bruton Parish churchyard attested, and was probably Scottish in origin. His mortgage recorded the interesting fact that a "Smiths Shop Forge Tools and Utensils [thereto] belonging"[119] were already present on the lot at the time of his purchase, although archaeological excavations failed to unearth signs of any extensive blacksmithing operations. Orr's widow, Catherine, inherited the property and still occupied it when she died in 1788.

Apparently the Orrs' dwelling was then dismantled, because archaeology confirmed that a square house (thirty-two feet by thirty-two feet) stood in exactly the same location as the existing residence until it was taken down deliberately during the 1780s. The present George Reid House was thus the second eighteenth-century house to occupy this corner lot facing Duke of Gloucester Street. It measured forty-two feet, three inches by nineteen feet, six inches, so its size was appreciably smaller than the earlier building.

George Reid, about whom little was known except fragmentary details, received the property from the widow Orr in 1789.[120] Since archaeological findings established that the present house was built around 1790, Reid must have constructed it between the date of acquisition and his own death in 1792. Some unknown close relationship of either blood ties or business connections linked the Orrs to Reid. Reid was a Williamsburg merchant who in 1775 served as an ensign in the local militia[121] and was elected secretary of the Society of Freemasons. In 1776 he furnished guns to the Revolutionary army.[122] Reid's store may have adjoined his house toward the northeast. His will left the lot to his wife, who soon remarried but continued to occupy the property until 1814. Thereafter it passed through a succession of owners.

---

[118] York Co. Recs., Deeds, V, pp. 89–91.

[119] *Ibid.*

[120] Williamsburg City Land Books, entry for 1789.

[121] *Virginia Gazette* (Pinkney), Sept. 4, Dec. 11, 1775.

[122] H. W. Flournoy, ed., *Calendar of Virginia State Papers (1795–1798)*, VIII (Richmond, 1890), pp. 85, 97, 195.

## CONDITION

The house was restored during 1930–1931. In many of Williamsburg's original houses, restoration entailed little more than refurbishment, whereas the condition of others necessitated almost complete replacement of original elements. The George Reid House fell into the latter category. Its structural framing had so largely deteriorated that the whole fabric had to be taken apart and rebuilt. Careful architectural investigation and recording, however, assured that replacements in new

*Figure 130*  George Reid House. North elevation.

materials were accurate reproductions of the unsound features that had to be discarded. Extensive substitution of all surviving interior and exterior details followed the same principles. The old wrought-iron lightning rod remaining on the west chimney is a fixture of particular interest. An unauthentic frame connection to the reconstructed kitchen just behind the house was added for residential convenience. Original outbuildings include the frame woodshed and the latticed wellhead, which had been moved to Richmond during the early 1920s, only to be returned during the restoration of the house.

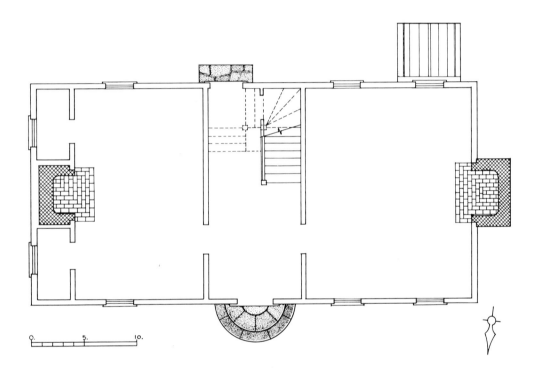

*Figure 131*   George Reid House. Plan.

*Figure 132*  St. George Tucker House. Southeast view.

# ST. GEORGE TUCKER HOUSE

WHILE the compact George Wythe House represented Williamsburg's domestic design at its most formal, the St. George Tucker House, with an elongated plan, varying roof line, and many gables, represented it at its most picturesque. Unlike others in town, the dwelling's sprawling, horizontal mass developed as the result of a series of late eighteenth-century additions. Its nucleus was a story and one-half dwelling, measuring forty feet by eighteen feet on plan, that stood a little way to the northwest facing Palace Street.[123] In 1788 St. George Tucker had it moved to face Market Square, where it thus formed the center of the present house. Between then and 1795 he added a second story and built the lean-to on the north, the wings at the east and west, and the west kitchen with its covered way.

The carpenter who moved and repaired the old house was John Saunders,[124] who, with Robert Saunders and William Pigget, undertook the

---

[123] Excavations in 1931 revealed the foundations.

[124] What appeared to be his estimate for the work contained the item "the Old Roof taken down & A New Dutch Roof [i.e., a gambrel] put on with 6 Dormond Wind^ws." Folder 28, Tucker-Coleman Papers. Tucker must have had second thoughts about the way to obtain more space and headroom on the upper floor.

woodwork of the additions, the three working for Tucker under individual agreements. Humphrey Harwood was the bricklayer who built the basement and chimneys in 1788–1789; William Harwood was responsible for brickwork after his father's death in 1789. Many of the building accounts survived, as did Humphrey Harwood's contract and an informative agreement between Tucker and Jeremiah Satterwhite concerning the painting of the house in 1798 (see Appendix II). Paint investigation verified that Satterwhite applied the colors Tucker specified, so the various parts of the exterior were once more painted straw color, yellow ochre, chocolate, dark brick color, Spanish brown, stone color, and pure white.

In the eighteenth century, the lean-to on the north side of the central section was referred to as the "shed," whereas in later years, that room on the main floor became known as the "great hall." An account rendered by William Pigget in 1791 showed that some lead was used on its roof. The kitchen, with its much admired massive chimney, was a reconstruction. In addition to the foundations and building accounts, the architects had a photograph of the original kitchen and the recollections of the then owner of the house, Mr. George P. Coleman, to guide its rebuilding. The covered way was also a reconstruction. Its originally open arches were filled in as a measure of modern convenience.

St. George Tucker, "the American Blackstone," was born at Port Royal, Bermuda, in 1752 and came to Virginia to enter William and Mary in 1771; he studied law at the College under George Wythe, whom he succeeded as professor of law in 1790. Tucker was a judge of the state General Court in 1785–1803, of the Supreme Court of Appeals in 1803–1811, and of the United States District Court from 1813 until his death in 1827. By his first marriage to Frances Bland in 1778, he became the stepfather of John Randolph.

## CONDITION

The house was restored during 1930–1931. Just one hundred years before, the west wing had been lengthened to take in the original covered way, and the first floor windows of the center were increased from two to four. More recently, the original kitchen had been replaced by a two-story structure on the original foundations, necessitating the reconstruction of that end of the house. In other respects, the house had been little altered. The framing was reinforced and replaced where necessary. The original brick nogging had to be removed during this process but was put back in place. The chimneys of the center were rebuilt above the roof. All eaves cornices on the old parts of the house, except that on the north side of the west wing, are original and repaired only. Many of the weatherboards, especially on the center section, are original, as are the endboards and bargeboards there. All first and second floor windows on the south side of the center section are original. Most of the other windows, including all dormers, were rebuilt. All shutters are new, but the front folding door is original. Floors in the old parts of the house are generally original, as is paneling in the first floor east room of the central section, which must be contemporary, or nearly so, with the earliest part of the house. A window remaining there (*Figure 133*), which once gave view to the outdoors, attests to the dwelling's informal, rambling growth.

*Figure 133* St. George Tucker House. Paneled east room in central portion.

*Figure 134*    Taliaferro-Cole House. Northwest view.

# TALIAFERRO-COLE HOUSE

STRUCTURAL, archaeological, and documentary evidence concurred in indicating that this house was built in two sections— the west twenty-two feet at an undetermined date, probably in the third quarter of the eighteenth century, and the east eighteen feet between 1815 and 1834.

In its first, unextended form, it was a unit house with a depth six feet greater than the length of the facade on Duke of Gloucester Street. The entrance was in the middle of the first front, that is, between the two west windows of the present front, and led straight into a large room. At the back of the room, on the axis of the entrance door, a door opened into a rear stair hall and one small room. Two rooms upstairs corresponded to those below, and a passage extended the full depth of the house. From the beginning, the house had two full stories, but in its original form, it was covered by a low-pitch gable roof whose ridge was parallel to Duke of Gloucester Street. The large room on

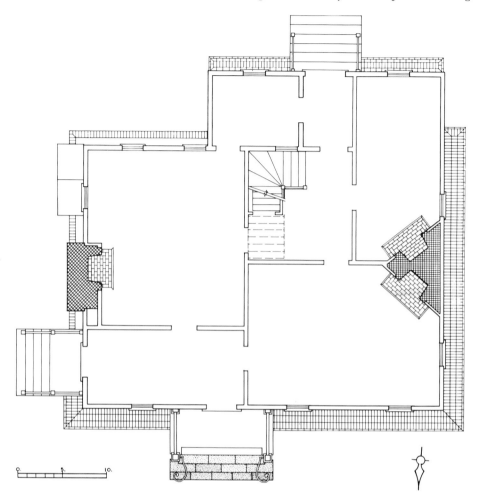

*Figure 135*    Taliaferro-Cole House. Plan.

the first floor probably was a shop, which would account for the plan. At a time when other unit houses were being built in Williamsburg with the side passage plan of the London terrace house type, it would also explain why so small a house was two full stories high. The south-west room on the ground floor would therefore have been the counting room.

An insurance policy of 1815 and a drawing by Charles Millington in 1834[125] substantiated that the east extension was constructed between

---

[125] Mutual Assurance Society, policies nos. 1516 and 7582, Virginia State Archives. The Millington drawing is at the College of William and Mary.

*Figure 136*   Taliaferro-Cole Shop before restoration.

those dates. Structural indications showed that one small addition, the south enlargement of the southwest room under a shed roof, had been made before 1805.[126] The asymmetry of the north elevation was forced on the builder by circumstances beyond his control; he spaced the new window and door openings to give it what balance he could and provided a spacious entrance hall in an attempt to counteract the inconvenient placing of the stairs.

The earliest mention of the shop to the east dated from 1782, when Charles Taliaferro, chairmaker, coachmaker, and general merchant, advertised in the *Virginia Gazette* that he had "an assortment of lines, shoes, saddles, bar iron, a few boxes of candles, nails and brads, and a large

---

[126] The southwest window in place in the shed at the time of the restoration belonged to the first building period and had evidently been moved from the corresponding position in the south wall of the original house.

*Figure 137*    Taliaferro-Cole Shop. Northwest view.

SEINE almost new" for sale "at his store opposite the Church wall."[127]
In the same year, the building was depicted on the Frenchman's Map.
Examination of the framing prior to restoration confirmed that there
had been two building periods, an inference already drawn from the
form of the street front and the breaks in the brick bond of the foundation walls. The insurance policy proved that the west, or shed, section
had been added by 1809.[128] Much of the building was clearly visible
in Millington's sketch, but a signpost that hid its northwest corner left
open to question the restored west roof overhang.

**CONDITION**

The house was restored during 1940–1941. A south extension was
demolished, and a columnar Doric porch was removed from the street

[127] *Virginia Gazette or Weekly Advertiser* (Richmond), Jan. 26, 1782.
[128] Mutual Assurance Society, policy no. 991, Virginia State Archives.

front then. Most of the exterior is old and original, including the weatherboards, the cornice (segments of which date from both building periods), almost all the windows with their sashes, second period shutters, and corner boards. The chimney caps, basement grilles, and north porch date from the restoration. The porch was reconstructed according to the evidence of the Millington drawing, the excavated foundations, and the paint line of the original pilasters, cornice, and roof as revealed by scraping the weatherboards. The south porch was added as a feature of convenience. Inside, the staircase is original, as are the floors, a number of doors, and the paneled wainscot in the northeast room.

Much of the original shop structure, with a late rear addition, was obscured until 1940 behind a false front added in the nineteenth century. Its condition was so poor, however, that much reconstruction was necessary. Among the features that were retained was the bulkhead ironwork.

*Figure 138*   Timson House. Southwest view.

# TIMSON HOUSE

THE oldest house beyond the limits of the Historic Area of Williamsburg probably was the Timson House, located on the corner of Prince George and Nassau streets. In 1715 the trustees of the city of Williamsburg deeded this lot, along with two others on the main street, to William Timson, a planter of York County. He evidently built the requisite dwelling house within the next two years,[129] but he probably never intended to occupy it himself. All three lots and the buildings on them were sold in 1717 to a tailor, James Shields,[130] whose family owned the property until 1745. That year the Timson

[129] York Co. Recs., Deeds, III, pp. 109–110.
[130] *Ibid.*, p. 185.

House changed hands twice. On May 16, 1745, when it was acquired by James Wray, a "Carpenter & Joiner," his deed contained an unusual clause to correct a "mistake" in a deed of sale dated the previous January that identified the wrong lot.[131]

Owing perhaps to its early date of construction, the Timson House was a building of small size and simple details. It measured thirty-two feet by seventeen, and consisted of a story and one-half gable-roofed structure to which two additions and a late porch had been appended. Former corner boards that remained in place, as well as its general configuration, indicated that the house may have originated as a one-room dwelling and then undergone successive enlargements over the years. It is unrestored.

---

[131] *Ibid.*, V, p. 134.

*Figure 139*　James Galt House. Northwest view.

# JAMES GALT HOUSE

THE James Galt House, which dates from the mid-eighteenth century, now occupies a compromise site on Tyler Street. It first stood on property that became part of the Public Mental Hospital in 1770. Given by Eastern State Hospital to Colonial Williamsburg in 1929, the house was moved first to a lot on Duke of Gloucester Street opposite Bruton Parish Church, where it was restored. The James Galt House was relocated on Tyler Street in 1954 as the result of a decision to remove houses inappropriately located within the Historic Area.

The James Galt House began as a sixteen by twenty foot single-room unit not unlike the Semple Quarter, the Nelson-Galt Office, and the original form of the Timson House. An atypically located room at the chimney end of the house and a lean-to addition at the rear were responsible for its present size and irregular shape.

*Figure 140*   Robert Nicolson House. South front.

# ROBERT NICOLSON HOUSE

O N York Street, at the eastern edge of town, stood the Robert Nicolson House. It was built by Robert Nicolson, Williamsburg tailor and merchant, who had a shop near the Capitol at the time of the American Revolution.

Nicolson built his dwelling house around 1751–1752 on a lot purchased for ten pounds in 1751 from cabinetmaker James Speirs, who had bought it from Benjamin Waller the previous year.[132] For a time Nicolson took in lodgers and operated a tailoring shop across the road. During the Revolution, he and his son provided uniforms for the American army. Nicolson lived here until his death in 1797.

The Robert Nicolson House was built in two sections, the east part being the earlier. This original section, with its double pile, side passage

[132] York Co. Recs., Deeds, V, pp. 363, 426.

plan, and gambrel roof, must have looked much as a contemporaneous Williamsburg dwelling, the Tayloe House (*Figure 76*), does today. The west wing was added late in the eighteenth century and increased the street front to its present five bay, almost symmetrical facade.

A preponderance of the original trim of the Robert Nicolson House remained intact. The building was partially restored by a previous owner. Now owned by Colonial Williamsburg, it awaits comprehensive restoration.

*Figure 141* Powell-Hallam House. Northeast view.

# POWELL-HALLAM HOUSE

WHEELWRIGHT and carpenter Benjamin Powell was thought to have built the Powell-Hallam House for himself on York Street sometime between 1753 and 1760. Powell bought this plot of land near the Capitol for ten pounds from Benjamin Waller, who had subdivided land that he purchased from Mann Page of Rosewell.[133]

---

[133] York Co. Recs., Deeds, V, p. 565, VIII, p. 219. The Waller suburb was incorporated by the city of Williamsburg in 1756.

The Powell-Hallam House was a handsome member of the same family as the William Lightfoot and Orrell houses, an isolated terrace house with a gambrel roof. Once a neighbor of the Robert Nicolson House, it also exhibited a strong resemblance to the earliest, east portion of that dwelling. Much of the original woodwork was still in place, the most distinguished feature being the pilastered archway in the stair passage.

In 1928, in order to make way for a bypass road around Williamsburg, the Powell-Hallam House was moved from its original location to a site on Francis Street and restored. It was moved to its present site in 1954 as a result of a decision that the Historic Area should contain only houses that stood there in the eighteenth century, or reconstructions of ones known to have existed there.

*Figure 142*   Griffin House. Northeast view.

# GRIFFIN HOUSE

THE unrestored Griffin House, probably built about 1770, is one and one-half stories high and two rooms deep, a rather uncommon combination in A-roof houses in Williamsburg. It was like a slightly larger version, in brick, of the frame Dr. Barraud House.

The house derived its present name from that of its earliest documented owner, Samuel Griffin, a member of the first United States Congress under the Constitution, which convened in New York in 1789. Griffin acquired the house about 1778, shortly before his marriage to

Elizabeth Braxton, whose father, Carter Braxton, was a Virginia signer of the Declaration of Independence.[134]

Several aspects of the interior of the Griffin House are noteworthy. The principal first floor room contains a handsome corner cupboard with an arched opening and a curved back that is comparable to niches of English design. The capacious central passage, running the full depth of the house, had a wide and well-designed stair that provided an easy rise to the second floor. The pilastered archway in the side wall at the rear of the stair passage was unique in Williamsburg. It provided access to a narrow passage and small corner room beyond. In the west bedchamber upstairs was an interesting and rather grand chimneypiece embellished with a carved basket-weave frieze and fluted pilasters.

---

[134] The marriage agreement between Samuel Griffin and Elizabeth Braxton is in the Corbin Papers, CWF.

*Figure 143*    Bassett Hall. North front.

# BASSETT HALL

STANDING well back from Francis Street near the southeast corner of the Historic Area was the plantation house known as Bassett Hall. Adjacent to the town limits of Williamsburg in the eighteenth century, the structure occupied part of a large plot of land owned by the Bray family as early as the seventeenth century. It took its present name from Burwell Bassett, owner from 1796 to 1839.

Colonel Philip Johnson was believed to have built the original house sometime between 1753 and 1766.[135] It consisted of the north portion, to which a one and one-half story wing had been added by 1782, as

---

[135] *Virginia Gazette* (Purdie and Dixon), June 6, 1766.

shown on the Frenchman's Map. The front section was probably one and one-half stories high originally, which was indicated by the contrast in window treatments on the first and second stories of the present two-story building. The roof of the south wing was also raised to two stories sometime in the nineteenth century.

Restoration of the house began in 1928 but was not finished until 1936. A fire in 1930 heavily damaged the gable roof, destroyed much of the interior of the second floor, and badly scorched the stairway. Despite extensive damage, the paneled wainscoting on the first floor and stair passage was mostly original as were the antique yellow pine floors. The south wing, however, was altered considerably in 1932–1933. First reduced from two stories to one and one-half, it was then rebuilt with a gambrel roof and made two feet wider. Modern service areas were also added. The dining room and bedroom in this wing contained eighteenth-century paneling not original to Bassett Hall.

Directly behind the house were the smokehouse, kitchen, and dairy. While original to the site, these outbuildings were relocated in 1931. A cottage east of the house retained some eighteenth-century framing.

# Part III

*Figure 144*    Carter's Grove. Southwest view. Riverfront.

# CARTER'S GROVE

SIX miles from Williamsburg stands the renowned plantation house built during 1750–1755 by Carter Burwell, a grandson of the mighty Robert "King" Carter of Corotoman, whose 1732 will decreed "that this estate in all times to come be called & to go by the name of Carter's Grove."[1] The exact date when Robert Carter acquired the parcel of property in James City County is unknown, but he specifically purchased it for the benefit of his daughter, Elizabeth Burwell, during her lifetime and afterward for the inheritance of her second son, Carter Burwell. Five generations of Burwells retained ownership until the house and lands were sold out of the family in 1838.

The site was first called Martin's Hundred and was composed of over

---

[1] *VMHB*, V (June 1898), p. 416.

21,500 acres alloted to its English patentees by a 1616 grant from the Virginia Company of London. The community of Wolstenholme Towne, located one-quarter of a mile southwest of the present plantation house, was established on the property in 1619 and thrived for three years, only to be abandoned after most of its inhabitants were killed in the Indian massacre of 1622. The property passed through several owners before Carter purchased it early in the eighteenth century.

Its walls built entirely of bricks, some of which were fired in kilns on the site, the mansion house today consists of five connected sections that extend more than two hundred feet in length. Twentieth-century renovations linked its flanking eighteenth-century outbuildings, the kitchen and laundry, to the central portion. Although a dwelling apparently existed somewhere on the property by 1750,[2] the dates of the earliest structures that remain, the former kitchen and laundry outbuild-

---

[2] Burwell definitely was residing at Carter's Grove by 1739, but extensive research and archaeological investigations have not located the dwelling that he and his growing family occupied until the present house was completed in 1755.

*Figure 145*   Carter's Grove. North elevation before restoration. Land side.

ings that now form the east and west wings, are uncertain. They are believed, however, to predate the mansion. Both hyphens that connect them to the main house were constructed during 1930–1931.

Carter's Grove is related stylistically to a number of eighteenth-century Virginia houses, from the early Marmion and the Governor's Palace, which might have served as design sources, through its tidewater contemporaries, including Westover, Wilton, Elsing Green, Powhatan, and the much smaller Lightfoot and George Wythe houses in Williamsburg, to Rocky Mills and Peckatone, which it possibly inspired. Carter's Grove bears the closest resemblance to Cleve in King George County, a great stone-trimmed brick house built by Burwell's uncle, Charles Carter, about 1750, but which no longer survives.

Carter's Grove today is admired for its superb brickwork, carved interior woodwork, and the sophistication of its original floor plan. One architectural historian has asserted that "the extraordinary parallel of the Carter's Grove plan to that of Cleve makes it seem certain that they were the product of the same designer," further claiming that these two mid-century houses represented a refinement in formality which first emerged in the academic quality of Marmion's plan.[3]

There is nothing in the account books or surviving documentary records to indicate that anyone other than Carter Burwell and the expert craftsmen that he hired served as the architects for Carter's Grove. The dwelling that Burwell created has many elements derived directly from William Salmon's *Palladio Londinensis, or the London Art of Building* (1734), a copy of which he purchased at the *Virginia Gazette* printing office in December 1751 when construction was in progress.[4] Interior details obviously based on designs in the book are found throughout the house. Other English handbooks of the period certainly were consulted during the planning of Carter's Grove. The designs of the parquet flooring on the landings of the stairway, for example, could easily have been duplicated from John Carwitham's *Various Kinds of Floor Decorations Represented Both in Plano and Perspective* (1739), two of whose plates illustrate geometrical configurations almost identical to the ones at Carter's Grove.

Carter Burwell contracted with David Minitree, a Williamsburg brick-mason, to construct the masonry shell of Carter's Grove for £115. Burwell was so pleased with Minitree's work that he gave him a bonus of

---

[3] Waterman, *Mansions of Virginia*, pp. 183, 77. Diagrammatic floor plans of Cleve and Carter's Grove are illustrated on p. 180.

[4] Virginia Gazette Day Books, Dec. 12, 1751.

£25.[5] Another Williamsburg craftsman, John Wheatley, directed the efforts of an unknown number of slaves and journeymen carpenters in raising the timber framework of the house between 1751 and 1753. Part of the carpentry was prefabricated in Wheatley's shop in Williamsburg. Burwell also made several payments to him for "Sundry goods from England."[6] In 1752 Burwell paid £23.13s.9d. for passage to America of an English artisan, Richard Baylis, and his family.[7] Baylis and other skilled craftsmen were responsible for fashioning in walnut and pine the magnificent woodwork at Carter's Grove. By the time final payments that marked completion of the house were made to the crafts-

[5] Burwell Ledger.
[6] *Ibid.*
[7] *Ibid.*

*Figure 146* Carter's Grove. South elevation.

men in late 1755, Burwell had paid out almost £1,300, about one-fourth of which was spent for materials.

Carter Burwell lived in the house only six months after its completion, dying in May 1756. The property passed to his five-year-old son Nathaniel, who inherited full authority over it in 1771. A superb feature that Nathaniel Burwell added to the house around that date was the Siena marble mantel obtained from England for the first floor southwest room. Although he made a few such improvements to Carter's Grove, Nathaniel Burwell built another house in Clarke County in 1792 and afterward lived there almost exclusively, placing Carter's Grove in the hands of overseers. While his son, Carter Burwell III (1773–1819), was born and died at Carter's Grove, he may actually have spent little of his adult life there. The property was inherited by his only son, Philip Lewis Carter Burwell (1817–1878), who sold it in 1838.

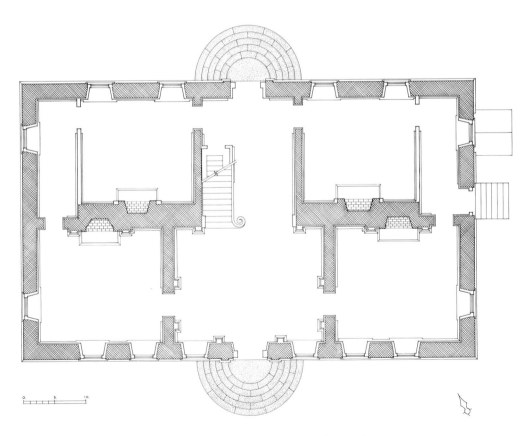

*Figure 147*   Carter's Grove. First floor plan.

The original house consisted of a two-story brick main block that measured seventy-one feet, eleven inches by forty-three feet, six inches. The low pitched hipped roof, devoid of dormer windows, had a slight flare or kick at the eaves that gave it lightness. Two interior chimneys with massive sculptural caps rose high above the wood shingled roof near the apexes of the ridge and hip junctures and were situated so that fireplaces could be centered on the inner walls of the rooms they served. A well-proportioned wood modillion cornice encircled the eaves. The two facades had contrasting fenestrations, with five bays on the land elevation and seven on the river front, a function of the elegant arrangement. The side walls were noticeably underwindowed. There may originally have been a doorway in the east elevation for access to the kitchen outbuilding, although it seems unlikely that one existed on the west, where the brickwork shows no sign of any correct type of eighteenth-century jack arch or architrave that would have trimmed

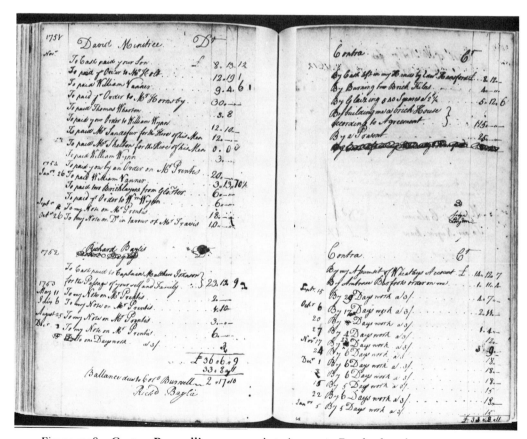

*Figure 148*  Carter Burwell's manuscript Account Book showing 1752–1753 entries for payments to David Minitree, brickmason, and Richard Baylis, carver.

a door there. Any doorway on either of the side elevations would have had to have been placed off center because of the position of the main east-west interior bearing wall through the middle of the house.

A high exterior foundation wall pierced by cellar grilles aligned beneath the front and back windows was capped with a heavy molded brick water table of the kind rarely used for domestic structures which, along with a four-stretcher-wide rubbed brick belt course at the second story level, provided emphatic horizontal definition. Nine over nine light sashes fitted into wood frames atop molded wood sills in the window openings of the first and second stories. An important divergence at Carter's Grove was the rare instance of the first and second story windows being exactly the same size rather than proportionally reduced on the upper level in the conventional manner. The superior workmanship of the rubbed brick dressings at all door and window openings, corners, and finely pedimented brick doorways lent importance to these rather modest exterior features. Significant details of the masonry finish included the absence of glazed headers, the evenly matched size of the bricks, and the maximum rubbing at the corners, which constitutes the only known domestic example in the tidewater area. Tall eight-panel doors with alternating square and rectangular molded panels filled the center doorways on both facades.

The entrance hall is Carter's Grove's distinguishing masterpiece. Its spaces and details were related with an unerring taste that reflects the artistry of a master craftsman's composition, although technically, when compared with the contemporary sophistication of woodwork at Gunston Hall and the rococo plasterwork at Kenmore, its superb ornamentation was a stylistic continuation of earlier fashions. Its distinction lies more in its richness than innovative urbanity. A simple paneled dado topped by a Greek fretted chair rail forms a pedestal base for the upper wall paneling that encases the entire passage. The river front door is flanked by projecting Ionic pilasters and the whole is crowned with a full entablature *en ressaut*. The elliptical arch has crowning carved keystones and molded archivolts that rest on plain Ionic imposts. The stairway ascends in a long flight against the west wall and then turns with two half-landings and short flights before reaching the second floor. It has finish details of round-shaft turned balusters, foliated brackets, geometric inlays, and a sweeping handrail that terminates in a scroll encircling the spiral newel post. The whole is trimmed with parallel dado paneling that boasts ramps and easings as well as spiraled pilasters at the landings.

The interior plan was an elaboration of the more familiar central passage, double-pile house in Virginia. It consisted of four rooms on a floor with full paneling downstairs and more conventional treatments of paneled chimney breasts in combination with cornices, chair rails, and baseboards that trim the plaster wall surfaces upstairs. The upper and lower north rooms originally had partitioned lobbies, or closets, along their end walls. Paneled interior shutters throughout fit into the window jambs. The flooring is pine. The first floor ceilings are thirteen feet, three inches high, while those on the second story are thirteen feet, two inches, echoing a similar peculiarity at the Lightfoot House in Williamsburg where the ceiling heights are also nearly equal on both floors.

Standing twenty-four feet from each end of the main house, the originally detached kitchen on the east side and the laundry on the west date from circa 1740. Both are story and one-half brick buildings whose walls have the embellishment of fully patterned glazed headers. The doors of the laundry were originally off center toward the west, which

*Figure 149*   Carter's Grove. Entrance passage and staircase before restoration.

reveals a plan having two rooms of unequal size on either side of a through passage, in this case a space adapted as a small entry in front of an enclosed stairway. A partial basement beneath the laundry was reached by a bulkhead at the northeast corner. The kitchen plan is problematical. Both outbuildings had pairs of end chimneys and one window on either side of the doorway in the north and south elevations. The fenestration of their end walls remains uncertain. Interior features of the outbuildings have been entirely lost, although the height of their ceilings is correctly measured at ten feet, five inches.

After Philip Lewis Carter Burwell sold the property in 1838, the house was occupied for the next seven decades by a series of owners and tenants who maintained it with few alterations except the addition of veranda-type porches. One late nineteenth-century resident, however, painted the entrance hall's carved woodwork "in shrieking tones of red, white, blue, and—*mirabile dictu*—green!"[8] Later observers hypothesized that this bizarre ornamentation might have been inspired by patriotic fervor engendered by the 1881 Yorktown Victory Centennial.

The first major twentieth-century preservation effort at Carter's Grove was begun by T. Percival Bisland soon after he purchased the property in 1907. Fire prevention equipment and mechanical systems to provide heat, water, and plumbing were installed and both the interior and exterior were refurbished. The kitchen was modernized and an early east porch on the main house was demolished to allow construction of a brick hyphen between the two structures. The interior hardware fittings were silverplated, while paneling in the dining room and upper and lower hallways was stripped of paint and given a natural finish. Elsewhere the woodwork was painted, white being selected for most first floor rooms. A large Victorian porch on the land front was removed so that the eighteenth-century circular stone steps that remained on the site could be put back in place, but another "piazza" extending the full length of the south river elevation was retained. Louvered shutters were attached at every window of the main building and the kitchen's first story. New slate roofing was applied on all three buildings. Bisland died shortly after he bought Carter's Grove, but most of the renovations were completed before his widow's trustees sold the house in 1911.

During the next seventeen years, Carter's Grove again had several owners, one of whom planted the grounds everywhere under heavy

---

[8] A. Burnley Bibb, "Old Colonial Work in Virginia and Maryland," in William Rotch Ware, ed., *The Georgian Period* (Brooklyn, N. Y., 1923), pp. 70–71.

cultivation that plowed deeply into the soil and therefore obliterated most of the original landscape and archaeological features. In 1928 Mr. and Mrs. Archibald M. McCrea purchased Carter's Grove and, with the assistance of architect W. Duncan Lee, embarked on an ambitious yet meticulously studious project of revitalization that culminated in the elegant country house seen today.

The sweeping changes introduced at Carter's Grove during 1928–1931 were largely compatible with the structure's eighteenth-century character. One major objective was to enlarge the interior space of the house for more convenient living and entertaining. To provide a full third floor for guest accommodations, the main roof was raised seven feet at the ridge, considerably heightening its original slope to a steeper pitch and necessitating rebuilding the chimneys and their stacks above the second floor level. Dormer windows were placed in each slope of the new hipped roof.

New stone pyramidal steps were constructed at the entrances to the main house, and semicircular stone steps were placed at all four exterior doors to the outbuildings. The Bisland shutters were replaced with new louvered wood ones hung at most window openings and at the laundry and kitchen doorways as well. The Victorian porch on the south elevation was dismantled. Apparently untouched since Minitree's crew of masons finished the brickwork of the main house in 1752, a nearly complete series of regularly spaced putlog holes was infilled.

The roofs of the two original outbuildings were raised five and one-half feet, although their pitch remained unchanged, and all three buildings were covered with new slate shingles. Old dormers on the outbuildings were replaced. The kitchen and laundry were enlarged nearly ten feet in depth toward the south, or river, side, and the south door to the office was relocated exactly in the center of the elevation. New fireplaces were constructed inside the walls at both ends. New one and one-half story brick connections, measuring almost the same depth as the two outbuildings and consisting of three brick arched bays with French doors (except on the north side of the kitchen hyphen where conventional windows occurred), were extended to link the kitchen and laundry with the main house in a manner similar to the east hyphen constructed during the Bisland tenure, which was replaced entirely. Ten doorways cut into the end elevations of all three buildings provided communication on the first and second floors.

Extensive interior alterations included the installation of mechanical equipment, luxuriously appointed rooms in the hyphens, and the provi-

sion of entirely new third floor guest rooms, but the building's eighteenth-century features were left relatively undisturbed. The stairway
in the main block was continued to the third floor level with the original
Baylis joinery and carving on the lower runs being duplicated almost

*Figure 150* Carter's Grove. Southwest room on first floor showing original
imported Siena marble mantel.

exactly. Perhaps the most significant interior change was the removal of three of the four eighteenth-century partitions that formed lobbies, which were believed originally to have been dressing closets and a serving pantry, in the north rooms of both stories. Layers of old varnish were removed from the entrance passages and stairway, and all old paint was scraped from the surfaces of the first floor rooms so that the woodwork could be stained to a natural finish, except in the northeast corner room where the paneling was repainted a cream color called "old ivory." The woodwork in all upstairs rooms was painted in accordance with the customary colonial practice.

The first floor of the laundry was opened into one room by the removal of all partitions. The original floor plan of the kitchen was disregarded for purposes of modern convenience, and it was subdivided by using the south wall as a longitudinal interior partition to allow an entryway and enclosed stair on the river side. The upper floors of both dependencies were converted to bedroom spaces.

Mr. McCrea died ten years after the restoration of the house was finished; Mrs. McCrea continued to live at Carter's Grove until her death in 1960. In her will, she stated a long-standing "hope and ambition" that the property might be maintained for the benefit of subsequent generations. Sealantic Fund, a Rockefeller-supported philanthropic organization, purchased Carter's Grove from Mrs. McCrea's estate in 1963. In 1969 it was transferred by deed of gift to the Colonial Williamsburg Foundation, which today preserves Carter's Grove and its grounds for exhibition to the public.

## CONDITION

Since 1969, architectural changes have been eschewed in favor of careful maintenance. Shutters were removed from the exterior of the mansion, and a new heat plant, electrical wiring, a fire prevention system, and air conditioning were installed in 1975. Structural reinforcement of the stairway carriage and landings, and repairs to the wood frame and brick architrave of the north doorway occurred in 1978. Limited architectural investigations were conducted simultaneously during each repair project.

# APPENDIX I

# *Excerpts from the*
# *Harwood Account Book*

THE following are two excerpts from the account book of Humphrey Harwood, bricklayer, and his son William. They relate to work done for, and materials supplied to, William Hunter and William Pasteur by Humphrey Harwood in 1776–1778. As noted earlier in these pages, the Harwood account book, now in Colonial Williamsburg Archives, was discovered by S. P. Moorehead in 1930 in the attic of a modern outbuilding behind the George Reid House.

Mr. William Hunter     Dr.

1776
October 23

    To 500 bricks 13/9.20 bush$^s$ of lime 15/– a Grate w$^t$ 74½
lb. @ 7½ d                               £ 3 · 15 · 3

    To Altering a Grate 6/3 by B.B. to laying a harth & Seting
up a Grate 10/–                                  16 · 3

    To lay$^g$ 2 harth 5/– & fixing a Grate 7/6. 18 bush$^s$ of lime
@ 9d & 1½ d$^o$ hair 2/3                           1 · 8 · 3

    To mend$^g$ Larthing & plastering 22/6 & 5 days labour @
2/–                                       1 · 12 · 6

    To Whitewashing Chamber & parlour 7/6 & 4 other Rooms
& a passage @ 3/9                              1 · 6 · 3

    To mend$^g$ Oven & Ash House 2/– to 200 larths 2/– & A
bushel of hair 1/6                                 5 · 6

    To cash lent you at Major Hornesby's to pay for a bowl &
2 Muggs 7/–                                     7 · –

November 25

    To half a Dozen Walnut Chairs 90/– & A Mahogany tea
table 36/6                                    6 · 6 · –

1777
February 1
    To 8 days labour @ 2/– Clean^g bricks. (8th). 15 days labour
    30/– dig^g Celler                                                   2 · 6 · –
[February] 15
    To 22 d^o lab^r @ 2/– Cart^g 4 loads of Sand 8/– 140 bus^s
    lime @ 9d                                                       7 · 17 · –
    To 3750 bricks @ 27/6. (20th) to 4000 D^o @ 27/6. & Cart^g
    1 load of Sand 2/–                                            10 · 13 · 1½
[February] 20
    To building Celler walls 100/– & 9 days labour @ 2/– &
    Carting a load Sand 2/–                                        6 · 0 · –
March 17
    To 100 bushels of lime @ 9d. 10000 bricks @ 27/6: 21
    days la^r @ 2/– & 5 lo^ds Sand @ 2/–                    20 · 2 · 0
[March] 22
    To building kitching Chimney & Oven 65/– & build D^o to
    Dwel^g House 80/–                                         7 · 5 · –
May 11
    To 20 bush^s of lime 15/– 230 bricks @ 2/9. ½ bu^l whitew^h
    9d. & Set^g a Grate with Rub^d bricks 20/–          2 · 2 · 3
    To turning 2 trimers & laying 2 harth 10/– & 1 Days labour
    2/–                                                     12 · –
[May] 15
    To 1800 larths 22/6 to 2 bushels of hair 4/– & 20 d^o lime
    15/– & 1 load Sand 2/–                                 2 · 3 · 6
    To Larthing and plastering Chamber below 70 yd^s @ 6d   1 · 15 · –
June 29
    To 40 bush^s of lime 30/– 2 d^o hair 4/–9 Days labour @
    2/–                                                  2 · 12 · –
    To 2000 larthes 25/– & larthing & plaistering 101 yards
    @ 6d                                               3 · 15 · 6
November 18
    To 2 bush^s of lime 2/– & altering a Grate 5/– & labours
    work 1/6                                          8 · 6
1778
January 4
    To 2900 Nails @ 20/– p^r M. 700 larthes @ 2/– & 28 bushels
    of lime @ 1/3                                   5 · 7 · –
    To 1 bushel of hair @ 2/6. 4 days labour @ 3/6         16 · 6
    To larthing & plastering 60 yards @ 7½d.        1 · 17 · 6
                                                            £91 · 9 · 11

    Doct^r William Pasteur         Dr.

1777
January 4
    To 8 bush^s of lime @ 9d p^d Oversear for D^r up the Country
    & a line 6/–                                     £ – · 12 · –

June 16

    To a Set of harrow howes 30/– (August 23rd) to 1½ days
Carting @ 15/–                                                 2 · 12 · 6

October 14

    To 1 day Cart hier 15/–                                          15 · –

1 /78

February 28

    To 1 days Cart hier 40/– (March 2nd) To 1 do Carting
plank to farm 40/–                                       4 · 0 · –

March 2

    To 200 bricks 3/– 12 bushels of lime @ 1/6. (4th) To 500
Do 25/– Carting them to Farm 40/–                   4 · 13 · –

    To working in 2 door frames to kitchg 12/– & building up
Old Door 12/–                                           1 · 4 · –

    To mendg Kitching Chimney 6/– & 2 days labour 6/–       12 · –

[March] 29

    To repairing well 10/– & 12 days Work of Old George @
2/6                                                   2 · 0 · –

    To 500 bricks 27/6. & Carting them to Farm & building
Oven 24/–                                           2 · 11 · 6

    To Repairing Chimney in Garrot 5/– & Do in landary
7/6. & Work in Doore Frame to landary. & Repairing
the wall 24/–                                     1 · 16 · 6

    To Working in 6 Celler window frames @ 12/–       3 · 12 · –

July 24

    To 400 bricks @ 5/– (Augt 24th) 300 bricks 15/–. 3 days
work of H. W. 15/– & 3 do George 12/–            5 · 10 · –

Septemr 2

    To 300 Do 15/– 1 days work of H.W. 15/– (24th) to 2000
larthes @ 30/–                                       4 · 10 · –

[Septemr] 25

    To 2500 4d. Nails @ 36/– pr M. 150 20d do 12/–      5 · 2 · –

    To 40 bushs of lime @ 1/6. & Carting it to farm 30/–     4 · 10 · –

    To ¾ of a days Carting Cole & Sault from Mr. Plumes     1 · 2 · 6

[Septemr] 30

    To 40 bushs of lime 60/– & Carting it to farm 30/–      4 · 10 · –

    To 1200 bricks pr Waggons 60/–                      3 · 0 · –

Octobr 10

    To 1000 larthes 30/– & 15 days work of Jack at 12/–; &
15 do of Moses @ 8/–                              16 · 10 · –

[Octobr] 17

    To 1200 bricks @ 5/– & 4 days of Hud Watkins @ 15/–.
2 do of Self @ 15/–                                 7 · 10 · –

    To 4 Days work of Phill, & 6 Do of Moses @ 8/–      3 · 4 · –

[Octobr] 24

    To 6 Days Do of Phill, & 6 Do of Moses @ 8/–      4 · 16 · –

[Octob^r ] 28
   To 2 Ditto. Self at 15/– & 2 D° of Moses 16/– 1 bushel
of Whitewash 3/– & 4 days of my horse plowing 24/–       3 · 13 · –
Novem^r 7
   To 6 D° Jack @ 12/–; 6 D° Mosses @ 8/– & 1 D° p^r Self
15/–       6 · 15 · –
[Novem^r] 14
   To 4 D° of Jack @ 12/– (19th) to 400 larthes @ 3/6     <u>3 ·  2 · –</u>
                                 £92 ·  8 · –

# APPENDIX II

# *Agreement Relating to the Painting of the St. George Tucker House*

T HE following agreement, in St. George Tucker's hand, is among the Tucker-Coleman Papers in Colonial Williamsburg Archives.

Memorandum of an Agreement made the thirtieth day of August 1798, between S^t George Tucker and Jeremiah Satterwhite, both of Williamsburg.

The said Jeremiah Satterwhite agrees & undertakes to paint the Outside of the dwelling house, & part of the inside, together with the Kitchen & Dairy, belonging to the said S^t George Tucker in the City of Williamsburg, as herein after mentioned, & in the most compleat, & workmanlike manner; taking Care never to paint but in dry Weather, nor at any time when the part to be painted is not perfectly dry.—The tops of the House, Kitchen & dairy are to be painted with Fish-oil mixt in the paint, the oil to be well boiled Linseed Oil, but if it should not be sufficiently boiled, it is to be boiled to a proper Consistency. Every part that is to be painted is to have two good Coats well laid on, in the best Manner. S^t George Tucker hath provided about 240-pounds of best white Lead; half an hundred weight of Spanish brown; and the like Quantity of yellow Ochre, all ground in oil, and about sixteen Gallons of boiled Linseed Oil; he is further to provide as much fish-oil as will be sufficient to paint the roofs, & sheds, as hereafter mentioned. He has also provided eleven bottles of Spirits of Turpentine, and a sufficient Quantity of Tar, and the said Satterwhite agrees to keep an exact Account of the Quantity of each of these Articles that he may expend in painting the House. The said Satterwhite is to find his own Brushes and a pot to boil the oil, and paint. S^t George Tucker will provide ladders, & furnish every necessary Assistance to him.

The top of the House, the roof of the Shed, and of the covered Way are to be painted with Spanish brown, somewhat enlivened, if necessary, with red Lead, or other proper paint.

The sides of the House, and of the covered way, & the Ends of the house are to be painted a pure White. The outer doors a chocolate colour—the brick underpinning and the other parts of the house below the floor of a dark brick Colour, nearly approaching to a Chocolate colour. The Chair boards, picture slips, Windows, & other parts of the front & back passage (except the doors & door Cases, which are to be of Chocolate Colour) are to be of a pale Stone colour, or straw Colour. The two small side passages of a Mahogany Colour, except the part leading in the dining room, which is to be of a stone colour.—The platform for the Steps, in front of the house, when finished, is also to be painted of a light stone colour.

The top of the Kitchen, and of the shed leading from the Cellar to the Kitchen yard, are to be painted with Spanish brown, mixed with Tar, & fish oil, & well boiled together. The sides of the Kitchen of yellow Ochre, with a very small mixture of White Lead: the window frames & Sashes of straw-colour, or white: the sliders to the windows in Imitation of the Sashes.

The dairy is to be painted as the Kitchen; the open work under the Eaves white.

When the work is compleated S$^t$ George Tucker agrees to pay fifty dollars for the same; but in Case he should concieve the work not to be well done, or in Case of disagreement on any other subject, he is to chuse one person & the said Satterwhite another, who, or in the Case of disagreement between them, any third person by them to be chosen shall determine whether any, or what abatement ought to be made, by reason of the work not being compleatly finished, in a masterly workmanlike manner, pursuant to the true Intent & meaning of this Agreement.

In witness whereof the parties aforesaid have subscribed their names to this present instrument of writing the day & year above—

Witness                                           Jeremiah Sattywhite
E. H. Dunbar.                                     S$^t$ G. Tucker

NB. The boiled Linseed Oil is not to be used for the Kitchen, the Dairy, or the top of the House.

# Index

Illustrations are indicated by *italic* type except when
they accompany illustrated accounts.

*THE EIGHTEENTH-CENTURY HOUSES OF WILLIAMSBURG*

*revised edition*

*Designed by Richard Stinely*

*Composed, printed, and bound by Arcata Book Group's*
*Kingsport Press*

*Printed on Glacto Matte manufactured*
*by P. H. Glatfelter Co.*

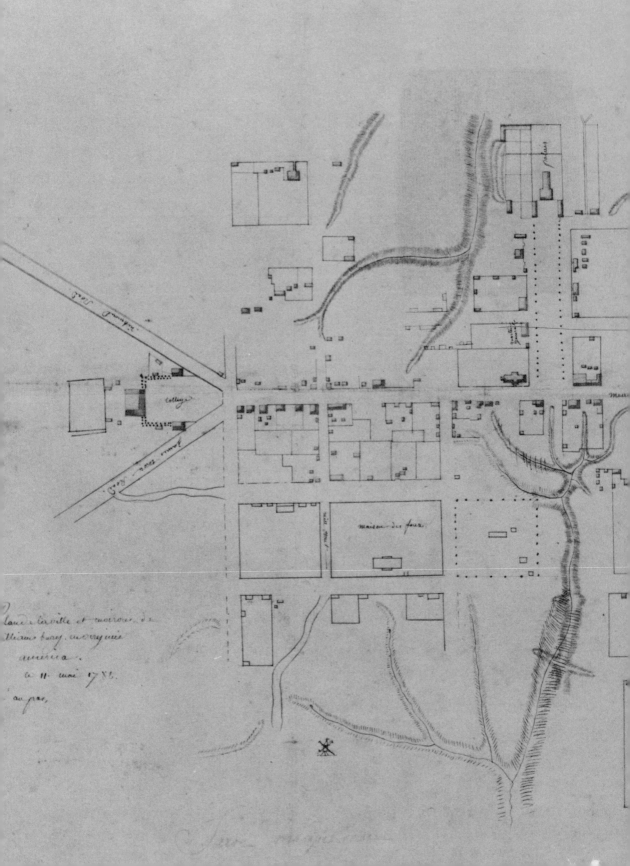

Plan de la ville et environs de
Williamsburg en virginie
amerique.
le 11 mai 1782.
au pas.